Civic Life in the Information Age

Civic Life in the Information Age

Stefanie Sanford

CIVIC LIFE IN THE INFORMATION AGE
© Stefanie Sanford, 2007.

First published in 2007 by
PALGRAVE MACMILLAN™
175 Fifth Avenue, New York, N.Y. 10010 and
Houndmills, Basingstoke, Hampshire, England RG21 6XS
Companies and representatives throughout the world.

PALGRAVE MACMILLAN is the global academic imprint of the Palgrave Macmillan division of St. Martin's Press, LLC and of Palgrave Macmillan Ltd. Macmillan® is a registered trademark in the United States, United Kingdom and other countries. Palgrave is a registered trademark in the European Union and other countries.

ISBN-13: 978–1–4039–7634–5
ISBN-10: 1–4039–7634–1

Library of Congress Cataloging-in-Publication Data

Sanford, Stefanie.
    Civic life in the information age / by Stefanie Sanford.
        p. cm.
    Includes bibliographical references and index.
        ISBN 1–4039–7634–1 (alk. paper)
        1. Generation X—United States—Political activity. 2. Citizenship—
United States. 3. Internet—Social aspects—United States. I. Title.

HQ799.7.S225 2007
305.2420973'090511—dc22   2006048318

A catalogue record for this book is available from the British Library.

Design by Newgen Imaging Systems (P) Ltd., Chennai, India.

First edition: February 2007

10 9 8 7 6 5 4 3 2

Printed in the United States of America.

To Madeline and Elizabeth, my
fabulous nieces

Whatever you can do or dream you can, begin it.
Boldness has genius, power and magic in it. . . .

Johann Wolfgang von Goethe

Contents

List of Illustrations

Figures

Tables

Acknowledgments

I am a part of all that I have met
Tho much is taken, much abides
That which we are, we are—
One equal temper of heroic hearts
* strong in will*
To strive, to seek, to find, and not to yield.

I have always loved the verse above and think it is especially apropos to open this tome and close this chapter of my life by thanking the people who helped make it possible. They are many. First and foremost, thank you to my adviser, Roderick P. Hart, a great intellect and teacher who fought cynicism on the gridiron of cool and won over and over again. Thank you for all of your help on this project, but most importantly for setting the conditions that make dedications like this possible. Annette would be proud. You do her memory justice every day and it has been a privilege to be a part of that.

To my immediate family—thanks to my mom and dad, their spouses and my siblings (David, that means you, too). Our familial stew has played a huge role in bringing me to this place. I come from a long line of unapologetically strong women. Their spirit runs through my veins and with each adventure I can hear the echo of their legacies in my mind: Mom, Nan, Meem, Aunt Bet, and Aunt "Louise" and of course the three great grandmothers I had the good fortune to know. I spent formative moments with each of these women and for as long as I can remember, I have been imitating them, stalking them, questioning them. They have taught me how to be the grown-up I want to be, how to chase dreams when everyone believes said dreams are nuts, and that, like all good southern women, one should always try to look great regardless of the weather. And in a more concrete and less romantic way, they have helped me finance these dreams through their direct investment, their pledges of support, their opportune checks, palmed $100 bills at holiday times and their last-minute loan cosignatures. Simply, I would not be here and this book would not exist without each of them.

To the teachers—I have been blessed with thoughtful, compassionate and patient teachers throughout my extended education. Mrs. Leaventhal in fourth grade at Lamplighter was the first to treat me differently because I loved to write. We recently reconnected in Washington—she hasn't changed since those days—and in some ways, neither have I. She admonished, "Please, call me Sheila." In my experience one can never call your greatest elementary school teacher by her first name, even as the fortieth birthday draws near. Dr. Hermann and Dr. Suzuki were violin teachers who gave me an early appreciation of excellence, commitment, and the power of practice and passion over mere memorization. Mr. Schultz taught AP history at Westlake High School and imbued in me forever a sense that history is a living, breathing thing and politics and civic life are its contemporary practices. Long before President Reagan toasted President Kennedy's memory at the rededication of his library, Mr. Schultz taught me that "[h]istory isn't about people, history is people . . . and it is as heroic as you want it to be, as heroic as you are." Dr. Warner even made me write about trigonometry and showed me that even *that* could be compelling. At TCU, I must thank Drs. Harris, Hall, and Babbili. Dr. Harris taught freshman comp and was the first writing teacher to ever make the apparently conflicting demands—write to the assignment and think hard. After years of glib improvisation in and around assignments, she forced me to risk, to put my real thoughts and philosophies on paper and defend them as an intellectual—not a satirist—would. Dr. Hall first said that she knew I would one day get a PhD—I couldn't fathom such a thing, but here it is—she believed it before I did. I can still see her determination for me as we had that conversation. And Dr. B—a good friend and mentor— always ready to take on the tough political challenges on campus and had a way of making writing, journalism, and politics all seem like noble pursuits. It's not so much that I pursued these tasks because he said I should as much as he showed all of us a professional that we could see ourselves proudly becoming. My heartfelt thanks to all of them. Their hair has grayed over the nearly 20 years since I sat in their undergraduate classes, but their wisdom stays with me to this day. Dr. Porter at The Kennedy School engaged me in the study of presidential transitions. That research became the fodder for my White House Fellow application (as his own story became my inspiration). He treated me as a scholar and supported this study even as it took me away from the rough and tumble world of public policy for a time. Most importantly, Dr. Porter taught me that in the game (said Teddy Roosevelt) ideas matter (no matter what the cynics say) more than ideology and that in order for good policy to be made, "honest brokers" must exist. I hope this effort has helped me become a better honest broker.

To my gal pals and critics—my best friends Colleen and Loree—for their always pushing me to think harder; for their fearless criticism of my ideas, my wine selection, and my tendency to respond to a social "How's the book going?" with an avalanche of specifics that could send even the most hearty social capitalist fleeing for the bar. Every successful person needs thoughtful, caring critics. I have been blessed with the best—they read and digested the ideas, challenged the principles, and endured the obsession that comes with successfully completing one of these tomes. Couldn't have done it without them.

To my doctorate-holding friends, helpers and cheerleaders, Drs. Sharon Jarvis, Bob Orr, Peter Fiske, and Stephanie Ferguson—many thanks for the late-night advice, strategic insights about the defense, the scope of the project, and the priority I must give to such enterprises if I ever hoped to finish. They were a source of inspiration and countless computer monitor post-it notes reminding me that some day this would be done, I would be glad and it would be a contribution to a national discussion I find vitally important. Obviously, this work could not exist without the my candid and thoughtful respondents and the insights of my mentor and friend, Mike Maples, whose generous spirit and long history in this field helped me sort through the idiosyncrasies of the tech world.

Special thanks must go to my most detail-oriented friend and colleague Ali Khedery. We traveled the postdefense last mile together, checking and rechecking formats, paginations, table numbers, and a host of minutia demanded by MAI 101. He has been in the Green Zone trying to help build a democracy in Baghdad since his days as my right hand in the Governor's Office and the Foundation. I think that if his likely career as a leading diplomat falls through, there could be a job as "margin police" in his future. You're the best—come home soon and safely. Like Ali, my colleagues at the Bill & Melinda Gates Foundation have been patiently supportive of this obsession since I walked through the door especially Tom Vander Ark and have allowed me to infuse our work with some of these ideas (but by no means all), providing a daily testing ground. It would not have been completed without their goodwill.

And finally, thanks to my tireless dissertation committee: Larry Leibrock, Daron Shaw, Chuck Whitney and Thurgood Marshall, Jr. I knew you all in some fashion before we gathered on either side of a potentially adversarial table and respected your intellects, humor, style, and professionalism. Geeky as it sounds, I wish we could have met over this topic many more times. Your disciplinary expertise and passion about these topics made each meeting exhilarating and memorable. It was your encouragement during the defense that led to this publication and the introduction of these ideas into a broader arena. Daunting as that proposition is, I will always be eternally grateful for your confidence.

Onward!

PS: There was no logical place to include them in the above acknowledgments, but this project owes a debt to a profound beginning and profound ending that took place over the course of this work. The profound ending was the passing of my grandfather, Dadoo, my feminist role model. He spent his life surrounded by ornery women and seemed to revel in helping us all find our place in the world and laughing along the way. Writing his eulogy helped me get my head around writing this dedication, which is really about being thankful for a lifetime full of smart, funny people. Dadoo helped me fully appreciate just how blessed I've been in that regard. The beginning was the birth of my fabulous nieces, Madeline Jeanne and Elizabeth Jayne Gillan to whom this book is dedicated. These little miracles of genetics carry the names of their ornery women ancestors, Dadoo's humor and wiry hair, and just perhaps the bold and entrepreneurial spirit of my other grandfather, GWF. At six years old, the twins were not even a glimmer when this inquiry began, but as it is complete, it occurs to me that this study is ultimately about them. We have seen a steady decline in the participation of young people in our democracy—and in some ways a systematic devaluing of their role in our continuation and our renewal. I believe to the very core of who I am that this must change and that some of the insights of this study could be catalysts to that sort of change. Magic Mad and the Little Clown give this study an urgency that scholarship or policy alone could never do. So my last dedication must be to them— that we do right by their dreams and bequeath them a democracy worth their tending.

Preface

The initial impetus of this work was to explore the intersection among generational change, technology, and civic participation. Over the course of completing this work, the first Baby Boomers have turned 60, sparking a renewed interest in generational themes. The 2004 presidential election was the first to truly use the Internet as a central strategy, raising unprecedented sums in smaller increments and helping to animate young people's participation in the failed Howard Dean campaign. The year 2005 saw the "blogosphere" flex its nascent muscles, weighing in to ultimately be the catalyst leading to the removal from consideration of Harriet Miers for the Supreme Court. Interest in the ideas explored here have only accelerated in the time I have been studying them. My respondents' thoughts, beliefs, and predictions have held up since our initial conversations.

Details and nuance are important in a qualitative inquiry such as this. I worked to balance the need for richness with the promise of anonymity. The names of respondents have been changed and I have worked to remove the details that would make identifying them easy, especially given the relatively small community that is high tech, political Austin.

The Problems of Citizenship in the Early Twenty-First Century

We are unsettled to the very roots of our being . . . there isn't a human relation, whether of parent and child, husband and wife, worker and employer, that doesn't move in a strange situation. We are not used to a complicated civilization; we don't know how to behave when personal contact and eternal authority have disappeared. There are no precedents to guide us; no wisdom that was not meant for a simpler age. We have changed our environment more quickly that we have changed ourselves.

—Putnam, 2000, p. 379

Sound familiar? Lippman's 1914 characterization of Progressive Era civic ennui in the face of industrialization bears eerie similarity to the documented unease of early twenty-first-century America. The events of September 11, 2001 only served to deepen and quicken American angst about the ways in which their nation had changed domestically and in the eyes of the world. At the turn of the past century, the Progressives grappled with new living patterns, new communication technologies, and the apparent disintegration of old ways of life. The industrialists' breathless rhetoric of progress stood in sharp relief against the unease that most Americans felt as vast sociological change bubbled around them. As people moved from rural hamlets to industrial cities for work, they found their old communication patterns changing. Work was away from the home. Interactions became less personal. People felt the decline of small-town interpersonal intimacy, a precursor to the *Cheers'* nostalgia for a place where "everyone knows your name." Though such progress brought existential angst, it also brought profound and unprecedented economic growth (Putnam, 2000; Marvin, 1988; Carey, 1988). Today, these same contradictory realities abound as contemporary technologies—the Web, the Internet, e-mail, instant messaging—are changing the way we communicate. Such technologies also have implications for how we define what it is to be a citizen.

Today, we are again in the midst of such change. In *Technopoly*, Neil Postman (1992) argued provocatively that "it is a certainty that radical technologies create new definitions of old terms and that this process takes place without our being fully conscious of it. . . . [T]echnology imperiously commandeers our most important terminology. It redefines 'freedom,' 'truth,' 'intelligence,' 'fact,' 'wisdom,' 'memory,' 'history'—all the words that we live by. And it does not pause to tell us. And we do not pause to ask" (p. 12). This book pauses to ask what early twenty-first-century technologies—and what those who lead it, create it, and use it—have done to the definition of citizenship.

The accelerating adoption of these new tools is undeniable. At the individual level, Forrester Research estimates that the number of households with Internet access more than doubled between 1996 and 2000 and through 2002, estimates that there are 662 million internet users worldwide, sending 60 billion e-mails a day according to the International data corporation. The Infoplease survey shows that over 135,000,000 Americans have accessed the Internet in the last 30 days. More than half a million households—about 18,000 every day—connect to the Internet every month. At the economic level, a recent University of Texas study found that the Internet industry added 650,000 jobs and increased its revenues by 62 percent and accounted for nearly 2.5 million jobs and almost $524 billion in revenues in 1999. Though only a fraction of the nation's roughly 129-million-member workforce and its $9.3 trillion economy, the Internet economy now employs more people than the insurance or public utilities industries and twice as many as the airline industry. Noting this aggressive growth, *USA Today* observed, "It's also a sign that an industry that barely existed a few years ago is growing at a virtually unprecedented rate. . . . The growth of Internet-related jobs is startling when considering that the Internet as a business driver is in its infancy." Drawing upon the infancy metaphor, in the mid-2000s, the Internet industry could be said to be in its "terrible two's" a tumultuous and difficult departure from the go-go days of the "dot-com bubble." Despite the setbacks in the telecom and Internet space, technological tools, though not an invincible sector as was once briefly asserted, still form an increasing part of our everyday lives and still serve as a catalyst to profound changes in the nature of work (Florida, 2002).

As with our Progressive Era forbears, a favorable economic condition does not necessarily yield interpersonal happiness. Observed Postman, "A new technology does not add or subtract something. It changes everything . . . surrounding every technology are institutions whose organizations [reflect] the worldview promoted by the technology. Therefore, when an old technology is assaulted by a new one, institutions are threatened. When institutions are threatened, a culture finds itself in crisis" (p. 18).

Studies of the culture of the Web result in two prominent and conflicting visions, both of which focus on interpersonal interaction (although much of this research is based in old studies of computer-mediated communication) generally studied in labs, in artificial experimental situations, and involving middle-aged respondents. In this research, one side claims that online relationships are "shallow, impersonal and often hostile," and that only the illusion of community can be created in cyberspace; the other side sees the "no one knows you're a dog" phenomenon of cyberspace relationships as liberating from social and geographical constraints, and thereby creating opportunities for new and genuine relationships and communities online. These opposing findings seem outdated in light of more recent research by the Pew Charitable Trusts (2001), which found that the Internet

- promotes social interaction, rather than "geeky isolation";
- enhances the spiritual life of religious people;
- has "enormous significance" to children and teenagers as they use the technologies (including instant messaging and e-mail) for "hours a day . . . to communicate with distant cousins, summer camp friends and the children next door."

Further, their more recent studies show that on any given day in 2005 over 40 million people were on the Internet for some purpose and that those from all age groups were logging on. Their habits are distinctive, with those older using the Web for commerce and those younger using interactive tools to socialize and stay in touch; however, the implication seems clear: the Internet is not an isolating instrument.

Regardless of the uncertainties, there are two consensus realities in the early years of the twenty-first century: Social capital is down. Technology use is up. Putnam (2000) provides exhaustive accounts of the ways in which Americans no longer vote, join Word War II era clubs, or socialize with each other over snacks or cards. The Pew

Charitable Trusts, Forrester Research, and an avalanche of popular accounts describe the ascendance of the so-called Digital Age. And nowhere are those two phenomena more frequently observed than among Generation X (Gen X), those born between 1960 and 1981. They are alleged to be postmodern slackers (Sacks, 1996), or self-centered, billionaire IPO survivors (Borsook, 2000). They vote at historically low levels (Bennett, 1997). Scholarly attention to this cohort has been nearly uniformly pejorative. As this generation progresses to middle age, and as the wealth generated by the tools of technology increases, parts of Gen X are emerging as an elite constituency. What does this portend for civic life in the early years of the new millennium? Will this maligned generation affirm Postman's observation that "those who cultivate competence in a new technology become an elite group that are granted undeserved authority and prestige by those who have no such competence" (p. 11)? Or will they construct a civic culture fundamentally new—the "changed everything" that a radical technology often brings about in widespread adoption?

This study focuses on the young and the new and how notions of citizenship are affected by emerging forms of interactive technologies. Specifically, I explore what distinctive civic attitudes are fostered in cyber-democracy and what those attitudes might mean for the future of our nation's civic life. Are we sensing changes that are the result of these technologies, which are changing our cultural values, as Postman argues, "embedded in every tool is an ideological bias, a predisposition to construct the world as one rather than another, to value one thing over another, to amplify one sense or skill or attitude more loudly than another" (p. 11)?

Before we can turn to those questions of a potentially new civic culture, we must first examine the old. Currently, the national civic consensus is that American citizenship is in *decline*—not in *flux*—and that decline is allegedly documented by a number of problems observed by a range of commentators and scholars. Those problems have been identified in myriad ways. In my view, they fall into the following broad categories:

- the problem of Bowling Alone;
- the problem of generational change;
- the problem of the Internet;
- the problem of technology and community;
- the problem of politics and young people; and
- the problem of old measures.

The Problem of *Bowling Alone*

In the mid-1990s, Professor Robert Putnam named the civic ennui felt by many Americans with a catch phrase so resonant that he was catapulted from obscure academic to the pages of *People* magazine. At the end of the twentieth century, he argued, Americans were *Bowling Alone*. His thesis: where citizens in the 1950s bowled in leagues with friends and coworkers, by the 1990s they were bowling increasingly with their families or by themselves. Of course, Putnam's point is larger than sport; his observations about how we bowl can be—and have been—generalized to how we live life itself. His argument and its made-for-TV catch phrase touched a raw nerve in the American psyche in the midst of unprecedented *economic* prosperity in the late 1990s, a prosperity largely animated by advances in information technology.

In response to considerable interest, Putnam completed a much longer, more thorough version of that initial article. His book, published in 2000, clung to the metaphor that proved so resonant. *Bowling Alone: The Collapse and Revival of American Community* is an exhaustive account of how American civic life has changed during the twentieth century. He examined a variety of social indicators, including traditional measures of voter turnout, party membership, political interest, volunteerism, and TV viewership. But he also turned to unexpected indicators of civic activity such as entertaining at home, joining clubs, and having a regular bridge game. From these varied measures of political, interpersonal, and group activities, Putnam constructed a detailed picture of the increasingly isolated, end-of-the-century American.

Perhaps because his initial thesis was constructed before the explosive growth of network technology, Putnam devoted surprisingly little time to the ubiquitous technological innovation of the 1990s—the Internet. He combined his brief exploration of this medium with a chapter on contemporary social movements, acknowledging that the advent of cyberspace might have implications for civic involvement, but spending very little time unpacking the notion. Here, I will attempt to take up where Putnam left off.

Whereas the late 1990s was marked by considerable discussion of declines in social capital, even more has been written in the past couple of years about so-called cyber-society. Amazon.com even created a separate cyber-society push e-mail service for its regular customers, recommending the latest thinking in space. These offerings, from the scathing and ironic *Cyberselfish: A Critical Romp Through the Terribly Libertarian Culture of High Tech* to the mercurial

Techngnosis: Myth, Magic + Mysticism in the Age of Information, claim to provide technology-related explanations for what Putnam named, and often blamed technology—and technologists—for our palpable social unease. By the immediate logic of Amazon's push list, Postman is old news. But he did raise a critical point well before the mass diffusion of Internet access that bears repeating: radical technologies do not yield a way of life plus the new technology; they often create something fundamentally new. The invention of the printing press did not yield Europe plus the printing press; it changed the way societies thought about the nature of knowledge. The invention of the television, Postman (1993) overtly argued (and Putnam implicitly claims) did not yield an old culture with a new machine at the margins. The television fundamentally altered the way we socialize and entertain ourselves.

It is from that argument that I take exception to Putnam's premise about the decline of social capital. Putnam argued, for example, that social capital is declining and he advanced a host of traditional 1950s American measures of citizenship and comradeship to support his thesis. He examined countless measures of old ways of socializing—even ways before television—and certainly ways before Internet communications. He defined social capital in terms of practices common prior to the widespread adoption of revolutionary technologies. It is a useful exercise to name and measure some ways in which a technology—in his case television—can change patterns of interaction. But he spends no time contemplating what this new culture might be. What if the fundamental nature of citizenship has changed? What if Putnam's measures are not the ones that increasing numbers of high-tech actors—especially young people—view as constituting citizenship? Do *changing definitions* of what it means to be civic result in a *decline* of civic life?

The Problem of Generational Change

There is ample evidence today that such a disconnect in definitions of citizenship exists within younger generations—Generations X and Y. Perhaps not coincidentally, those are the people who also dominate the ranks of the high-tech sector. Putnam actually blamed the declines in social capital on several broad factors, but the two most prominent are generational effects. The first explanation he advanced was specifically aimed at the behavior of younger Americans: social capital has declined because the young do not do the communal things that older social capitalists once did. His second culprit was television.[1] Though Putnam blamed electronic entertainment, particularly television, for 25 percent of the decline in civic engagement, generational change was his primary culprit. He argued that the "long civic generation" raised Baby Boomer children who were less engaged than they were, who then passed down their dissipating social cohesion to their Generation X children, who in turn allegedly showed even lower levels of civic and political participation than their parents. These generational effects account for half of Putnam's decline in social capital.

In essence, Putnam argued that social capital was high within the WWII generation and has been steadily declining with each successive generation. Spending time in front of the television screen has exacerbated this decline. Putnam worried that the Internet simply creates another screen for people to watch, especially the young, at the expense of other forms of participation and connection. Was Putnam overly dismissive of the young when judging them by the measures of the old? Did he miss the fundamental difference between the two electronic screens that gave him pause: that one is inherently passive and almost exclusively used for entertainment, whereas the other, newer one is interactive and rife with substantive information?

The Problem of the Internet

Putnam expressed concern that where television—the radical technology of the 1950s—contributed significantly to the decline of social capital, the Web technologies of the new millennium would prove equally damaging. Certainly, Internet access and Web usage have dramatically increased in recent years. Numerous studies and surveys describe the demographics and usage patterns of the Web by citizens. One study explored the content of congressional Web pages and theorized about what sort of citizens are hailed by those pages (Jarvis, 1998). The John F. Kennedy School of Government at Harvard University also held a conference on the topic in which several papers addressing the use of the Internet in politics were presented. One reviewed active Senate and gubernatorial races, fostering campaign Web sites (Kamarck, 1998). Another study debunked one of the most common perceptions about Internet users with the surprising findings that the Internet is not dominated by elite, affluent well-educated

---

[1] Putnam also points to 2 other factors, each accounting for 10% of the decline: work pressure and suburban sprawl.

males, but is increasingly diverse and progressive in its orientation (King, 1998).

A more recent study of the Pew Internet Project found that women and children are the fastest growing demographic of Internet users (Pew Charitable Trusts, 2000). Pew found that 21 million Americans (12 percent of the voting age population, or more than half of those with online access) obtained political or policy news from online sources in 1996. Some 7 million (4 percent) used the Internet or commercial online services for information about the presidential election. On Election Day, 3 percent of voters went so far as to say that the Internet and online sites, especially the World Wide Web, were their "principal election news sources" (Pavlick, 1998, p. 298). Still others claim that those who use the Web for political purposes are those who were already politically active and politically interested, persons who had high media use as well.

Tempering some enthusiasm for a democratic renaissance ushered in by online politics is the emergence of the so-called Digital Divide, a concern that new technologies will widen the rift between the information rich and the information poor in American society. A 1995 survey of household computer ownership by the U.S. Department of Commerce found broad discrepancies based on ethnicity. Asian American households had a 36 percent computer penetration; this ratio dropped to 28 percent for white households, 12 percent for Hispanic, and 9.5 percent for African Americans (Dizard, 1999, p. 25). The most recent installment of *Falling through the Net* (LeBlanc, 2000) found that though the gap is narrowing in some ways, there are still causes for concern. The percentage of American households now having Internet access is 41.5 percent, with over 50 percent owning a computer, yet the technology gap between the rich and poor grew by 25 percent.[2] The most current data on access is the late 2005 Pew data, which found that sixty-eight percent of American adults, or about 137 million people, use the Internet, up from 63 percent one year ago. Thirty-two percent of American adults, or about 65 million people, do not go online, and it is not always by choice. Certain groups continue to lag in their Internet adoption. For example,

[2] In the years since 1998, a significant movement toward increasing "public access" to information, especially the Internet, has been undertaken by community organizations, such as Austin FreeNet, public libraries (largely funded by municipal governments, the Telecommunication Infrastructure Fund and the Bill & Melinda Gates Foundation), and NGOs.

- Twenty-six percent of Americans aged 65 and older go online, compared with 67 percent of those aged 50–64, 80 percent of those aged 30–49, and 84 percent of those aged 18–29.
- Fifty-seven percent of African Americans go online, compared with 70 percent of whites.
- Twenty-nine percent of those who have not graduated from high school have access, compared with 61 percent of high school graduates and 89 percent of college graduates.
- Sixty percent of American adults who do not have a child living at home go online, compared with 83 percent of parents of minor children.

Other work shows that the information poor may opt increasingly for entertainment diversions rather than personal enrichment in the form of educational and other cultural resources, essentially mimicking Putnam's television effect. The result could be further fragmentation of community, an increasing sense of disengagement, and greater distrust of government and other institutions that need broad consensus to be effective (Dizard, 1999, p. 25). Certainly, we see remnants of all of these predictions and descriptions at play in communities today. But do these descriptive studies of "Netizen" behavior ignore more fundamental changes in communication patterns among citizens and the broader use of e-mail and other interactive Web tools in creating other kinds of communities?

The Problem of Technology and Community

While academics are comfortable describing who surfs and what they surf toward, they are less certain about the impact of this new technology on individuals, institutions, and communities. Because of its explosive development in the past ten years, claims about the Web's political impact have fallen into two broad camps, similar to those occupied by prophets and critics of older technologies. Some, for example, make populist claims that the Web will erode the influence of organized groups and knowledge elites, that the Web will cause a restructuring of community and social order (Bimber, 1998). Others see the Internet as protecting freedom: "Advances in the technology of telecommunications have proved an unambiguous threat to totalitarian regimes everywhere," argues media mogul Rupert Murdoch (Pavlick, 1998, p. 296). One wonders about cyberspace in Iraq.

A similarly exuberant vision describes Byte City, a postmodern, populist *Infosphere* where people from all over the world exchange ideas and thoughtfully govern themselves without national borders or confining social roles and expectations (Vlahos, 1998). Another describes new "flowering communities . . . where individuals shape their own community by choosing which other communities to belong to" (Jones, 1994b). A more negative prediction envisions the Web imitating the less savory elements of current political communication, creating a "centrifugal force in social organization" by encouraging more narrow specialization and fragmentation among factions of the electorate (Carey, 1998). Which way will it go? Are these utopian and apocalyptic visions our only options? Illustrating the pace of so-called Internet time already, some writers are lamenting the "taming of the frontier" of cyberspace. Are these studies confined by their attempts to show a reality that is simply today + technology, rather than Postman's observation that radical technologies ultimately yield something totally new and often unexpected in our social organization?

For good or ill, Pavlick (1998) argued, as the adoption and diffusion of new media technologies accelerate, social institutions are inexorably altered. The influences are varied and unpredictable, although certain common patterns emerge. These patterns include the sometimes contradictory forces of decentralization and multidirectional communication, as well as a drive for increased efficiency, productivity, and adaptability.

Writers in the nation's trade press claim that the Web will revolutionize the practice of politics (Noble, 1999; Selnow, 1998). Vendors, philanthropists, and political leaders at all levels claim that the "Information Superhighway" will change the nature of education as we know it (Ehrmann, 1999; Gates, 1999).

Expectations of revolution abound. Optimists also argue that new technologies hold the promise of improving public participation in the political process and reducing political alienation. On a practical level, they say, new technologies can make it easier to register voters using electronic means, or even allowing voting or public opinion polling by online methods (Pavlick, 1998, p. 293; Strama, 1998). Though some of these predictions seem silly in retrospect: the television as the national classroom; the life of armchair leisure as a result of electricity; a revolution in social organization as a result of the telephone—the way we live and communicate did change as a result of these new tools. People are generally incorrect when predicting what the future will look like as a result of technological change. Postman argues that our failure to make accurate predictions results from our adopting technologies (and the logic of its experts) without question, analysis, skepticism, or theoretical underpinning.

This unpromising track record in prediction has not stopped the proliferation of the expected utopian and dystopic literatures. From Gutenberg to Morse, and from ARPANET to Netscape, advances in communication technologies have always spawned these avalanches of prediction. And yet, technologies have always ultimately altered the geography of politics, governance, and social life through their widespread adoption. Communication technologies are not the only ones that result in impressive, unexpected change. Who could have predicted the revolutions in social life brought by such unlikely inventions as the stirrup, the telescope, and the clock? Postman (1992) convincingly argued that without the stirrup, there would have been no modern warfare; without the telescope, there would have been no physics or astronomy; and without the clock, there would have been no industrial capitalism. Each invention spawned a new way of thinking about time, space, theology, and communication. In essence, each of those innovations fundamentally altered our conception of acceptable social life and threatened old moral definitions.

Each innovation was met in its time with skepticism and fear by some and embraced with idealism and passion by others (Stephens, 1998). Each innovation demanded a reconsideration of communication, regulation, ownership, and conduct. And each innovation inevitably led to a series of related sociological changes. At the turn of the nineteenth century, Americans grappled with industrialization, the telephone, the telegraph, and electricity (Marvin, 1988). Today, we grapple with cyberspace. And we must grapple quickly.

The Problem of Politics and Young People

Those at the tip of the spear of technological innovation and adoption are Generation X, the young group said to be most disaffected from those activities likely to produce social capital. Douglas Coupland, the young author who named Generation X in his cult classic, *Generation X: Tales for an Accelerating Culture*, calls such derogatory comparisons *clique maintenance*. Clique maintenance is the tendency of one generation to malign the one that follows. The popular press and the political science literature give substantial credence to his theory. With such titles as *After the Boom* and *13th Generation: Abort, Retry, Ignore, Fail?* the die appears to be cast. The scholarly literature casts a similarly disparaging light on the younger generations, generally using voter turnout as the defining measure.

Crystallizing these derogatory approaches, Hart (2000) observed four prominent views of young people in politics, all of which operate on the assumption of youth as a threatening "other." Those models are as follows:

> *Youth as stranger.* Young people constitute a culture completely removed from adult society. They have their own values, language, tastes and interest—all of which cause them to be culturally disenfranchised and politically disinterested.
>
> *Youth as ideologue.* Young people cannot be trusted with democracy. They have bizarre political values and adopt extreme points of view; therefore, they are best left out of mainstream politics.
>
> *Youth as egocentric.* Young people care about nothing but themselves. They are rooted in the momentum and interested only in maximizing pleasure. As a result, they are immune to political appeals aimed at making society better.
>
> *Youth as distracted.* Young people are neither children nor adults but live in a borderline world devoid of serious concerns and moral obligations. According to this model, when young people come of age, they will regain their senses.

These models are persistent in discussions of "lifestyle effects" for low voter turnout among the young (Hout and Knoke, 1975; Cavanagh, 1981; Bennett, 1997; Lijphart, 1997). They are certainly at play in the laments of Boomer academics regarding Generation X (Bennett, 1997; Sacks, 1996). And, finally, all four models are encompassed in the persistent characterizations of young people as a lost political constituency (Hart, 2000). In essence, conventional political wisdom holds young people to be at best a hostile political audience, and, at worst, completely irrelevant to the political process. Though more subtle, these generational accusations echo through Putnam's tome as well. This dynamic is especially interesting as "youth" is a longer period of time than it used to be—with Baby Boomers characterizing "60 as the new 40," Generation X as deferring marriage and children until after 30 and middle-class Millennials "boomeranging" home from college to live with their parents as young adults.

Yet while the young are certainly refraining from voting and perhaps joining WWII era social clubs, numerous studies show a more complicated picture of this generation and perhaps foreshadow a new and emerging definition of citizenship. For example, studies from UCLA and Pew show that Generation X members volunteer in their communities at higher rates than previous twentieth-century generations (UCLA Higher Education Research Institute, 1998; Pew

Charitable Trusts, 2000). Hays (1998) conducted a focus group study of college students, finding that, contrary to more popular accounts, young people are not overwhelmingly angry, frustrated, and alienated. Rather, they are concerned about civic affairs and social issues but discouraged from participating by a lack of political experience and civic connectedness, and by the absence of galvanizing issues. The study also found a link to notions of efficacy—young people want to participate when they believe they can be effective. Further, recently published research on the so-called Millennial generation predicts an even greater community involvement among young people born after 1981 (Howe and Strauss, 2000).

While the literature on voter turnout shows a persistent downward trend since 1960, especially among younger cohorts (Bennett, 1997; Lijphart, 1997; Hays, 1998), recent UCLA data show that volunteerism, especially among the young, is operating at higher levels than in previous generations. Another study found that the "Generation X" cohort comprises at least two distinct camps of nonvoters, persons who differ markedly in their attitudes toward, and actions within, the public sphere—Doers and Uplugged (Shearer et al., 1998).[3] Unlike most nonvoters, Doers were substantially involved in either philanthropic work or political activity, ranging from contributing money to writing letters to the editor to expressing their views to their local congressman. Thwarting the popular image of cynical alienation, this group had a relatively upbeat view of institutions and of their own efficacy. They were not disengaged from public life, *only from the political act of voting.* "Traditional politics" and "engagement in public life" were not synonymous for this generation.

This dynamic—separating political involvement from civic involvement—is also present in nascent deliberations among the emerging High-Tech Elite, through such organizations and forums as the Austin 360 Summit and the Joint Venture Silicon Valley Network. Like their Industrial Era predecessors, some of the elite leaders of the high-tech sector are now turning to philanthropy. Early press accounts of their forays belie the bitter characterizations of their laissez-faire attitudes, but also point to the fundamental question for this study: are basic notions of citizenship changing, rendering Putnam's observations valuable but his metrics outdated?

[3] The other categories outlined in the study were Irritables, Don't knows, and Alienated. The majority of these categories comprised older Americans who choose not to vote.

The Problem of Old Measures

Forbes Magazine featured the young billionaire founder of Ebay on its cover, with the title "Ebay's Radical Do-Gooder: The Dot Com World Takes on the Charity Establishment." In describing his approach to philanthropy, Pierre Omidyar explained, "The idea of a community with difference and common responsibility has been lost in America. We want to bring it back." Yet he and other newly minted elites in their thirties are eschewing traditional Industrial Era charities in favor of building "social entrepreneurs," more consistent with their own values and incorporating the pace and metrics of the high-tech economy. Like the college students in Hays's study, they are interested in genuine personal involvement, a sharp distinction from the evolution of political and membership organizations during the twentieth century. Perhaps telegraphing the difficulty in new elites changing institutions, *USA Today* on September 19, 2002, ran an extensive article (by their standards) describing the frustrations of new corporate philanthropists in trying to change the Industrial Era public school system (Jones, 2002).

Richard Florida, who coined the phrase "creative class" as director of Carnegie Mellon's Software Industry Center, found that "[i]n an insecure, temporary, free-agent world, the crusaders of the new economy increasingly take their professional identities from where they live. . . . [P]eople are finding community in the real world . . . virtual communities are not enough, talent seeks out places with real assets" (Florida, 2000). He quotes one of his students as saying, "My work is a series of projects. My life is a series of moves. My parents had institutions that they connected to. What can I connect to? My community." Florida features the intensity of community, the notion that the young seek places "that feel the energy that fuels creativity around them." Florida's work portends an evolving definition of community— one that is intensely tied to work, to place, to friends, and to technology. Postman argued that culture ultimately surrenders to technology. Florida argues that the people who are living and working in the new technology fields are not surrendering. Rather, they are defining community in a fundamentally distinct and intense way.

This intensity stands in sharp contrast to Putnam's historical descriptions of formal and informal interactions within mid-century communities and more recent work by Skocpol (1999), who observes that patterns in American civic life have dramatically changed, from an emphasis on membership organizations to *advocacy* organizations. Where the great social clubs of the early part of the century were national, largely male, organizations with active local chapters whose members met regularly, they have been gradually replaced by national advocacy groups with professional staffs in Washington, DC, and large memberships characterized by persons who make annual financial contributions rather than attend weekly meetings. Akin to Hart's (1994) observation that television equates watching with participating, this move from local meetings to mailing a check equates *contributing* with participating. Early accounts of Gen X elites find that this abstract type of participation neither appeals to nor engages the young.

As members of the high-tech leadership explore their civic responsibility, their entrepreneurial roots demand action and tangible results from their personal and monetary investments. In my own work studying a group of High-Tech Elites assembled in Texas in 2000, their most common complaint about the political system was its abstractness and lack of accountability for measurable progress. Sentiments of this sort could also be found in the Progressive Era. Putnam found that civic actors at the time *created* the new civic institutions to help allay their discomfort with the impersonal nature of industrializing cities. The WWII generation *joined* those institutions rather than creating them reflecting their unique values about citizenship. Curiously, the most recent installment of Howe and Strauss's (2000) work on generations opined that Generation Y (the offspring of the "self-absorbed Baby Boomers") would be the new "civic generation." Like their WWII grandparents and great grandparents, they are allegedly going to be optimistic joiners. Someone will have to create those new institutions for them to join. This study indicates that it may well be the entrepreneurial members of Generation X.

And so we return to the basic question of this study: Are new citizenship values driving the participation, involvement, and philanthropy of these "cyber" generations and thereby changing how they live, what they value, and how they govern themselves? Have earlier scholars attempted to judge civic life by the scale of old life + technology, rather than adopting the insight Postman provides, which says that revolutionary technologies yield something fundamentally new? Do these changes require a theory of what it means to be a citizen in the twenty-first century?

To thoughtfully answer these questions, we must first examine traditional notions of citizenship and social capital. How has citizenship been conceived thus far? What standards do people use when judging what it means to be a "good citizen?"

2

History's Standards of Good Citizenship

To meaningfully assess the concept of citizenship in the age of the Internet, we need some idea of what citizenship has meant historically. That is, we need answers to the questions that have occupied the attention of philosophers, political scholars, and social scientists for thousands of years: What is citizenship? What constitutes a citizen? What do good citizens do? What do good citizens believe? These questions are wracked by tensions between ideas of individual entitlement and attachment to a particular community (Kymlicka and Norman, 1994) and a persistent mismatch between democratic theory and modern practices (Mueller, 1999). This section will attempt to outline a manageable set of propositions—useful for auditing conceptions of citizenship.

While some scholars have focused on citizenship as a legal construct—one measured by birth status, nationality, identity, or immigration—this review will focus on citizenship as a normative *activity*, a reflection of the attitudes, behaviors, and values present in the "good citizen." In particular, it will focus on the citizen as a *participant* (with varying degrees of responsibility and agency in the affairs of governance) rather than the citizen as *subject*, one who simply obeys the edicts of the state.

The literature on citizenship, democratic theory, and social capital is voluminous. This study will focus on two particular components. The first view is that of classic democratic theory, which addresses the relationship between *citizens and the state* and their respective responsibilities to each other, thereby wrestling with this question: what do citizens and states owe each other in a democratic system? The second view not only addresses those same democratic concerns, but also contemplates the relationship that citizens have to one another and to community organizations and institutions, drawing from the landmark work of the *Civic Culture* (1960) to more contemporary observations about social capital in the United States (Putnam, 2000).

In his concise history of democracy, Dahl (1999) explores the dilemma of citizen participation versus system effectiveness: the smaller a democratic unit, the greater its potential for citizen participation and the less the need for citizens to delegate government decisions to representatives. The larger the unit, the greater its capacity for dealing with problems important to its citizens and the greater the need for citizens to delegate decisions to representatives. These questions are persistent questions in democratic thought: What is the role (or should be the role) of the individual citizen in a large, mature democratic system? What is the appropriate level of citizen participation in the affairs of state?

While Dahl focused on citizen *activity*, Galston (1991) explored what animates citizen behavior, positing a set of virtues allegedly guiding civic behaviors (table 2.1).

The *Civic Culture* combines the approaches of Dahl and Galston. Using survey data and conducting interviews in five democratic countries, the authors sought to define and quantify the nature of "civic culture." They defined civic culture as the actions and beliefs that citizens in these nations felt were a part of their responsibilities to their democratic regimes. More specifically, "political knowledge and skill and feelings and value orientations toward political objects and processes—toward the political system as a whole, toward *the self* as participant, toward political parties and election, bureaucracy and the like" (Almond and Verba, 1960, p. 27, emphasis added).

Table 2.1   Galston's Virtues of Citizenship

Virtues	Attributes
General	• Law-abidingness • Courage • Loyalty
Social	• Independence • Open-mindedness
Economic	• Work ethic • Capacity to delay gratification adaptability to economic and technological change
Political	• Capacity to discern and respect the rights of others; • Willingness to demand only what can by paid for • Ability to evaluate the performance of those in office • Willingness to engage in public discourse

The study examined cognitive, affective, and evaluative characteristics of citizens. *Cognitive* refers to knowledge about government and politics. *Affective* refers to feeling toward political objects. Finally, *evaluative* refers to judgment about political objects that combine cognitive and affective elements. All three elements are inherent in Galston's political virtues. Further, citizens in stable democracies have high levels of subjective political competence (people believe they know enough about the workings of the political system to affect it) and interpersonal trust, believing in the inherent honesty of their fellow citizens.

In addition to citizens' possessing Galston's virtues, Dahl's political knowledge and Almond and Verba's evaluative characteristics, authors have found that the viability of democracies and democratic institutions depended on *certain* civic attitudes, particularly a sense of efficacy about an individual's ability to affect the workings of government. In addition to this sense of efficacy, they found that in stable democracies people generally felt that the system was legitimate (consistent with enunciated democratic values) and that other citizens were essentially trustworthy.

Subsequent authors have found that elements of citizenship concern the ability to tolerate and work together with others who are different from oneself; a desire to participate in the political process to promote the public good; a willingness to hold elected officials accountable and a willingness to show self-restraint and exercise personal responsibility in their economic demands in personal choices (Kymlicka and Norman, 1994).

From *Civic Culture*, the attitudes that citizens must have toward one another and to the regime are

- interpersonal trust;
- political efficacy;
- political knowledge;
- desire to participate toward the public good; and
- belief in the legitimacy of the regime.

Work in social capital adds another element—participation in voluntary associations. Putnam argues that these informal webs of human connection are closely tied to personal satisfaction and to the ability of communities to function. Beyond participation in the political affairs of the nation and community, Putnam sees more general participation in a broad range of interpersonal and social interactions as key to building generalized social trust, a conclusion that echoes Almond and Verba's finding that interpersonal trust is a key to civic culture and increases civic participation.

Within each of these traditions are explorations of what good citizens *do*, what good citizens *know*, and what good citizens *believe*. Drawing from those literatures and informed by a small focus group, I have constructed the following categories of historically "good citizens" in the United States. These categories fall along a continuum based on the level of civic and political activity and political knowledge demanded of citizens, beginning with a definition that requires very little activity from citizens, progressing through categories that demand much more activity and knowledge. The categories are as follows

- passive minimalists;
- attentive minimalists;
- typical citizens;
- civic leaders; and
- activists.

Passive Minimalists

Within democratic theory, a minimal level of citizenship is posited—citizens should obey the law and vote. This notion of citizenship is a component of the most passive tradition, that of social citizenship. This theory enunciates an obligation on the part of the state not found in the liberal tradition and broadens the scope of "rights." This position argues that because citizens are loyal to the state, the state owes certain services to the citizen as a right in return (Oliver and Heater, 1994). In Kymlicka and Norman (1994), citizenship rights are divided into three categories: (1) civil rights; (2) political rights; and (3) social rights.

In this context, the perfect expression of citizenship is the liberal-democratic welfare state, because it ensures that every member of a society *feels like* a full member and is able to participate in and enjoy its common life. Therefore, citizenship in this tradition requires a state to provide a minimal standard of living for its citizens and to afford them a sense of efficacy within their society.

In essence, this view of citizenship is inherently passive, focused on the rights of the citizen ensured by the state and the services it provides, rather than on the responsibilities of citizens to participate in their own governance. Within Galston's framework of civic virtues, the minimalist citizen explicitly possesses the general virtues of law abidingness and loyalty. Combining this notion of democratic citizenship with the baseline attitudes of civic culture, the most basic elements of democratic citizenship are

- belief in democratic values;
- trusting the legitimacy of the regime;
- voting;
- obeying the law; and
- being tolerant of other views.

Attentive Minimalists

Next on the continuum of activism is the liberal tradition. This approach suggests that a "legal contract" exists between a government and its people in which governments must allow citizens two important things—access to just laws and the right to vote. While this definition requires that states provide citizens with rights, it does not instill a reciprocal obligation in citizens that they use these rights by actively *participating* in the system of governance (Oliver and Heater, 1994). Here, a good citizen is one who simply abides by the law and who votes but does not expect the state to provide extensive services or financial security.

Pateman (1970) characterizes liberal theory as espousing "institutional arrangements," observing that "[t]he social inequalities of the political culture of the liberal democracies are treated as separate from, and irrelevant to, the formal equality of citizenship" (p. 59). The political culture—the informal space where citizens interact with each other when discussing the issues of the day outside of formal structures—is not contemplated in this tradition, nor is the obligation of the state to provide services to citizens. Rather, the citizen is ascribed a well-defined but minimal role focusing on the role of selecting representatives and exercising the vote as protective device against overreaching or corruption by the representatives (Pateman, 1970). Essentially, citizens/voters seek to *influence* public decisions rather than *participate* in them.

A more contemporary offering within the liberal tradition is Schudson's (1998) notion of "the monitoring citizen." As he traced notions of democratic participation in the United States from the time of the American Revolution to the present, Schudson noted an ebb and flow of participation and, as a result, advanced a current definition for the Information Age—a citizen is one who *follows* public affairs, even if he does not actively participate in them.

In his critique of classical democratic theory, Schumpeter (1943) argues that it simply demands too much of citizens. He asserts what he believes is a more realistic model in which democracy becomes a method whereby dynamic leaders *compete* for citizens' votes and where citizens respond to the alternatives presented to them. In his view, this method works because it places responsibility for the effectiveness of a regime on its ambitious leaders (acting in their self-interest) and requires just one action from citizens—that they vote.

Skocpol (1999) recently noted that political organizations in the United States have evolved from local meetings to national membership organizations, where citizens across the country make monetary contributions but where professional staffs based in Washington, DC, conduct political *activities* on their members' behalf. While these active minimalist citizens are perhaps not living up to the Aristotelian ideal of civic virtue, they are *intellectually* (if not physically) engaged in the political life of the nation. This category also adds social and political values from Galston's framework—independence and ability to evaluate the performance of those in office. Building activity from the passive minimalists, the attentive or active minimalists engage in the civic activities such as

- believe in democratic values;
- trust the legitimacy of the regime;
- vote;
- obey the law;
- are tolerant of other views;
- make few demands on the state;
- are aware of political affairs; and
- join/contribute to organizations.

Typical Citizens

Ordinary, middle-class Americans are the topic of countless political speeches. In political discourse they are the backbone of the democracy and the workhorses of communities. They are the Americans studied by Almond and Verba. Several scholars have observed that the expansion of the middle class creates a more hospitable environment for truly participatory democracy. Aristotle called for political friendliness, partnership, and political restraint. Dahl observed that the middle class tends to be efficacious without having large claims on the government. Habermas (1991) argued that the expansion of the bourgeois class—a propertied class that actually has the education, experience, and leisure time to meaningfully engage in deliberation—is central to the development of the public sphere. De Toqueville (2001) observed that middle-class Americans exhibited the "temperance, moderation and self-command" and "animated moderation" necessary for successful democratic engagement. This view of citizenship as civic virtue, broad and thoughtful participation of the middle class in their own governance, is perhaps the most typical characterization of American notions of citizenship.

A central finding of Almond and Verba (1960) was that in essence a myth of efficacy existed in mature democracies, especially in the United States. This sort of myth is a delicate balance between belief in the ability of the common man to impact governmental affairs but without the willingness to test that belief by actually attempting to participate. This balance, they argue, is key to the stability of modern democracies and is rooted in individual perception more than in systemic concerns. "If an individual believes he has influence, he is more likely to use it. A subjectively competent citizen, therefore [in the original] is likely to be an active citizen. . . . The extent to which citizens in a nation perceive themselves as competent to influence the government affects their political behavior. . . . [F]urthermore, the existence of a *belief* in the influence, may affect the political systems even if it does not affect the activity of the ordinary man" (p. 139).

This myth appears to explain the persistent mismatch between classical democratic theory and the relatively efficient operation of stable democratic governments. Citizens believe that they *can* participate in their own governance but seldom feel compelled to do so. Therefore, the ideological benefits of classical theory are compatible with the practical realities of the operation of the state. In such a scheme, democracies realize the benefit of efficacy and the legitimacy it creates in the minds of citizens without the disruption caused by widespread participation and activism on the citizens' part. Some argue that the immediacy of Internet communication could jeopardize this balance.

Conover et al. (1991) used focus groups to understand citizens' perception of citizenship. They found that the meaning of citizenship is far more complex and ambiguous than suggested in the common delineation between liberal (individualistic) and communitarian (collective) ethics. According to their findings, American citizens actually combine these two ethics, participating in community and political activities but participating for mainly individualistic reasons rather than for civic motives. This finding led to the observation that it is possible to have some of the benefits of communitarianism in a basically liberal, individualistic polity. This broadest category of citizenship not only encompasses the activities of the more minimal views, but it also adds additional economic and political virtues from Galston's matrix: the economic virtue of the work ethic and the willingness to engage in public discourse and community involvement. Typical citizens show their citizenship by engaging in the following:

- believe in democratic values;
- trust the legitimacy of the regime;
- vote;
- obey the law;
- are tolerant of other views;
- make few demands on the state;
- are aware of political affairs;
- join/contribute to organizations;
- personally participate in community organizations; and
- participate to some degree in their own governance.

Civic Leaders

The responsibility of citizens to *participate* in public affairs—civic virtue—is imbedded in the classical tradition of democratic theory. This conceptualization moves beyond the passive citizen who abides by the law and who ratifies the action of the state and demands *intellectual activity* on the part of citizens (Oliver and Heater, 1994). The classical tradition also emphasizes a sense of *obligation* not contemplated by the social model, which focuses on the state's provision of goods and services.

This view features normative constraints on the behavior of citizens, imploring them to embrace "civic virtue." Aristotle and Rousseau, in particular, advanced definitions illustrating these reciprocal obligations. Citizens are those who share in the civic life of ruling and who are being ruled in turn, said Aristotle. Those who are associated in (the body politic) take the name of a *people* and call themselves *citizens* in so far as they share in sovereign power, said Rousseau.

The notion of *shared power* and responsibility first appears in this tradition, requiring more from citizens than mere voting participation (liberal tradition) or the exchange of allegiance for social benefits (social model). The ability to meaningfully engage in true citizenship is often tied to the emergence of a broad middle class, which is ironic given the Greek's contempt for labor and economic virtues (Aristotle, 1943).

Fishkin (1995) provides a more specific operationalization of citizenship. He takes these values and applies a particular deliberative structure to citizen participation in public affairs. His ideas encourage a system of small-scale politics. Such a system is reminiscent of the definition of citizenship in classical tradition: citizens should (1) become educated on political topics; (2) deliberate on current events; and (3) act as a recommending force in national politics. Scholars evaluating the outcomes of Fishkin's National Issues Convention found various effects, but two of the most promising were as follows: first, that participants' views became more moderate as a result of their deliberations; and secondly, that their language grew appreciably more *collective* the longer they discussed issues with their fellow citizens (Hart and Jarvis, 1999).

Sartori (1987) views the quality of elites (what he calls the *vertical* dimension of democracy) as the more important goal of democratic processes, as opposed to the mobilization or participatory models that feature increased voter participation (horizontal aspects). While voting and participation are important, Sartori asserts, it is more important to the functioning of a democratic state that their participation yields *the selection of competent and effective leaders.* This most sophisticated category of citizen encompasses all of Galston's virtues and represents the ideal democratic citizen. Civic leaders, in this model:

- believe in democratic values;
- trust the legitimacy of the regime;
- vote;
- obey the law;
- are tolerant of other views;
- make few demands on the state;
- are aware of political affairs;
- actively participate in political affairs;
- lead community organizations;
- participate to some degree in their own governance; and
- select competent leaders.

Activists

Activists are those citizens who spend the most time engaged in community and political pursuits. In her study of political "sophisticates," Herbst (1998) found that while cynicism had increased among political actors, the most optimistic were partisan political operatives and volunteers. By examining "lay theories" of democracy, she uncovered "stereotypes" that these actors deployed in their political lives: "The interpretation of meaning in the political world is individual and cultural at the same time" (p. 24). Even those operatives who were in minority parties or chronically on the losing side of elections were found to have a strong sense of optimism and patriotism. This finding is consistent with literature on social capital, which finds that social involvement breeds increased feelings of efficacy. Brehm and Rahn (1997) found a "tight reciprocal relationship" between participation and interpersonal trust, where the stronger causal effects are from participation to trust (i.e., the more citizens participate, the greater their levels of interpersonal trust). Interpersonal trust is a critical component of civic culture.

While these activists exhibit many of the attributes of democratic citizenship, some theorists argue that such high levels of activism are actually damaging to democracy. For example, Huntington (1975) argued against the "excess" of democracy and urged a *moderation* of democracy. He and Sartori (1987) cited examples from the United States in the 1960s, where governmental *activity* was expanded but where governmental *authority* declined. Concurrently, street-level democracy among the young increased, in their view, thereby damaging the stability of democracy. Huntington christened such a confluence as a "democratic distemper." Because democratic procedures can undermine the *efficiency* of a regime, Huntington believed, "the effective operation of a democratic political system usually *requires some measure of apathy and noninvolvement* on the part of some individuals and groups" (p. 37).

By Galston's criteria, activists, while engaged, sometimes do not exhibit the democratic virtues of less active citizens. In the name of resistance and dissent they disobey the law. In pursuit of their views, they can be politically narrow and myopic, closing their minds to the arguments of others. While they exhibit willingness to engage in political activity, they often ignore the rights of others, make unrealistic demands on the state, and mistake activism for discourse. Thus, activists represent a unique segment of the citizenry—engaged, participatory, and often optimistic—yet, missing other virtues *classically* required for good citizenship.

These studies show notions of citizenship to be a complex mix of roles and responsibilities with respect to the state, tied to a belief in an individual's capacity to bring about change, but also related to interactions that have little to do with politics or governance. The activist

- believes in democratic values;
- votes;
- is aware of political affairs;
- organizes citizens in pursuit of political/social change;
- creates community organizations; and
- actively participates in political/legislative activities in pursuit of specific policy goals.

As these definitions and models suggest, political thinkers have varied in their conceptions of citizenship as well as the desirable amount of participation in a democratic system. While some hold that citizen involvement helps to legitimize a democratic system through voting, others claim that democracies run more smoothly—and efficiently—without much citizen participation. There is an acknowledged mismatch between ideal characterizations of citizenship—and the demands it places on individual citizens—and the reality of the attention span and capacities of citizens to meaningfully engage as democratic theory opines they should. Table 2.2 summarizes the categories of citizenship advanced in this chapter.

Table 2.2 Categories of Citizenship

Category	Virtues	Civic Activities
Passive minimalist	• Law-abidingness • Open-mindedness	• Vote
Active minimalist	• Law-abidingness • Open-mindedness • Independence • Work ethic • Ability to evaluate the performance of leaders	• Vote • Awareness of political affairs • Contribute to organizations
Typical citizens	• Law-abidingness • Open-mindedness • Independence • Work ethic • Ability to evaluate the performance of leaders • Willingness to engage in public discourse	• Vote • Awareness of political affairs • Contribute to organizations • Personally participate in community affairs • Personally participate minimally in political matters
Civic leaders	• Law-abidingness • Open-mindedness • Independence • Work ethic	• Vote • Awareness of political affairs • Contribute to organizations • Lead community and political organizations

Continued

Table 2.2   Continued

Category	Virtues	Civic Activities
	• Ability to evaluate the performance of leaders • Willingness to engage in public discourse	• Select competent leaders
Activists	• Willingness to engage in public discourse	• Vote • Awareness of political affairs • Contribute to organizations • Organize in pursuit of political/social change • Create organizations

There is obviously something complicated going on within notions of citizenship at the turn of the twentieth century. Where even the most limited conception of classical citizenship posits that citizens should vote, more contemporary realities shed light on a kind of citizenship not necessarily linked to traditional political activity or relations with the state. In a number of studies, it was found that although contemporary young people were chronic nonvoters, they served as volunteers. High-Tech Elites are creating innovative new philanthropies but cannot name their U.S. senators. Is the definition of citizenship in the United States now something different than it was in the past? What does it mean for the nation when the slogan "Think Globally. Act Locally" leaves no room for acting as a nation or in relationship to a state?

While these varied definitions of citizenship are disparate and confusing, a common element lies within each: *reciprocity*. In democratic theory, reciprocal obligation exists in varying degrees between citizens and the state. In civic culture and social capital approaches, reciprocal obligations exist between individuals and institutions—and among individual citizens themselves. While reciprocity is a deceptively simple concept, a review of the wide-ranging literature shows it to be a powerful norm and present in countless human interactions, and, as such, it may provide insight into changing conceptions of contemporary citizenship. This research also illustrates that discomfort ensues when the norms of reciprocity are violated, perhaps providing some insight and explanation for the negativity that Americans feel about civic life at the turn of the millennium.

Reciprocity

At its most basic level, reciprocity is the rule that says one should try to repay, in kind, what another has provided (Cialdini, 1984). This simple idea has spawned a wide-ranging literature, from dyadic interpersonal encounters to geopolitical concerns of international trade and super-power negotiations. Scholars have studied the concept in areas such as game theory, economics, biology, sociology, and psychology.

In his seminal article exploring the concept, Goulder (1960) claimed that reciprocity is at the heart of all human cultures, a "primordial imperative, which pervades every relation of primitive life" (p. 161). He christened it a powerful social norm and maintained that reciprocity connotes rights and duties for each party that embraces two interrelated demands: (1) people should help those who have helped them; and (2) people should not injure those who helped them. The key social engine of this norm is a sense of obligation or indebtedness that arises from a gift given or deed done.

This obligation perpetuates norms of negotiation (Fisher and Ury, 1983), is related to attitude change (Groves et al., 1992), and is often illustrated through examples of game theory (Sopher, 1994; Axelrod, 1984). These theorists also underscore a host of political norms, from reciprocity of concession (Cialdini, 1984) to reciprocity in social norms and dilemmas (Komorita and Hilty, 1991). Basically, this norm operates among individuals, within communities and societies, lies at the heart of political negotiation, and is addressed in a range of literatures, including interpersonal, conflict resolution, self-disclosure, negotiation, bargaining, and leadership (Boyle and Lawler, 1991).

Research on individuals has found that reciprocity is a basic norm of interaction, undergirding concepts such as altruism, social responsibility, bargaining, and exchange (Komorita and Hilty, 1991)—the very building blocks of social capital and the most basic tenet of democratic citizenship. Cialdini (1984) reminds us that one of the positive byproducts of the act of concession is a feeling of greater engagement and a heightened sense of responsibility, enabling people to fulfil agreements and engage in further agreements. Obviously, the primary and secondary effects of this norm play a considerable role in individual citizenship and in the more generalized reciprocity (not person-to-person, but person-to-society) that builds social capital.

This more generalized concept of reciprocity lies at the heart of arguments about both democratic citizenship and social capital. Quigley (1996) argues that social capital and trust develop though norms of reciprocity and successful cooperation in networks of civic engagement, which provide the necessary human sinew for democracy to work, activity that becomes a socially stabilizing exchange mechanism.

Putnam sees social capital built through the reciprocal exchange of involvement among individuals in civic and social pursuits—from political organizations to the now famed bowling leagues. He characterizes these arrangements as a dense network of secondary associations that builds trust and cooperation among people and that lays the groundwork for a liberal democracy of reasonable people to function (Strike, 1988).

Civic Culture found that people organize politically in informal groups and that the ability to create those associations and engage them to affect a political decision is key to political efficacy. Further, Almond and Verba found that some sort of participation was integral to building interpersonal trust, a fundamental building block of social capital and stable democracies.

Rucinski (1991) defined reciprocity somewhat differently, as more the shared knowledge of the perspectives of others and also the interests underlying those perspectives. Rather than a tit-for-tat arrangement among individuals, she operationalized reciprocity as the ratio of perspective and underlying interests known to the members of a collective. In a sense, she argued that political knowledge—especially that of others' views—is a necessary condition for societal reciprocity. Here, rather than a gut-level norm, reciprocity becomes a knowledge-based negotiation of shared political power and influence among social actors, individuals, and groups. The bottom line appears to be that the norm of reciprocity—whether individual favors or generalized social trust—requires *activity* and *trust* on the part of social and political actors. Interpersonal trust and participation are the key findings of the *Civic Culture* as fundamental components of a healthy democracy—and are inherent in Galston's matrix of civic virtues.

While these scholars make a compelling case for the virtuous cycle of reciprocity and social capital, can norms of reciprocity also explain the cynical cycle that Americans seem to have embraced with respect to civic activity today? The notion of "citizen as free rider" (Olson, 1965) was recently explored by Raadschelders (1995), who claimed that contemporary citizen participation, particularly the demand and rights-oriented activism of special interest groups, highlight the "true problem of our time"—*a lack of reciprocity between government and citizen.* This dearth of reciprocity, he argues, explains dissatisfaction with government, declining participation and demand overload for governments. In a sense, he argues that the welfare state that provides communal benefits yet asks little from citizens in return has changed citizen participation from a moral duty to a civil right, a right that does not necessarily imply a sense of mutual responsibility. Recall that several scholars have found that civic engagement breeds additional engagement and activity. Might this insight predict the inverse? That is, if reciprocity animates social capital, could this same norm accelerate a decline in social capital as "entitled" people make demands without concessions? Thus, does this "free rider" phenomenon then elicit a reciprocal response—equally entitled and uncivic? In the same way that reciprocity animated by generosity builds social capital, does reciprocity animated by cynical sentiments of entitlement deplete social capital for the very same reasons? Could this deceptively simple norm help explain the cause for the conditions Putnam described? Could the changing definitions of citizenship and participation, attended to by technological innovation provide the mechanisms to reverse this vicious cycle of decline in social capital?

These questions can only be addressed by comparing the definitions employed by new, young constituencies to traditional conceptions of citizenship. To recap, the following are traditional American civic actors:

- passive minimalists;
- active minimalists;
- typical Citizens, Putnam's league bowlers;
- civic leaders; and
- activists.

Although the level of knowledge and civic activity encompassed in each of these categories vary, they all include a basic belief in democratic values, a willingness to vote and to obey the law (with the exception of the activists).

Informed by these auditing standards, we can now consider how best to assess contemporary young citizens in the Information Age. Where do these new elites fall along this continuum of citizenship in the United States? Do young high-tech actors employ similar attitudes, attributes, knowledge, and values as traditional democratic citizens? Or are they, like their Progressive Era forebears, creating new definitions and institutions of civic life that reflect a fundamentally different era?

Popular accounts portray a young, disengaged monolithic high-tech community—passive minimalists ostensibly—disengaged from public life and focused on the pursuits of youth. Yet similar accounts show a near obsession with technology—whether games, toys, or tools—that might cast them more in the mold of single-minded activists who are focused on their own narrow interests and convinced of the superiority of their priorities and causes.

While coverage of young tech workers tends toward the pejorative, recent articles of High-Tech Elites—leaders such as eBay Omyidar and Papermaster's Alpha 360 Summit—perhaps portend a move into civic leadership. These leaders are starting philanthropic foundations. They are publicly pondering their civic duty. High-tech names are turning up on boards for the art museum, symphony, and opera. In Austin, Texas several prominent high-tech leaders have been visible and active in a recent (unsuccessful) campaign to fund light rail. Tech leaders are even beginning to launch civic institutions such as the Austin Entrepreneurs Foundation and Silicon Valley Action Network. Could these activities animate a contemporary virtuous cycle of reciprocity among the young?

While these activities may seem the nascent enterprises of fledgling civic leaders, some have accused these leaders of being self-congratulatory and self-serving. Critics see tech companies giving away computers in order to increase the demand for their company's software or espousing an expensive light rail solution, hoping that others would take public transportation so that the highways would be clear for them to more freely drive their new Porsches. Perhaps they are minimalist capitalists—or capitalist/activists—lacking the civic spirit of their Rotary Club predecessors, exhibiting the wealth of civic leaders, but maintaining the juvenile temperament of activists. What kind of new citizens might these actors be?

While I worked on this book, I gave a speech to the Sunrise Rotary Club at quarter to seven in the morning in Georgetown, Texas. There, about 40 Baby Boomer men between the ages of 45 and 60 had gathered for their weekly ritual. There were two women as well, one a guest of her husband; all assembled to hear from "the girl from the Governor's office." They began the meeting promptly with the pledge of allegiance and a short Christian prayer. Then they took turns putting a dollar in a basket accompanied by a testimonial about a good thing that had happened that week. Then, business. Pledges for the golf tournament to raise scholarship money. The raging debate about whether to open a second high school. Then me. There was a nostalgic sweetness and sincerity to them. They seemed to me to embody

Putnam's notions of social capital—gathering regularly. Doing good. And there was absolutely no connection between their leisurely sunrise rituals and the world I live in. Is it a national tragedy (as Putnam asserts) that these morning gatherings of Rotarian men have declined? Might a new generation be creating new institutions and norms more reflective of their values and life experiences? Could they be creating a new definition of citizenship?

As cynicism grips our national psyche, fed by a steady diet of late-night television hosts well schooled in the language of ironic detachment, mere descriptions of mass disengagement are not enough. To name and quantify changes in the patterns in which we communicate and socialize is only part of the work. As Postman so elegantly argued in *Technopoly*, radical technologies ultimately change everything—they do not yield the status quo plus a new technology. Are we experiencing a revolutionary change akin to those of the printing press, the clock, or electricity?

In the words of Barbara Jordan at the Democratic National Convention in 1992, the convention that nominated the nation's first Baby Boomer president, "Change. Change. All this talk of change. The question is 'from what, to what?'" From what? We know. To what? This study asks.

3

Assessing Contemporary Citizenship: The Case for Qualitative Methods

Assessing citizenship is a complicated matter. As the literature I have reviewed here suggests, citizenship involves a complex interplay of virtues, attitudes, knowledge, and behaviors. Such complexity and depth invites a qualitative approach to studies in this area.

Why Qualitative Methods?

Studies on the Web, social capital, and Generation X have been awash in a range of quantitative data. For example, more recent research on the Web has been quantitative in nature, focusing on who is on the Web, who is not on the Web, the demographics of surfers, and the content of Web sites. What little scholarly work that has been undertaken on Generation X has largely focused on either voter turnout or basic survey instruments, such as analyses of the National Election Survey. Such studies have generally provided support for the conventional wisdom of "clique maintenance" and lifestyle effects. Those studies that have yielded more insightful and original findings have been qualitative in nature, employing either focus groups or long interviews.

According to Meloy (1994), qualitative methods are most useful and powerful when they are used to discover how a respondent sees the world.

Because this study seeks to understand how high-tech actors think about citizenship, qualitative methods provide the most effective mechanism.

At the heart of Postman's critique of the contemporary "Technopoly" is that the "hurried and mindless" adoption of radical technologies—especially computer technologies that leave us "awash in information"—happens in the absence of new theory. In essence, he argues that in a Technopoly, "[our] [culture's] available theories do not offer guidance about what is acceptable information" (p. 8). Further, he argues, the "experts" in technology unconsciously imbue the culture with their own ideology, which in Postman's mind is driven by the technology in which they are most skilled and privileged. This study attempts to build a theory of citizenship and civic life in the Information Age. To do so requires listening to those who are animating the radical technology of our times—and listening to them in a fashion that enables them to speak their own language and enables us to discern their implicit theories and philosophies of citizenship.

In their study of political attitudes, Conover et al. (1991) argued that what is needed now is research that explores the *actual self-understandings of citizens* and that directly addresses the contemporary debates in political philosophy, particularly the tension between liberal and communitarian claims. This tension is implicit in writings on social capital. The most effective qualitative tool for such a complex exploration is the long interview.

The Long Interview

The purpose of this study is to determine the "cultural logic" that high-tech actors bring to politics, particularly with respect to traditional notions of citizenship and social capital (McCracken, 1988). Said McCracken (1988), "The long interview is one of the most powerful methods in the qualitative armory. For certain descriptive and analytic purposes, no instrument of inquiry is more revealing. The method can take us into the mental world of the individual, to glimpse the categories and logic by which he or she sees the world. . . . The long interview gives us the opportunity to step into the mind of another person, to see and experience the world as they do themselves . . . and to allow respondents to tell their own story in their own terms" (pp. 9, 34).

Because one of the central hypotheses of this study is that Putnam and others have used outdated measures to judge contemporary actors, such a personal approach is critical. Accordingly, this study will focus on three subsets of the "high-tech community" and a group of young people who have grown up in the age of ubiquitous technology—college-educated people born after 1975.

Respondents

According to McCracken (1988), the first principle is "less is more": it is more important to work longer and with greater care with a few people than more superficially with many of them. The reasoning here is that a more in-depth approach provides one with a glimpse of the complicated character, organization, and logic of culture. Further, as methodologists in grounded theory observe, the "right" number of respondents typically presents itself during the data collection process—theory development halts when the interviewer is no longer hearing anything novel (Herbst, 1998).

To create a topology of the high-tech community, I created four categories of respondents, three of which represent occupational segments of the high-tech sector. These are largely a priori categories, but represented natural professional demarcations among a larger list of high-tech actors. To operationalize the notion of high-tech actor I created a list of high-tech occupations drawn from the weekly technology section of the *Austin American Statesman*. This section featured news and human interest stories about people in high-tech professions as well as an employment section that included want-ads for technology sector occupations. I grouped these stories and job categories by the nature of the work demanded. There were high-profile entrepreneurs who had started companies. Those who were active in technology-related policy and civic and community debates who were frequently covered by the paper. Finally, the want-ads provided a laundry list of hands-on technical occupations. Essentially, I wanted to examine both elites and workers of the contemporary high-tech economy. Once a list was drawn from that coverage, I contacted the office of each member of that list, and frankly, those who agreed to answer the survey by e-mail and undertake an in-depth interview that promised to take between 60 and 90 minutes became my Cyber-democrat and Tech Elite respondents. Elites were those who had started companies or who held executive-level positions in technology companies. Cyber-democrats were those who either led civic enterprises related to technology or who held government-related positions in technology companies.

This convenience sample could certainly indicate a bias toward those who were interested in these topics. However, this study does not claim to a representative sample of Generation X or the High-Tech community. Rather, it aims, through deploying a more qualitative methodology to a subset of a generational and occupational group that had been studied only in cursory and quantitative ways historically—to unearth a more complicated story that seemed to play out in popular accounts of young high-tech actors, but had been largely ignored in scholarly accounts to date.

In creating a list and contacting respondents for the Wirehead category, I listed the types of hands-on technical work described in technical want-ads in the same section of the local newspaper. These tasks were more varied: consultants, network administrators, information systems coordinators, software developers, Web designers, technology support, and even "Geek Wanted" solicitations. I sought to find a representative of each type of hands-on technical work, then asking other respondents (and a committee member) for recommendations from those categories. As with the Cyber-democrat and Tech Elite respondents, there was a "convenience factor"—I called and explained the project, and those who agreed to participate became respondents. Where Tech Elites were difficult to recruit because of their stature and schedules, Wireheads were difficult to recruit because they had some reservations about the topic. In two cases, other Wirehead respondents "vouched for me" and encouraged those they knew who fit the demographic and professional profile to participate.

The fourth category comprises young people, born after 1975, who would have no recollection of life prior to ubiquitous access to contemporary technology in the United States. These respondents were drawn from an undergraduate course at the University of Texas and from the undergraduate intern pool at the Office of the Governor.

I interviewed 10 respondents per category, with demographic diversity being sought within categories where possible. To recap, the categories are as follows:

Cyber-democrats. These are individuals who are working with contemporary technologies in the civic or political space, including entrepreneurs leading election-related enterprises and those holding government-related positions with technology companies.

Wireheads. These respondents are mid-level to junior, nonmanagerial technical workers, including corporate and public sector programmers, technical support personnel, technology consultants, Web designers, and network administrators.

High-Tech Elites. These are corporate leaders of high-tech enterprises (hardware, software, Internet, etc.) who have been featured in local newspaper accounts over the past year for entrepreneurial leadership and civic involvement.

Trailing Xers. Like asking fish to describe the experience of being in water, this category comprises the youngest cohort of Generation X-Y; they are respondents under the age of 26 who have grown up with ubiquitous access to contemporary technologies. Simply put, these young, college-educated respondents have no knowledge or experience of a home, school, or community without the presence of contemporary information technology.

By parsing the high-tech community, this study can explore questions such as these:

- Compared to other accounts of demographically similar actors, how do Generation X high-tech actors differ in their civic, social, and political attitudes, behaviors and knowledge?
- Within the high-tech community, how do these groups compare to one another?
- While conventional wisdom and popular accounts portray a monolithic high-tech community and Generation X, are they, in reality, diverse in their civic attitudes and behaviors?

To explore those questions, I used an interview guide that had two sections.

The Interview Protocol

The interview protocol used for this study was divided into two basic sections, each designed to explore different aspects of civic outlook, attitudes, and knowledge. It begins with a survey guide of approximately 30 questions, which included basic demographic data and questions on a range of political variables drawn from Delli Carpini (1996) and the National Election Study. In some cases, these were answered by e-mail. These responses also generated data that have been compared to national norms, including data for the following variables:

- demographics;
- political knowledge;
- political efficacy;
- voting; and
- participation.

The second section of the interview guide allowed for deeper exploration of a respondent's worldview, civic behaviors, attitudes, and beliefs about citizenship and civic participation. Many of the questions were drawn from *Civic Culture* and from the measures used by Putnam to illustrate his views on the decline of social capital in the United States.

This mix of closed and open-ended questions helped flesh out critical questions, such as these: What kind of citizens are these high-tech actors? As what kind of citizens do they see themselves? Do they fit into one of the categories of traditional American approaches to citizenship outlined in chapter 2? Or are they creating their own definition of twenty-first century citizenship?

Analyzing the Data

The interview data was analyzed using an approach to qualitative research that draws from Glaser and Strauss's (1967) work in grounded theory. I employed an emergent coding process, defined as a process of identifying categories of meaning by looking for similarities in the data. I augmented this process with two focus groups representing two of the sample categories, which were used to help derive coding categories for the long interview data. From these data, I have attempted to advance a contemporary theory of citizenship and social capital among younger generations for the Information Age.

Grounded Theory

As Glaser and Strauss argue, grounded theories are produced inductively, with the researcher engaged in multiple tasks simultaneously—data collection, analysis, and theory building. These multiple activities move this study well beyond description. Rather than simply an account of an interesting group of people at a point in time opining about things public, this study attempts to employ concepts that tie responses, stories, and narratives together in a coherent fashion, searching for relationships among those concepts through intensive and ongoing interpretation of the data. This process allowed for both in-depth exploration of their responses and the weaving of those responses with larger theoretical concepts to uncover a perhaps nascent new theory of citizenship among young people.

What might this picture of citizenship look like? Will it reflect the "changed everything" that Postman describes and Putnam laments? Might it reveal something new, resonant, and engaging that captures the energies alluded to by Howe and Strauss (1993) in their prediction that Generation Y is heir to the "long civic generation"? Will these actors fit into traditional categories or combine in unexpected ways?

My cohort–Generation X-Y—surely are minimalists, voting at an anemic 18 percent in the 2000 election. Yet despite eschewing the ballot box, they exceed many Rotarians in their commitment to hands-on community service. While this cohort exhibits deplorable voter participation, even by minimalist standards, they show the voluntary tendencies of traditional civic leaders. The recent experience with the rise and fall of the Howard Dean presidential campaign in 2004 seems to affirm that young people are enthusiastic volunteers but perhaps not dependable voters.

Perhaps the quirkiest case will be the Cyber-democrats. These technophiles show an activist impulse to participate in political life even as they take to the Web rather than the streets. While their technology tools implore more people to get involved and while they promise greater access and influence for "the people," many Cyber-democrats see potential profits in such engagement. Where might such attitudes fall on the traditional continuum of citizenship? Such persons are making democratic promises, providing political information, but they do so for a profit and through a medium still dominated by those affluent enough to own computers.

Are these actors in the high-tech sphere—Elites, Wireheads, Cyber-democrats, and Trailing Xers—recreating what it means it means to be a citizen in the United States? Are they mixing and matching old behaviors and commitments in new and original ways that more accurately reflect their life experiences rather than the views of the post–WWII social capitalists or omnipresent Baby Boomers? Are they forcing us to rethink the relationship between business, technology, politics, and philanthropy? Could they be recasting reciprocal obligation in a way that better reflects the reality of their world rather than the nostalgia of Putnam and the Rotarians?

Rather than projecting preconceived notions onto such measures and thereby perpetuating the conventional wisdom, the time has come to ask such persons: What kind of citizens are you? What kind of civic life do you foresee in the future? Are you and your cohorts floating a new theory of what it means to be an American citizen? Is the Web helping you do so?

We begin with the most curious and overlooked of both the technology sector and Generation X—Cyber-democrats—those young people who are already politically active and engaged and using contemporary technology tools to work within the democratic process.

4

Cyber-Democrats and
Just-In-Time Social Capital

A *New York Times* headline lamented what Cyber-democrats already know, that the Web is less about entertainment and more about work: "As the Web Matures, Fun is Hard to Find." In this article, author Lisa Guernesy (2002) recalls with misty nostalgia the good days of 1994 when the Web was full of "bizarre, idiosyncratic" sites such as the Coffee Cam; a live image of a coffeemaker at the University of Cambridge; and Jenni-Cam, the first Internet peep show. "The Web was like a chest of toys, and each day bought a new treasure." Mindless treasure in many cases, no doubt. Guernesy's observation noting the shift from mindless fun to more serious fare is supported by recent findings from the ongoing Pew study on Internet practices. Researchers found that users reported little or no growth in demand for online hobbies or game playing, although the time spent online "just passing the time" has grown. As it turns out, the Web is evolving from a toy to a tool—the very opposite evolutionary curve of television. For Neil Postman (1985), given his concern that television has caused all of us—and the post-Sesame Street crowd especially—to amuse ourselves to death, this news must come as both a surprise and a relief. For Robert Putnam (2000), who worries that the flickering computer screen will displace as many social capital-building activities as the television set, additional findings that Internet use is displacing TV—must be welcome news.

All technologies have their implicit biases, Postman repeatedly argued. Notably, midlife accounts of the Web seem to reflect biases more akin to text in a book than an image on a screen. This phenomenon is certainly reflected in the habits and views of Cyber-democrats, persons who are a curious subset of Generation X residing within the emerging intersection of Internet technologies and American politics.

To date, no comprehensive studies of politically active Generation Xers have been conducted. Shearer et al. (1998) investigated young nonvoters and found a category of "Doers," persons who were active in their communities and aware of political issues but disengaged from voting. Hays (1998) conducted focus groups with college students to understand notions of political efficacy, and several NES survey studies have shown political apathy to be rife in this generation. While scholars have largely ignored this subset of politically active young people, some popular authors have implicitly addressed the group. And yet, of each of the subsets of Generation X characterized in this study, Cyberdemocrats seem to be the most overlooked and yet most intriguing.

The Generation X scholarly literature, largely based on analyses of national survey data, paints a pejorative and apathetic picture of this generation as a whole. In those studies, Gen Xers are maligned for *not* participating in the public life of the nation. Opined Hill (1997), "Generation X is the anomaly: an atavistic, even slightly reactionary group of Americans who have thus far been unable to cope with the mostly positive changes occurring in a nation now run for the most part both politically and financially by boomers" (p. 123). Yet as young actors in the political system, especially during the Clinton era, they were maligned by popular authors for their youthful political and policy involvement. In scathing accounts of the disorganization witnessed during the early days of the Clinton administration, Boomer stalwarts Bob Woodward (1994), Elizabeth Drew (1994), and others chastised members of this generation *for* participating in the political system and worried about their civic and political incompetence operating at such a high level in the public sector.

In the early 1990s, Richard Linklater's classic film *Slacker* painted a picture of Austin Gen Xers as eccentric wanderers through the streets of the Texas capital, killing time and peddling Madonna's Pap smear in lieu of more rigorous employment. In that account and in Coupland's classic that named the generation, Gen Xers were either seen as aimless and unemployed (or underemployed) and ineffectual in the *private* sector. Finally, Borsook, in her book *Cyberselfish* (2000)—an account of the dot-com crowd penned a scant five years later—characterized the young techno-elites as rich, self-absorbed, and status-obsessed workaholics.

These readings portray Gen X as apathetic and thus unsuited for the role of citizenship in a democracy. If, however, Gen Xers are *actively* involved at the highest levels of government, they again are viewed as a threat to democracy. If they reject the private sector, they are accused of threatening the country's economic health. If they are successful in the private sector, their actions are again seen as negative—for the economy, for politics, and for public life. While Boomers may have cut their teeth on "Don't trust anyone over 30" they seem to have matured to a space that sees little of value in anyone under 40. In defiance of these judgments, Cyber-democrats have a much richer and more hopeful story to tell.

Cyber-democrats embody many of the conflicting characterizations of Gen Xers, however. As Drew and Woodward lamented, Gen Xers do not dress in accordance with traditional professional norms. While I interviewed all but one of these young people during the standard workday (and many of them in and around their workplaces), only one was dressed in traditional business attire. As *Cyberselfish* describes, they have made money and they have achieved relatively high status for persons so young. With only one exception, a man who had left a political job to start a new consulting company, my interviewees all remarked about their good fortune to have made more money—and made it younger—than they had imagined possible. They are in their twenties and thirties often doing the work that was previously reserved for those in their forties or fifties in the political world, a world that in earlier times privileged seniority and relationships over rigor and intellect.

Like Coupland's "microserfs," Cyber-democrats work a great deal. Those I interviewed all carried a range of the latest technological devices and often noted the irony of marketers' promises that these innovations would make them more efficient and leave more time for the "things they really wanted to do." All conceded that, in effect, these devices created a 24/7 workweek. In different ways, they credited technology for the pace of their professional upward mobility and the increased influence they wielded. With information and intellectual sophistication being privileged, seniority and relationships matter less than they once did in this notoriously insular profession. As all parts of the policy world grow more data-driven, those with info-centric skills become more influential. Echoing Postman's caution about biases implicit in certain technologies, the online political world privileges the young, the intelligent, the rigorous, and the insomniac.

This decidedly impersonal take on politics may make one long for the glory days of the Senate in the 1950s. But as John Gardner, founder of Common Cause observed shortly before his death, U.S. politics is cleaner and more meritocratic than ever before—although recent high-profile scandals in the Congress may make such a claim harder to believe in 2006. As Postman argues, with every technological innovation there are winners and losers. It appears that in the case of technology and politics, the losers are the backslapping gray eminences of legislatures past and the winners may be Gen X Cyber-democrats.

Generations and Cyber-Democrats

Generational marketers argue that distinct life experiences will determine the messages that best appeal to respective generations. For example, Gen X grew up amid a rising divorce rate and economic uncertainty, while Boomers grew up in more intact families surrounded by talk of unprecedented opportunity and prosperity as the children of doting parents, power nesting after their profound sacrifices in World War II. Where Boomers rebelled against domestic tranquillity by creating a range of dramas and movements, they developed a perverse idealism that, when frustrated, crystallized into a cynicism that now corrodes our public discourse. For Gen X, economic insecurities and broken families led to a more tempered set of expectations about what life would be like and what others, including the government, should provide. For Boomers, a pampered childhood fed an entitlement mentality—the world owed them something (Hicks and Hicks, 1999). In the eyes of Gen X, by contrast, the world owes nothing to anyone. Each individual is responsible for taking care of himself. They must create their *own* lives, communities, and workplaces. Said one Boomer during an informal focus group meeting, "It's not that we are cynical, it's that our standards are so high that no one can meet them." These unrealistic expectations lead to chronic disappointment and likely disdain for imperfection. In life, perfection is often in short supply.

According to Bagby (1998) and Hicks and Hicks (1999), Gen X understands imperfection and seeks to embrace and build upon it while also working to improve things. Cyber-democrats especially bring this sensibility into the political world. This orientation, combined with the democratization of information catalyzed by the Web, is subtly changing how people interact in political and community life. This quiet evolution, overlooked by Putnam (2000) and others and generally lost amid the boom and bust coverage of the Information Age, is largely unreflected in national survey data. Most civic culture and social capital measures are concerned with joining old institutions rather than building new ones. Further, these measures do not contemplate organizing over the Web or identifying an immediate discrete need around which a group can quickly organize, accomplish the task, and then disband. Current definitions and measures of social capital fail to capture the instance or value of these activities for the social health of communities. Must an effort be static, constant, and lasting to animate reciprocity and hence social capital? New Economy Cyber-democrats certainly think not.

When I set out to create a subsample of Cyber-democrats, I envisioned them to be individuals who were working with contemporary technologies in the civic or political space, primarily entrepreneurs leading election-related companies (e.g., election.com, votehere.net, speakout. com); nonprofit political offerings (e.g., e-thepeople.org, getheard.org, Moveon.org); and Web masters for political campaigns. I certainly found some of those individuals, but I also found that almost anyone seriously working at the intersection of politics and technology in Austin would also be involved in working with the state legislature. Those activities included working to introduce technology tools to the political process and to change laws to better reflect the pace and unique attributes of technology organizations. All of the Cyber-democrats who I interviewed were involved in lobbying interactions (either official as lobbyist, citizens or legislative staff). As a result, this group was the most monolithic in their views on citizenship, public virtues, and the role of technology in public life, largely because they were—inadvertently—the most professionally cohesive of the groups studied.

The Cyber-democrats I interviewed ranged in age from 25 to over 40, representing the largest age span of the groups studied here. The Cyber-democrats included 9 males, 1 female (not terribly different from the overall ratio in the technology field and electoral politics), 1 Asian, 1 Hispanic, and 8 Anglos. As Herbst (1998) found with legislative staffers, they were efficacious, optimistic, well-informed, and active consumers of news. But they also held a rather dim view of those outside the political process—the general public—whom they viewed as lazy with respect to politics.

The Cyber-democrats' stories are varied, compelling, and occasionally inconsistent, but they also paint a picture of an emerging elite that is defining a distinct sense of civic responsibility. This group looks *structurally* different from its predecessors while nonetheless displaying many of the *virtues and behaviors* of classic civic leaders from previous generations. However, Cyber-democrats do *not* particularly honor the *institutions* created by their generational predecessors.

As Ted Halstead (1999) observed in his provocative cover story in *Atlantic Monthly*, this group does appear to have a "radically centrist" or nonideological view of political issues. They view themselves as problem solvers rather than activists (whom they often view as problem makers). Unlike Halstead, however, I found the ways in which individual Cyber-democrats *approached* politics and civic life to be very similar to one another, although I did not find consensus around specific public *policies.*

Meet the Cyber-Democrats

Let us now meet these 10 thoughtful, often intense, exceedingly verbal and very active young Cyber-democrats. Sam, 34, grew up as the child of hippies. He remembers passing out fliers at a McGovern rally as a toddler while his parents organized their graduate school campus. He shies way from partisan labels but is comfortable with the designation "left of center." After several years working in the State Capitol and now armed with a public policy degree, he runs a technology and education interest group.

Maurice, 31, is an unabashed liberal who had worked on several campaigns for the Democratic Party, is suspicious of many things corporate, but did not want to miss the chance "to win the Internet lottery." He combined his passion for politics and broader participation with his belief that the Internet "didn't have to be a tool of The Man." He started two companies, one featuring an online voter registration tool and the other that facilitated charitable giving. Both companies having been acquired by larger companies, Maurice now works as an executive with the acquiring company, bent upon infusing new voting technology into states, with Florida clearly emerging as an obvious priority. As he observed, "The real story of online voting is not whether we should vote online and whether that will be secure or it will work. The real story is the false sense of security we have about our current systems." This first observation occurred in an interview on October 12, 2000, several weeks before the fateful presidential election of 2000. In a subsequent interview, he recalled his prescience and analyzed the Bush victory this way: "The margin of error of our current paper systems is 2%. The margin of victory in this election was one-tenth of one percent. By our own current technology, the race was a tie. You recount 10 times—5 times Gore wins, 5 times Bush wins. We would have been better off flipping a coin. . . . I think our company can make sure that something like that never happens again."

Billy is a 26-year-old Asian staffer who has worked at the Capitol since he was 16. He is chief of staff of an influential House member who is the leading voice on technology issues. His sense of efficacy was evident throughout our interview: "I think if people choose to be involved they can make a difference. I know that sounds hokey but I can't tell you how many times we've passed legislation because constituents brought something to our attention . . . something changed because they were able to give us a personal story which allowed for there to be positive change. I think people can make a difference . . . I think that a lot of folks have the ability to do that. More than know about it."

Kate, 35, is a Republican who grew up in a small town "where everyone looked after everyone else." She goes to church every Sunday, volunteers in the evenings and lobbies for a technology advocacy group based in Silicon Valley. "Can you believe that John Doerr calls me on the phone?" she enthuses about her access to the nation's top technological minds and venture capitalists. Her office features photos of top leaders of the Republican and Democratic parties but she confides, "We just can't look to government to do everything." She "loves" her work, but at the same time aches to get back to her small town to raise a family. Each day, she surfs the tension between a high-powered job where "I get to make a difference" and the tug of Mason, Texas, and the traditional life that she and her parents always thought would be hers.

Ted, 32, is a Hispanic father of three who commutes to Austin from San Antonio each day. He lobbies for an edgy, top-tier technology company, among other clients, and underpins his advocacy with serious research. "Brain research is going to revolutionize how we think about learning. Technology is not only going to be the way we express those new means, it's also going to be the way that we investigate and test what works." Ted's father was an enlisted member of the military and a devout Catholic who is still involved in community work. Ted's faith echoes throughout his responses, as does his amazement that at such a young age he makes "more money that I ever could have imagined."

Tommy, 30, is an Anglo father of two who lives in the outer suburbs of Austin. He works in technology for a state agency and commutes to law school in San Antonio, hoping to complete his law degree at night and pass the Bar Exam by the end of the year. In his early twenties, he worked as an intern for the legendary Texas political figure, Bob Bullock, mentor to George W. Bush. It was there that Tommy wrote a memo to his boss, in 1993, alerting him to the potentially revolutionary implications of this thing called the Internet. In this memo, he advocated a system for both internal and external citizen use that would enable ordinary people to dial in and track legislation during the session. It would "give Joe Six Pack access to the same information that high powered lobbyists had." Nearly a decade later, the system he envisioned, including a full service online portal to state government services, are used by hundreds of thousands of Texans each year.

Robert, 40, was elected to Congress in the Newt Gingrich landslide in 1994. Today he leads a national technology organization and hopes to bring greater policy and political sophistication to the technology sector. "We all talk about efficiency in government. I tell people that government was never supposed to be efficient. It is supposed to be fair." Robert was defeated in the following Republican primary but is not cynical, seeing himself being able to make a bigger difference in the interface between politics and tech community by teaching new leaders. As he says, "the thing is government sets the environment for which all these things can happen . . . there's a lot of things our government can improve on but frankly there probably has never in the history of the world been a government that's as conducive to the growth of technology companies and technology as the United States government today. I mean, it's probably better than it's ever been so we need to understand why that is and what we can do to preserve it and improve it."

Dirk is a longtime fixture around the Texas Capitol, a large, boisterous, and funny man who spent years in religious life before signing up for partisan politics. He works for an influential state senator who was an early adopter of technology issues. Together, they authored much of the most innovative technology legislation passed that year. While talking about the camp for dying children he founded in the Hill Country several years earlier, this deeply spiritual man was interrupted by a barely audible (but apparently not unpleasant) vibration on his belt. He then showed me his new Blackberry (the now seemingly ubiquitous wireless e-mail device) with great enthusiasm, "I'm the senate guinea pig on this—is this cool or what?"

Leon, 35, is a Republican partisan who started his own education technology consultancy after seeing the troubles that agencies and schools were having maximizing the impact of technology to match the efficiency gains of private enterprise. He wants to be the president of the United States someday and sees both technology and the private sector as the way to get there. His company is currently run out of his quaint bungalow in a fashionable part of town; his "commercial vehicle" is a well-worn 1987 Honda Civic parked at the curb.

Colin, 34, is the son of a well-respected elected official. He is among the youngest of the top-tier "hired gun" lobbyists in Texas and represents a number of technology clients. He explicitly tells clients and potential clients that he will not lobby his father on any matters. There is nothing in the law to prohibit him from "talking business over Thanksgiving turkey," he observes, but such an arrangement "just wouldn't be right." Despite his considerable success in the realm of hardball politics, Colin still takes public cynicism about politics personally: "It's like they're talking about my Dad."

Much to the chagrin of my tireless transcriber, I interviewed these characters in a range of different places—at the state Capitol, in coffee shops, over a beer near the lake if the weather permitted. My interviewees were candid, witty, and rarely cynical. While much of this study contradicts Putnam's (2000) views on social capital and Sacks' (1996) and Bennett's (1997) views on Generation X political views and behaviors, the Cyber-democrats did offer some important insights about animating social capital in 2002. Further, Cyber-democrats reflected the well-documented relationship between political knowledge and efficacy and echoed the harsh criticisms of the mainstream press leveled by Fallows (1997), Patterson (1994), and Cappella and Jamieson (1997), among others. In addition to the critique about "pathetic" press coverage of political issues, Cyber-democrats felt that the press was perpetuating the negative stereotypes about Generation X. Curiously, the language that the Cyber-democrats used to describe the press mirrors the characterizations of Gen X found in the work of Bennett et al. In the eyes of Cyber-democrats, it is not Generation X that is without civic virtue; rather, it is the American press.

Exploring Virtues of Citizenship

The picture of the classic "civic leader" found in many American communities is a familiar one. Such persons populate the Rotary Clubs and Chambers of Commerce, frequently playing golf in support of worthy causes. In a more scholarly context, civic leaders are those who, through lifestyle effects (Lijphart, 1997; Bennett, 1997; Miller, 1992; Cassel and Luskin, 1988) have "aged" into their prime citizenship years—finished school, married, started a family, bought a house, and gotten the kids out of school (or at least away at college). Conventional wisdom says that this high level of citizenship is the purview of elite 40–60-year-old couples. Even the title Civic Leader found on the left-hand side of the stationery for nonprofit entities is generally reserved for wives of successful businessmen. Cyber-democrats, in contrast, certainly undertake multiple roles and activities within their various communities (work, neighborhood, virtual), but they largely eschew the traditional organizations attended by previous generations of civic leaders.

Although their community work is significant (and will be discussed later in this chapter), Cyber-democrats are mostly political animals. If table 4.1 below is taken to represent public virtues from the inside out—that is, from the most basic and popular to the most

Table 4.1   Galston's Political Virtues

Virtues	Attributes
General	• Law-abidingness • Courage • Loyalty
Social	• Independence • Open-mindedness
Economic	• Work ethic • Capacity to delay gratification adaptability to economic and technological change
Political	• Capacity to discern and respect the rights of others; • Willingness to demand only what can by paid for • Ability to evaluate the performance of those in office • Willingness to engage in public discourse

external and rare (akin to Maslow's hierarchy from sustenance to actualization)—Cyber-democrats have it all backward.

Cyber-democrats' conceptions of citizenship are inexorably bound to their views of *politics*. In essence, Cyber-democrats see citizenship as inherently political, with involvement and knowledge as its key elements. They are unanimous and passionate in this belief; thus, they stand far apart from typical characterizations of Generation X.

However, a different way to look at this phenomenon would be through Richard Florida's (2000) observations of the economic geography of talent and the Generation X tendency to create social and community spheres revolving around the workplace. In his work, Florida found that creative people tended to congregate, bonded most closely with those with whom they worked, and located themselves in communities with pleasing aesthetics and a liberal sensibility. In this view, Cyber-democratic political interest, knowledge, and efficacy are more about *professionalism* than citizenship. While this may be a useful frame to help analyze the potential lessons in Generation X involvement, this is *not* how Cyber-democrats view themselves. Although they view political life as a profession, they also believe that all people who live in a democracy should have some knowledge and expertise in public policy areas as well.

While they are relatively firm in their prescriptions for good *political* citizenship, Cyber-democrats are closer to their generational comrades in their squeamishness about more general virtues, affirming Wolfe's (2001) findings in *Moral Freedom*. While Cyber-democrats say that a good citizen should be informed and should vote, they stop short of saying that a good citizen should always obey the law.

Across the political spectrum, Cyber-democrats struggled and equivocated when asked about general virtues. When dealing in the world of economic virtues (what does it mean to be a good worker or employee) or political virtues, they talked at length. However, when moving to more general virtues, those that grew closer to questions of morality, authority, and obligation, they grew equivocal. Said one moderate,

> You know, again I'm uncomfortable saying "thou shalt" when it comes to these things. I think it's going to be depending on each person. That, you know, I'm going to go by a set of values and things that I have and someone else will do the same. Those values are going to be different. So uh, you know, it's difficult to say but I think generally speaking uh, there is a higher level of responsibility for those who have been successful to uh, give more. And uh, that's your money and time. Just as much as it is through time just as much as money. Uh, but some will give more than others. I can't give you set rigid, you know, requirements because I don't think you should.

Such discomfort in prescribing normative absolutes about moral conduct was not restricted to nonideological moderates. One Cyber-democrat self-described as conservative was equally reluctant to impose an external standard on the duties required of good citizens:

> I personally think that I have a duty and that is to help others. Whether it's a mentor of a child . . . [w]hether it is to coordinate a, you know, bill to help out kids that need reading materials. I think that I have a sense of duty and I will act on that but I don't require that of everybody. I don't expect everyone to be that way.

And one self-described liberal reflected this "legal relativism" in even stronger, more specific terms:

> Yeah. Well, I will tell you that I don't necessarily think that if you disobey the law that you're a bad citizen in all cases. I speed all the time.
> And so yes, is that hypocritical or is that, yeah, I mean, yeah. Or do I think if you, you know, I mean, it depends on where you come from and what your culture's like. I grew up in an environment if you were 16 and you wanted to have a beer. And, you know, your mom and dad gave you a beer because what's wrong with that? . . . [and] I don't know why, you know, we're so big on putting people in jail for smoking marijuana. . . . It just amazes me that we would spend money on harassing people for personal consumption of marijuana.

While Cyber-democrats from across the ideological spectrum recoiled from prescribing norms of moral or legal conduct, they expressed no hesitation when speaking of the responsibilities of citizens to be informed and participate in a democratic polity and of their view regarding the relationship between knowledge and efficacy:

> I think if more people could watch how the government acted there wouldn't be as much cynicism about it. . . . It's like anything, you know, there's so much misunderstanding when you look at something from afar and you get closer into it. You know, it's easy for somebody to sit there and pop shots about how the state spends a bunch of money on a bunch of useless things and you get them in the room and say OK, tell us what you'd cut.

Another expressed an even harsher view of both the personal and institutional level:

> I don't think that politics and government are complicated at all. This country does a pathetic job [at educating people about itself]. And that's being charitable at training people to use its democratic institutions. That's why you have the institution. I mean, that's why you have the professional lobbyists. They make a dollar because they understand a process that seems labyrinthine and Byzantine to the average individual. The reason it seems Byzantine to the average individual is that if you look at any basic high school curriculum there is very little there about civics. There is very little there about democratic institutions and how to actually interact with them on a day-to-day basis. And, in fact, look at those institutions themselves. They do very little self-promotion to the public about how the public should interact with them. Ironically uh, they don't exist without public interaction. So I think that the institutions themselves and the complexity of them frankly haven't changed very much since democracies were first founded. Now there may be a greater volume of things that they deal with. Maybe more people associated with them but the basic processes are still very much the same and the opportunities to affect them are very much the same. We just don't teach people how to use those opportunities.

In his concise history of democracy, Dahl (1999) explores the dilemma of citizen participation versus system effectiveness: the smaller a democratic unit, the greater its potential for citizen participation and the less the need for citizens to delegate government decisions to representatives. Conversely, the larger the unit, the greater is its capacity for dealing with problems important to its citizens, but also the greater is its need for citizens to delegate decisions to representatives. This question persists throughout democratic thought: What is the necessary role for the individual citizen in a large, mature democratic system? In other words, what must citizens do to exercise their responsibilities within the affairs of state?

Where Dahl focused on citizen *activity*, Galston (1991) explored what animates citizen behavior, positing a set of virtues allegedly guiding civic behaviors (see table 4.1). I would argue that these values are cumulative. For example, the very least a good citizen should do is obey the law. Echoing Oliver and Heater's (1994) useful taxonomy of citizenship, these virtues lie along a continuum ranging from a minimal (or liberal tradition) of citizenship through a more demanding sort of citizenship posited by those who advocate a more participatory vision (Fishkin, 1995). Within this vision, the traditional notion of citizenship begins with a minimal expectation about obeying the law and voting and culminating with a willingness to engage in public discourse. In other words, the traditional view looks rather like table 4.1. For Cyber-democrats, however, the chart is *inverted* in that they view political virtues as more important than general ones (see figure 4.1 below). This dynamic might help explain the persistent popularity of former President Bill Clinton among this cohort. *In essence, quality citizenship is determined more by one's political knowledge and participation than it is by obedience to the law for Cyber-democrats.*

Traditional Citizens	Cyber-democrats
• Law-abidingness • Courage • Loyalty • Independence • Open-mindedness • Work ethic • Capacity to delay gratification, adaptability to economic and technological change • Capacity to discern and respect the rights of others • Willingness to demand only what can by paid for • Ability to evaluate the performance of those in office • Willingness to engage in public discourse	• Willingness to engage in public discourse • Ability to evaluate the performance of those in office • Willingness to demand only what can by paid for • Capacity to discern and respect the rights of others • Capacity to delay gratification, adaptability to economic and technological change • Work ethic • Independence • Loyalty • Courage • Law-abidingness

Figure 4.1   Classical Attributes and Behaviors of Traditional Citizens Versus Cyber-Democrat Views of Quality Citizenship

- Willingness to engage in public discourse

- Willingness to demand only what can by paid for

- Ability to evaluate the performance of those in office

- Work ethic/independence/open-mindedness

- Capacity to delay gratification, adaptability to economic and technological change

Figure 4.2   Cyber-Democrat Continuum of Good Citizenship

Willing to make value judgments about what a good citizen is *through a political lens,* Cyber-democrats turn the model of traditional virtues required for good citizenship upside down. In some ways, they track Wolfe's observations even more closely. Whereas Wolfe argues that Americans have had consensus about ideas of political and economic freedom for a long time, their views of moral freedom are just now taking hold. Cyber-democrats implicitly argue that for political freedom to exist, it must be tended, used and taken seriously. As a result, their conception of quality citizenship is intimately tied up with their notions of political virtues. They see moral issues as being individualized and personal and are therefore reluctant to make value judgments about people. Given that dichotomy, a specific Cyber-democrat view of quality citizenship can be depicted in figure 4.2 below, beginning with a minimal willingness to engage and then growing cumulatively to a definition of what an especially good citizen does and believes:

Willingness to Engage in Public Discourse

Cyber-democrats harbor particular disdain for those who "sit on the sidelines" and disparage the political process. They therefore part company with Susan Herbst's legislative staffers, who generally discounted the involvement or input of the individual citizen. Herbst (1998) found that in staffers' conceptions of "public opinion" the public was often curiously missing. Instead, they relied on newspaper accounts and interest group lobbyists to provide them with aggregate notions of public opinion. Said one of her staff informants, "We don't really care about what the average Joe thinks. . . . [I]f you want to have influence up here [in the legislative process] then you need to care enough to work hard and get organized" (p. 53). In contrast, while my informants often talked in tactical terms such as these, more traditional notions of the "efficacy of the common man" and the capacity for a single person to make a difference was a cornerstone of their political vision. Typically, their critique of the individual citizen was not that he could not make a difference or that a single voice did not matter. Rather, they felt that individual citizens did not take the time to read the newspaper, "get smart on the issues," understand the process, make a coherent and compelling argument, and make fiscally reasonable demands. Cyber-democrats view citizen attitudes as more accurately reflecting widespread *apathy* rather than cynicism. Two of my respondents Colin (C) and Billy (B) were in near total agreement on the matter:

> COLIN: I just think people are just generally distrustful of government because all they read about is the scandals and they're so busy running their business or their family they don't pay attention to the issues.

* * *

> BILLY: I think the average person can understand but their willingness is a different story.
>
> SS: And why do you think that?
>
> BILLY: You know, it just goes with that whole thought that voters are more apathetic these days . . . that uh, they're not as motivated. They don't try to stay abreast of what's going on as well as they used to. They don't follow newspapers as well as they used to. Uh, even with so much new information available to them on the Internet and everything else it doesn't seem like the majority of the electorate is getting more educated. It seems like some folks are really using those tools to their advantage but not everybody . . . we live in a more complicated time where folks are working harder longer hours and they choose to not prioritize [work] over their personal life. Which is, you know, very valid if they have a family and raising children and sometimes don't know have the luxury of having an hour and a half or two hours a day to read the paper like they once did. Or just sit around the family table and talk about the issues as we once did in this country.

Willingness to Demand Only
What Can be Paid for

Apathy regarding the political process is directly related to what Cyber-democrats see as a byproduct of citizens' ignorance, an ignorance often stoked by sensational media coverage. This combination, in their view, concedes power and influence to special interest groups that, by definition, advocate for their interest and privilege to the exclusion of other interests. According to Cyber-democrats, this dynamic leads to reduced citizen involvement and an absence of any collective notion concerning "general interest."

One of my informants, Maurice, offered one especially compelling example during deliberations about a potential airline bailout in the wake of the attacks on the Twin Towers on September 11, 2001. At that time, the airline industry had been lobbying Congress for significant cash grants and government-backed loan guarantees. Layoffs were in the tens of thousands; flights and routes were being canceled. In the midst of all this, Maurice observed this:

> Why would we give them money not to fly? That's ridiculous. They are talking about having taxpayers foot the bill to cut flights and lay off workers . . . why don't they just take the $15 billion and give everyone in the country a voucher or two and tell them to go fly somewhere? That way, people get to travel, you create a market for airline travel so that the good ones survive and crappy ones like Midway tank instead of being put on life support by taxpayer money.

Obviously, this example not only shows a significant awareness of news and politics on Maurice's part, but it also shows a problem-solving orientation transcending traditional ideological definitions of Right and Left. Although a Progressive, Maurice was willing to support governmental intervention to help a critical industry and believed that the best approach would be to use governmental policy to create a market. And although Maurice held the traditionally conservative belief in the power of market to provide high-quality solutions to some policy problems, Maurice argued for a more progressive approach to supporting individuals and workers over the larger corporate interests.

While this example is especially vivid, such a nonideological synthesis was prevalent across all of my Cyber-democrat respondents. Whereas Herbst's group placed their faith in lobbyists and interest groups for efficiency's sake, this group sees that relying on organized interest groups in the complete absence of the engaged citizen yields approaches that privilege existing power structures, especially corporate interests.

Ability to Evaluate the Performance of Those in Office

Closely tied to the virtues of being informed and of demanding only what can be paid for is the ability to evaluate the performance of those currently in office. Almost all of the Cyber-democrats lamented that political officials are often grouped under a cynical label of "scoundrel." This is not to say that the Cyber-democrats were naive about the frailties of the human beings involved in the political system or about the disconnection between idealized notions of democracy and the distinctly human ways in which it is often carried out. Even Colin, one of the most eloquent and sensitive of the Cyber-democrats, conceded,

> Privately the closer I've gotten to politics sometimes the more cynical I've gotten about it. Because by and large we've got a very good system but there are people in it for their own reasons. And it makes you sick when you see it.

The Cyber-democrats believed that the politicians who "make you sick" get all of the coverage from a lazy media, which makes the system seem inaccessible and intractable to the general public. That paralyzing effect relegates the political process to the special interests and activists, which in turn makes politics seem alien to citizens' everyday concerns.

This disconnection is further exacerbated by television, in their opinion. Like Neil Postman, Cyber-democrats observe the short attention span of a body politic raised on television: "[A] person who has seen one million television commercials might well believe that all political problems have fast solutions through simple measures—or ought to . . . or that complex language is not to be trusted, that argument is in bad taste" (Postman, 1985, p. 126). Cyber-democrats are not afraid of argument: they engage in it all day, every day. This appreciation of argument and the grasp of the necessity for well-managed conflict sets them dramatically apart from other members of the Generation X cohort.

As I will show in subsequent chapters, one of the many political elements that makes young people uncomfortable is the presence of conflict. Because many Generation X members grew up in divorced households, conflict and argument are seen by them as disrespectful at best and frightening at worst. Thus, recasting argument and conflict in the policy and public spheres will likely be a critical component of any strategy designed to engage young people in the political process.

This group also reflects Mueller's (1999) observation in *Democracy, Capitalism and Ralph's Pretty Good Grocery* that the inflated promises of democracy often lead to unrealistic expectations about how it can—and should—operate. Mueller claims that the idealized stories that Americans tell each other about how democracy should work set the stage for cynicism. In other words, cynicism is derived from unrealistic expectations.

Satisfaction—whether in marketing or in politics—is determined by performance relative to expectations (Fountain, 1995). Citizens who know only the idealized precepts of democracy and the cynical, episodic frame of the contemporary news media understandably become chagrined by the mismatch. Add increasingly busy lives and multiple information sources and you have a disengaged polity and a vicious circle of ignorance and paralysis. That is the bad news. The good news is that in the Cyber-democrat's view of citizenship, efficacy is just a phone call or a modem away. All it takes is a little work—and the right technology.

Work Ethic

One of the most curious disconnections between my Generation X sample and conventional wisdom about that generation is the question regarding its members' work ethic. In their written surveys, my respondents were asked to rate important qualities of good citizenship, using the scale from Almond and Verba (1960). Most all of my sample rated hard work or "does his/her job well" among the top three qualities. In the professional world, Gen Xers believe that people should work hard and that good citizens should avail themselves of the available information to become informed about political and civic life.

There are a number of potential explanations for this belief, starting with social desirability. For one thing, the work ethic is a key component of American lore; thus, respondents might be tempted to overstate its importance. Yet the popular attack on Generation X is that they have no respect for traditional norms. Another possible explanation is the generational "entitlement gap" mentioned earlier. Generation X was raised on lower expectations and so did not grow up to expect the level of success promised to Boomers. Finally, as outlined by numerous researchers, Generation X is currently redefining what *work* is. It follows, then, that a Generation X individual possibly "works hard" and "does his job well" in a way that other generations do not understand or appreciate. If one is wearing shorts, sipping a latte, talking on a cell phone, and reading data from a laptop plugged in at Oyster Landing pier overlooking Lake Austin on a sunny day, is that work?

Independence

The primacy of independence runs throughout my interviews with the Cyber-democrats when they talked about citizenship and their work. Mostly, they valued independence in their schedules, independence in their political views, and expected independent thought on the parts of citizens. Accordingly, they have disdain for activists and special interest groups but also for ill-informed and straight-ticket voters:

> Voter turnout is pathetic. When you look at other countries where people are given the right to vote, [then] voter turnout is just way up there. . . . And you look in Texas. I actually did a study just as a stupid hobby. I had some time on my hands and looked at the straight ticket voting in Texas in the top 10 counties. Over 50% of the votes cast are straight ticket. . . . And I'm sorry but you can't just punch one box that includes Clayton Williams and Bill Ratliff or Ann Richards and Bill Simms. . . . It just doesn't work. And it's just lazy and its pathetic. And, you know, so even the people that vote aren't necessarily doing the correct thing because if they go in and check one box.

Curiously, this most politically active cohort of my respondents appear to also be aggressively "postpartisan"—eschewing such labels and blind loyalty, privileging instead independent thought and a problem-solving orientation. This dynamic could have significant implications for political parties in the future.

Capacity to Delay Gratification, Adaptability to Economic and Technological Change

This virtue is a particularly ironic one given technology's promise to give one access to everything, any time, anywhere. It is also ironic given the common lament about the MTV attention spans of young people.

With respect to technology, Cyber-democrats see it as a tool for the good, a tool they need to master and one that creates a twenty-first-century professional mobility for them in the public policy world. They see the increased access to legislative information as potentially empowering for citizens, but they worry that only those with extreme views will use it. Further, this group implicitly understands Postman's caution about technology worship. As in political battles, they reason, there will be winners and losers in the wake of innovation and technological change. For a group of tacticians, Cyber-democrats were often surprisingly thoughtful, deliberate, and concerned about the potential detriments of a Web-based society, forecasting such double-edged developments as the blogosphere's response to the Harriet Miers Supreme Court nomination:

> The Internet has revealed and unleashed all sorts of genies . . . information is power, but I know this sounds weird, it's a double-edged sword. It's liberating to be able to communicate and learn, but you can be bombarded with so much information that it can cloud your judgment. We need to be wise and discerning so we don't lose our anchor.

More specifically, this group uses technology to animate other kinds of activity. Far from seeing technology as *replacing* old ways of interacting in communities, they generally use the Web to more efficiently and effectively accomplish specific community tasks. Each of them could cite examples of organizing an effort through an "e-mail tree" or keeping in contact with people with whom they had lost touch in the days prior to ubiquitous e-mail. The following was typical of their views:

> Does it (technology) break it (community) down because people spend less time with humans and more time on chat rooms or e-mail or whatever else? I don't think it will ever take over. I think it makes business more efficient and it makes commerce more efficient but I just don't see anything replacing a neighborhood or a community. . . . I'm sure there's online churches but it's hard to imagine people getting up and turning on the computer and watching a church service versus going and sitting in a pew. And in terms of political accountability I think that, you know, you can now watch it on the Internet. You can track the bill. People have a lot more tools to be informed than they used to. Whether they will have the interest level to do it is anybody's guess.

Behaviors of Good Citizenship

In addition to civic virtues, one can also imagine particular behaviors comprising the definition of a traditional civic leader. From the taxonomy previously constructed, those behaviors include the following listed in figure 4.3.

The Cyber-democrats also shuffle the order of priority in this behavioral model, with most of them putting awareness of public affairs above voting. For them, the idea of straight-ticket voting, single-issue voting, or other "thoughtless" approaches to elections were seen as more problematic than not voting at all.

This finding is curious and raises some interesting points regarding technology and politics. Michael Schudson (1998) coined the term "monitoral citizen" to describe those who keep up with public affairs but who do not necessarily translate this information into *action*. Cyber-democrats are far more than monitoral citizens and in this respect especially differ from my other respondents. Within the technology world and Generation X, much has been written about the "action-bias"—don't just sit there, do something. Several scholars have discussed this action/inaction paradox. Hart (1994), for example, argued that television often confused watching with participating. Skocpol (1999) argued that contemporary interest group politics equates contributing with participating. Cyber-democrats implicitly raise the question: does being informed matter if it does not translate into even minimal action, such as voting? From their perspective, Cyber-democrats tentatively answer "yes." This belief differs from traditional notions of citizenship, which posit voting as the minimal act of citizenship. Cyber-democrats believe *that being informed is not only the minimal act of citizenship, it must be a precursor to the vote.* In other words, to Cyber-democrats, an uninformed vote is worse than no vote at all.

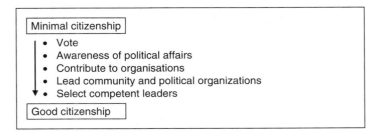

Figure 4.3   Traditional Nations of Citizenship

Neil Postman explores the relationship between information and citizenship in a number of his books where he poses the question: *what problem does "more information" solve?* He is skeptical that modern news coverage and the ways we talk about the "news" actually provide information that is useful to promoting quality citizenship. As he puts it in *Amusing Ourselves to Death*, "What does all of this alleged news give us except a bunch of facts without context about things we can do nothing about? News serves no other purpose than to provide more useless information so we know more about things we cannot do anything about." But Cyber-democrats typically escape Postman's dilemma by very much believing in their own efficacy and in the efficacy of those who take the time to learn processes and issues and then to make cogent and realistic arguments to those who can effect change.

For example, all the Cyber-democrats in my sample voted, both in the current election and in the first one for which they were eligible. They all were aware of political affairs and noted that they had been interested in politics since childhood. While they were convinced that informed voting was a minimal act of civic participation and that individuals can—and do—make a difference, when asked on a written survey if they thought that how people voted determined the way that things actually got done, a number of them said no. It is not clear whether these opinions reflect their sophistication about the political process (i.e., that voting is merely one of many elements that affects how things actually get done), or that they are not quite so idealistic about the influence of the common man.

Cyber-democrats were also equivocal about whether people *must* vote. They all agreed that good citizens cast informed votes and that informed voting is a minimal act of good citizenship, but they were not willing to say that citizens had an *obligation* to vote. Affirming Wolfe's thoughts, one of my respondents mused as follows:

> Uh, I think a citizen has a duty to, you know, be the best possible citizen that they can be. So what does that mean besides being active in the form of government that we have? Voting, I think that's what good citizens ought to do. Uh, I don't think they ought to be compelled to do it because again I'm a big believer in freedom and if I don't want to vote, no one should make me vote.
>
> But citizens again have a responsibility in this country to uh, I think, raise their children in a way that promotes civic responsibility and that doesn't necessarily mean running for office or you have to run for city council or whatever. But it means just trying to, you know, to be uh, to be a good citizen. I don't know how else to say it. I really don't.

Awareness of Public Affairs

In this area, Cyber-democrats are completely different from typical accounts of Generation X. The former were commonly immersed in news, using multiple channels to access it. They were also sophisticated in their understanding of political issues, especially those related to their work. This is consistent with studies that show that those who use the Web for news are also avid consumers of other kinds of news. Further, Cyber-democrats' news consumption has evolved over time as new technologies have come online. They read newspapers, watch CNN, and listen to NPR. They also augment those sources by surfing to news sites on the Web and join headline services and newsgroups; however, their behaviors have not yet evolved to the state of the "Daily Me" posited by Sunstein (2002), in which the Web enables a narrow casting of news based on a user's special interests and provides an efficient filter to remove alternative points of view. Indeed, Cyber-democrats were not afraid of alternative points of view and in many cases sought them out as a part of doing their jobs well. However, because of busy schedules, strenuous jobs, and a need to balance their lifestyles, the risk for Cyber-democrats is that they will eventually use these filtering devices to confine their news consumption only to the areas related to their work. While this means they would still be aware of political affairs broadly, they would likely lose some of the more collective benefits of community awareness that comes from reading newspapers more generally.

Select Competent Leaders

Sartori (1994) makes a controversial distinction in his revised theory of democracy, arguing that vertical democracy is more important than horizontal democracy. He defines horizontal democracy as the broad participation in the democratic process, while vertical democracy is the result of the vote—the quality of the leaders selected. Many democratic theorists claim that broad participation is a good in itself and that their choices must be, de facto, the best ones. Sartori disagrees. One can hear Sartori in the concerns of Cyber-democrats. Unlike Sartori's more paternalistic view, Cyber-democrats see the selection of quality leaders as a function of being informed about political affairs and casting an informed vote. Whereas other respondents held a generally dim view of politicians and those in government, this group saw them as an extension of the human race—some good, most trying to do the best they could.

Said one conservative,

> I think elected representatives are highly enthusiastic about their jobs and I think they take very seriously the sense that they are there to represent uh, their opinions but not only their opinions but also the opinions of others from home. And I think they also have a much better sense quite frankly of the . . . [t]he lack of permanence . . . [and] the gift that is the position that they hold. . . . And that means that they are just as easily unemployed as they are employed if an election is an employment. So I think that gives them a healthier sense of responsibility and responsiveness. Uh, the further you go down the food chain the less likely you are to find anybody that's attached to the notion of being elected and therefore, content.

Interestingly, a liberal (L) takes up a similar theme:

> L: My general impression is very positive of people who are in government. I think it is a form of public service and I think it is a calling. Uh, as somebody who has been a staff person myself I think staff people are terrifically talented, hard working and under appreciated.
>
> SS: Why do you think that?
>
> L: Because I don't think most people well, I don't think most people are as impressed with government or with what it takes. With the effort that lies behind the seemingly effortless delivery of services to people . . . I think many of us as citizens take for granted things like everything from the fact that our streets are paved to that clean water comes out of our tap to electricity coming out of a light bulb to national defense being provided for and we don't realize the effort that goes into that and therefore, we don't tend to appreciate the people who make careers and lives out providing those services. Or making those things happen. Uh, elected officials, I think are a very strange bunch. I think it takes a lot to be an elected official and uh, both in the good sense and the bad sense. . . . I think that the stresses that are placed upon elected officials, you know, in our modern society are such that you have to be a little bit crazy.

Cyber-democrats recognize not only that citizen participation matters in the political process, but that the quality of those who are elected and serve also matters.

Respond to a Community Need

Like their Generation X counterparts and the middle-class respondents in Wolfe (2001), Cyber-democrats are uncomfortable with notions of transcendent obligation. However, they are conscious of the norm of reciprocity—the duty to respond. Many scholars have explored the concept of reciprocity in a range of contexts from interpersonal interactions to geopolitical concerns. At the core, reciprocity—the norm that demands that a gift given be repaid, whether individually or socially—is a key animator of social capital. This dynamic is also a critical component of an updated definition of social capital. Putnam observed that younger Americans were no longer joining older organizations. Cyber-democrats reflect this shift as well. However, this does not mean that civic capacity does not exist for them. Rather, Cyber-democrats were involved in a series of small projects in which they responded to specific needs, emergencies, and events. This dynamic helps explain the phenomenal outpouring of civic activity after September 11. When a need exists, when someone asks for help, Cyber-democrats organize and activate. They address the problem and then disband the organization. Akin to e-commerce promises, this dynamic may represent "just-in-time" social capital.

From these findings, a Cyber-democrat's view of good citizenly behavior emerges, one that encompasses some of the classic qualities of good citizenship but that changes the order of a number of those behaviors. For Cyber-democrats, quality and substance matter. Therefore, being aware and informed about political issues and candidates is a necessary precursor to voting. Further, the result of greater understanding of issues and candidates will result in the selection of better leaders. Finally, moving from politics to social capital, Cyber-democrats are not joiners like Putnam's social capitalists of the 1950s. Rather, they are actively involved in a range of activities that respond to community needs. Like the technology tools that have enabled Cyber-democrats to become young elites, they embrace community activity of a "just-in-time" sort, activity that responds effectively and efficiently to a specific community need. Therefore, the Cyber-democrats' view of quality citizenship looks like what is presented in figure 4.4.

Cyber-Democrats and Technology

A striking finding in my study is that Cyber-democrats do not appear to watch much television for entertainment. According to popular accounts, the typical American watches approximately 20 hours of television per week. Most Cyber-democrats mentioned watching CNN, but not a single one mentioned watching television for fun nor did they make allusions to a specific TV show, with the exception of *West*

Minimal citizenship

- Awareness/knowledge of political affairs
- Vote
- Select competent leaders
- Respond to a community need

Good citizenship

Figure 4.4   Cyber-Democrat Citizenship Behaviors

Wing. Certainly, some of this could be attributed to social desirability, since there is a bias among political sophisticates against the fare served up by contemporary network television. However, the respondents' self-reported online behavior indicated that they spent up to half of their workday and between one and three hours of their personal time online, interacting with business associates, friends, and family and researching political issues. In other words, the flickering screen of television and the flickering screen attached to an interactive keyboard appear to be used in substantially different ways. Affirming the most recent Pew (2005) findings, technology use is increasing at home and work, conflating the two spheres of life—personal and professional but is still fundamentally *interactive.*

From a policy perspective, Cyber-democrats think a great deal about the role of technology in politics and public life. They see these new tools as being democratically useful, giving the public free access to a wealth of information about the workings of their government. They also see technology as making the business of politics more substantive, thereby offering additional influence to young professionals in the field. As one of my respondents observed, the "old boy network" was largely personal and closed, based on personal relationships and access. With the increased availability of information, both to decision makers and voters, things have changed considerably. Now, "data-driven" decision making in education or cost-benefit analysis of capital or technological expenditures is a critical part of the "inside-the-Beltway" political conversation. Similarly, Postman argued that all technologies privilege one set of skills over another. In the view of Cyber-democrats, the new privilege animated by the infusion of Web technologies into the political process privileges content over relationships, intellect over shmooz, thereby creating a new competition based on ideas and arguments rather than liquor and money.

Is this an egalitarian development? In a way, it is because it opens up the political process to those who wish to arm themselves with arguments and data. In such a world, the system ceases to function on the basis of secret handshakes exchanged by insiders. However, these developments have made the policy/political sphere more complicated, necessitating the need for technological competence by would-be citizens. Where "Harold Smith" from Ozona, Texas, could leave the farm and represent his constituents in Austin with wisdom derived from common sense and historical perspective, the business of legislating now requires knowledge of statistics, the law, and the ability to use technological tools as well. As a result, power has been shifting from the rural hamlets to the more sophisticated cities and suburbs, an evolution assisted dramatically by new technologies. The old bias was the bias of the small town—a cheaper race, a longer term of office. The new bias is the bias of higher education and intellectual sophistication, a bias that may widen the divide between the educated and the uneducated.

Digital Divide

The top policy issues facing the Cyber-democrats in Texas during the period comprising this study were (1) the question of access to broadband technology; and (2) the proper role of government in providing it to citizens across the state. Broadband deployment—or "closing the Digital Divide"—became a New Economy proxy for old debates about economic justice. The preoccupation of rural legislators with technology as a way to reverse the economic and political power migration from rural areas underscores the power of technological progress and innovation in the public realm. A similar gestalt was present in the African American caucus of the Texas House: if only broadband were made available in the inner cities, equal opportunity would be realized. While the tool itself certainly affected the ways in which Cyber-democrats did their day-to-day work, it is the *metaphor* of technology that becomes the major story for this group. As one influential rural legislator put it in a hearing on the subject, "We have been waiting and waiting for advanced services. We don't even have caller ID. We're dying out here." It is hard to imagine that the economic decline of rural Texas is the result of Knox City residents not yet being able to avoid annoying phone calls at dinnertime. In any event, this sentiment underscores Postman's caution that technological progress inadvertently creates winners and losers.

Cyber-democrats are conflicted about the role of government in overseeing technological progress. This conflict comes from all ideological perspectives. On the right, one finds concern about "meddling in the market" and the notion that governmental intervention would ultimately slow the very progress that would bring caller ID and DSL to rural and underserved areas. From the Left, a more complicated angst is in play. Lessig (1999), for example, persuasively argues that technology is not organic; it does not grow on its own. Rather, it is the result of deliberate human agency. Therefore, the government, as the expression of a nation's collective interest, has an obligation to act on this technology and assure that it serves a broader public purpose. More Left-leaning Cyber-democrats understand this impulse instinctively. However, they worry, perhaps paternalistically, that the expansion of broadband services will undermine the intellectual and community functions that the Web currently provides. The most cited benefits of broadband accessibility are speed and the ability to download large files, generally streaming video. The result of this development, noted by a number of my sources, is the convergence of the computer and the television set. While the Web is, for most people, an interactive, text-based medium currently, broadband makes it a more visual entertainment-oriented source. Is this a desirable development? Should a democratic government be in the business of quickening the shift from text to images in the name of economic justice?

The Cyber-democratic Left believes in equal access to resources and benefits but is concerned that the civic and political benefits they currently see the Web facilitating would evaporate in the entertaining wake of video-on-demand.

This chapter began with the *New York Times* lament, "The Web is no longer a frontier." It is not fun anymore. Where Netizens once explored the Web for hours for fun, finding a range of different views and quirky sites, the Web is now just another appliance that people use to find information, book travel, and communicate with people they already know. The Internet began as an intellectual highway between research universities. It then evolved—or rather, exploded—into an egalitarian frontier of free expression, where everyone became his or her own individual publisher. What we have today emerged from that fun frontier: an increasingly commercial appliance.

A revolution? Not to the Cyber-democrats. But certainly an evolution for good, one that gives them professional mobility, enables them to participate in their communities in new ways, and democratizes—for the moment and for those who care—the legislative process. Still, several questions emerge. Will increased commercialization and entertainment be animated by broadband access? Does the government have a duty to maintain common space on this new medium? Will this preoccupation with technology and change mask the older problems of social and economic justice that the policy sphere needs to address? My Cyber-democrat informants worry about such things and are beginning to write laws and policies to deal with them. This is serious business undertaken by serious people who have fun in their work.

Conclusion

Contrary to most accounts of Generation X, Cyber-democrats advance an active definition of citizenship, one that encompasses traditional virtues and behaviors but that shuffles the order of priority and infuses the smart use of technological tools. These individuals are not cynical about politics. They work hard. They are aware of the pejorative characterizations of their profession and generation while believing that both sets of misperceptions can be attributed to a single source—the news media. Cyber-democrats feel that reporters and news outlets serve the public poorly by covering only scandal, instead of substantive issues. Further, they felt that the persistent coverage of "ulterior motives" created increasingly cynical public opinion about the nature of political people. One took the matter especially personally, but his view pervades attitudes of the other Cyber-democrats as well:

> Well, it affects my family's life because the way the national government behaves makes so many people cynical about the process that it bleeds over to how they view my father or what I do for a living. And I think unfortunately I don't think the national government is viewed on their substance but they're viewed on what they read in the paper or they read about the scandal. You know, they don't care about anything but the scandals or the hot issues that newspaper reporters write about. But they just don't care enough to read about the Medicaid reforms or anything else. All they do is read the semantics or the crap parties spew at each other. . . . And the only thing that they hear is when somebody really throws it up at them and that's a scandal. . . . And then they, you know, make statements like they all do it. And that's when it stings a little. And, you know, Phil Gramm's record of achievement as a U.S. Senator doesn't sell papers. If Phil Gramm was caught in bed with an intern, *that* sells papers.

As the only elected official in the group, Robert also had a more personal view, a view tied to the belief in the kind of political efficacy that comes from being knowledgeable:

> I would say that what really drives [cynicism] is, this is maybe a little biased, but I think it's the tone of the national debate, which really is driven in large part by the media. . . . You know, it has a big impact on it. You know, the way the media operates you've got a little bit of a lowest common denominator going. . . . They have to do what they have to do to get news, you know, and so that tends to have a little bit of a spiral of decline over a period of time. . . . And as I say its so much easier just to uh, be cynical about everything and so I think that you're a sophisticated person because you're not going to be fooled by anything . . . there's people who play politics and there's some people who are really trying to do the right thing in the political process.

The irony in the Cyber-democrats' descriptions of the news media lies in their strong resemblance to how Generation X is often characterized by scholars and the media: lazy, cynical, and vacuous. Cyber-democrats certainly do not fit the typical characterizations of Generation X nor do they fit the descriptions that most people offer of political actors. They are doubly misunderstood yet profoundly interesting in what they suggest for the future of civic participation and the growth of social capital. Cyber-democrats are politically knowledgeable and active. Cyber-democrats are passionate about their work and draw much of their social activity from work-related pursuits, affirming Florida's (2000) work predicting an evolving definition of community intensely tied to work, place, friends, and technology. Cyber-democrats have been involved in a series of episodic, need-based community activities. For example, a coworker contracts an illness and her colleagues organize to watch her children during the hospital stay. Or a vacant lot is overgrown and causing a hazard, so one Cyber-democrat sends out an e-mail and organizes friends to spend a weekend cleaning it up. Postman argued that culture ultimately surrenders to technology, but Cyber-democrats show that this culture is using technology to help the work of the community, just in time. Where Putnam argues that civic life is in decline because membership in a range of organizations is down, Cyber-democrats show that community capacity exists to address large and small problems. That capacity simply uses technology to organize around a task rather than meet at the Elk's Lodge every month just for the sake of meeting. Like Florida's respondents, Cyber-democrats are not surrendering to technology or contributing to civic decline. Rather, they are defining "community" in a distinct, intense way. Cyber-democrats are high-energy creative people, animated by work and willing to blur the lines between work, community, and family. They choose to mix up these worlds, to change definitions of work and community in the process. Technology enables this blurring and, like all prior inventions, produces both anticipated and unforeseen consequences. These insights, drawn from the most civically active and informed element of Generation X, yield a host of new questions having implications for how we think about and measure social capital, engage young people in democratic and civic life, and characterize this much maligned generation of young people.

Where Cyber-democrats were using technology to add vitality and intellectual heft to the political process, another group of Gen X actors were animating technology with their own hands, and coming up with very different definitions of good citizenship, a definition as tied to economics as Cyber-democrats are to politics. These young technologists, the Wireheads, are the subject of the next chapter.

5

Wireheads as New Minimalists: "I gave at the office"

Introduction

In May 2002, VH1, the venerable music video television station ran a customary Memorial Day list of the most influential pop songs of the 1990s. Top of the list? *Smells Like Teen Spirit* by Nirvana, the quintessential Seattle grunge band. The program followed this announcement with a gauzy portrayal of lead singer Kurt Cobain, a scruffy young poet/musician. In the ensuing clip and commentary, the host of the program christened Mr. Cobain a spokesman for Generation X and his suicide one of the great artistic traumas for his generation. Cobain's cynical aloofness combined with countercultural scruffiness and tragic denouement helped solidify the public picture of disaffected Generation X sensibility. Wireheads are his technological heirs. In these early days of the millennium, they are too old to smell like teen spirit; however, they stand in grubby opposition to traditional workplace and civic conventions.

Professionally, Wireheads are mid-level, nonmanagerial technology workers. They work in a range of sectors, including high-tech companies large and small, as well as public sector and university programmers and support personnel. My sample ranged in age from 29 to 40; in education from GED to doctoral candidate; two females, eight males; one Hispanic. The remainder were Anglo, again reflecting the inherent racial and gender bias in high-tech professions. While they are certainly knowledge workers,[1] Wireheads also still work

---

[1] A knowledge worker is anyone who works for a living at the tasks of developing or using knowledge. For example, a knowledge worker might be someone who works at any

with their hands—more than any of the others in my study. In the postindustrial American economy now dominated by service and increasingly involving the use of technology, Wireheads would seem to best reflect the contemporary version of Putnam's (2000) postwar social capitalists—nonelites. While this group shares some characteristics of typically middle-class Americans reflected in earlier literature about political knowledge and civic attitudes, Wireheads also reflect many of the modern demographic shifts of Generation X. Despite being in their late twenties to late thirties, only half were married and only three had children (Strauss and Howe, 1993; Smith and Clurman, 1997).

Paradoxically, Wireheads embody many of the classic Generation X characteristics (recall Coupland's [1992] "microserfs") and yet also seem to be the clearest reflection of what an emerging technological middle class might reflect—a sort of evolution from Joe Six Pack to Joe Keyboard. They encompass a range of cubicle-dwelling functionaries, modern-day trekkies[2] animating futuristic technologies. Some spend their days "pounding out code" to keep the digital trains running on time in other large public organizations. The code they write can create "middleware" that helps different high-dollar computer systems talk to one another. Their code can also build "elegant" Web sites, a feat that allows some Wireheads to fancy themselves as a new generation of artists, using the tools of technology to create a new art form—the "skip intro" followed by a highly "user-friendly experience." Others are the "tech support guys" who field calls from knowledge workers who cannot find an important document on their hard drive, install a printer, or put a video clip into their Power Point presentation for the upcoming professional conference. Wireheads are in high demand when companies are growing but are often the first to go when the layoffs come, as they often do in this volatile sector of the

---

of the tasks of planning, acquiring, searching, analyzing, organizing, storing, programming, distributing, marketing, or otherwise contributing to the transformation and commerce of information and those (often the same people) who work at using the knowledge so produced. A term first used by Peter Drucker in his 1959 book, *Landmarks of Tomorrow*, the knowledge worker includes those in the information technology fields, such as programmers, systems analysts, technical writers, academic professionals, researchers, and so forth <http://searchcrm.techtarget.com/sDefinition /0,,sid11_gci212450,00.html>.

  [2] "Trekkie" is a slang term used to describe devotees of the 1960s science fiction television show *Star Trek* and its contemporary successors.

economy. Their profession demands toleration of change, a constant refreshing of skills, and a viable exit strategy.

Broadly, Wireheads are best aligned with much Generation X literature in their political knowledge, interest, and participation. They are often cynical, eschewing newspapers and traditional news sources and holding a dim view of politics (Bennett, 1997; Smith and Clurman, 1997; Thau and Heflin, 1997; Howe and Strauss, 1993). However, despite these surface similarities to earlier characterizations of Generation X, Wireheads have a more complicated story to tell, a story of changing norms and attitudes about citizenship. In this new story, technology plays a critical role in what they think about and how they interact within their communities. This account begins with the conception of an attentive minimalist, a citizen who subscribes to modern, albeit minimal, tenets of democratic citizenship.

Defining Attentive Minimalists

As discussed in previous chapters, when compiling a taxonomy of citizenship, different schools of democratic thought fall along a continuum based on the amount of activity required for citizens to fulfill their democratic duties. The notion of *social democracy* posits a sense of activism on the part of the state and passive acceptance of collective benefits on the parts of citizens. Next on the continuum of activism is the *liberal tradition*. This position suggests that a "legal contract" exists between a government and its people such that governments must allow citizens access to just laws and the right to vote. Although this definition requires that states provide citizens with rights, it does not instill a reciprocal obligation that citizens use these rights by actively *participating* in the system of governance (Oliver and Heater, 1994). Instead, a good citizen is one who simply abides by the law and who votes, but who does not expect the state to provide extensive services and financial security.

Thickening the notion of the liberal tradition, Pateman (1970) characterizes liberal theory as espousing "institutional arrangements," observing that "[t]he social inequalities of the political culture of the liberal democracies are treated as separate from, and irrelevant to, the formal equality of citizenship" (p. 59). The political culture—the informal space where citizens interact informally when discussing the issues of the day—is not contemplated in this tradition, nor is the obligation of the state to provide services to citizens. Rather, the citizen is ascribed a well-defined but minimal role focusing on the vote as protective device against an overreaching or corrupt system (Pateman, 1970). Essentially, citizens/voters seek to *influence* public decisions rather than *participate* in them.

A more contemporary offering within the liberal tradition is Schudson's (1998) notion of "the monitoral citizen." As he traced notions of democratic participation in the United States from the Revolutionary period to the present, Schudson noted an ebb and flow of participation and, as a result, advanced a current definition of citizenship for the Information Age—a citizen is one who *follows* public affairs, even if he does not actively participate in them.

In his critique of classical democratic theory, Schumpeter (1943) argues that participatory democracy simply demands too much of citizens. In his model, he defined democracy as a method whereby dynamic leaders *compete* for citizens' votes and where citizens respond to the alternatives presented to them. In his view, this method works well because it places responsibility for the effectiveness of a regime on its ambitious leaders (acting in their self-interest) and requires just one action from citizens—that they vote (or exercise their *choice*).

Skocpol (1999) recently noted that political organizations in the United States have evolved from local meetings to national membership organizations where citizens across the country make monetary contributions but where Washington, DC-based professional staffs conduct political *activities* on their members' behalf. While these active minimalist citizens (those who follow and contribute) are perhaps not living up to the Aristotelian ideal of civic virtue, they are *intellectually* (if not physically) engaged in the political life of the nation.

In addition to those behaviors of citizenship, attentive minimalists also possess certain social and political *values*: independence and the ability to evaluate the performance of those in office (Galston, 1991). In sum, the active minimalists engage in the following civic activities:

- They believe in democratic values;
- They trust the legitimacy of the regime;
- They vote;
- They obey the law;
- They are tolerant of other views;
- They make few demands on the state;
- They are aware of political affairs;
- They join/contribute to organizations.

Based on this framework, let us now view the Wirehead respondents in light of this model of citizenship to discover what it means for them to be a "good citizen" in the Information Age.

Meet the Wireheads

Before exploring these implicit theories of citizenship, let us meet these "iron majors"[3] of the postindustrial economy.

Byron reflects many of the classic characterizations of Generation X. He is the negative, cynical character that populated Sacks's (1996) account of teaching college in the early 1990s, a person who claimed repeatedly to know little—and have even less interest—in politics. Byron asserted that he had no duty to his government, community, or country and refused to prescribe standards for good or bad behavior, claiming implicit right to Wolfe's (2001) moral freedom:

> Uh, do people owe the government anything? No, absolutely not. I would tend to think its more one sided. Uh, the government owes the people something. The government is in purpose the administerer (as in one who administers) the country and the people have all given up a share of their own personal freedom and personal power to make sure that the government is there and doing its business . . . . Why is that? . . . The two types of government that I see as either the bureaucracy or the political side. Uh, the political side is guided purely by self-interest, in my opinion. Uh, these are people who could probably care less about their country. Uh, less about their community than others might. And then, of course, they would let you believe that they're guided primarily by self-interest.

Yet despite his professed ignorance about politics, Byron had strong, cynical opinions about politicians and journalists. When pressed, he cited his sources for information as television and often used popular television shows as examples and analogies to illustrate his points. For example, when asked what his "ideal community" would be like, he managed to be nostalgic and cynical at the same time, reflecting not only a physical and intellectual complacency but

---

[3] "Iron major" is a military term for mid-level army officers who, according to army mythology, are the highest level of officers to actually "work for a living." They walk the line between tactical and strategic work.

also a longing for what television had shown ideal communities to be like. His view was the ersatz community explored by Freie (1998):

> Oh, gosh. Uh, you want to say that an ideal community would be like Logan's Run or the Stepford Wives or something which is everybody always has their great Truman Show. Where, you know, the sun always rises. Its always a nice sunny day. And everybody goes to work for 2 hours a day and they're doctors and make $100,000. And come home and play with their kids.

Simply, for Byron, real life is a pale approximation for the perfection he repeatedly saw on television.

Susan is married to Byron. They met at one of the area's largest employers and a company that enjoyed enormous growth throughout the 1990s. Byron was laid off in 2000 in the mass firings at the edge of the dot-com bubble, but Susan remained employed there. She reported feeling the strain of being both a family breadwinner and mother to two toddlers as Byron surfed the volatile ups and downs of contemporary Wirehead corporate life. At work, Susan is a product tester, a job she prepared for by obtaining a technical certification from a proprietary school. She likes her job because she gets to "try out all the new stuff," and she gets most of her community or political information by listening to those in the cubes around her. She does not read the newspaper or watch television news but feels little dismay at missing out on issues of national or local import, knowing that if things are important enough, people in her workplace will discuss them and she will overhear the discussion. Her vision of citizenship is both close to home and focused on her children, reflecting the lifestyle effects found in political literature (Lijphart, 1997; Bennett, 1997; Miller, 1992; Cassel and Luskin, 1988), and some of Putnam's (2000) small acts of civic engagement.

During our interview, we discussed Susan's view of citizens' duties, and here she displayed a mix of civic minimalism and a community-based social capital orientation:

> SUSAN: Uh, certain duties. Well, to work and pay taxes. To uh, contribute to the community in like uh, you know, buying stuff from children selling stuff for their schools to raise money. And doing food drives and stuff like that. . . .
>
> SS: If you think about people who vote regularly, they kind of keep up with what's going on, they do volunteer work like you talked about do you think that those people are extra good citizens or they're behaving as all citizens should?

SUSAN: I think they're behaving as all citizens should.
SS: Do you think people do?
SUSAN: I think more do than do not. Especially people who have children. I think uh, I know I do since I've had children.

When asked about her vision of the ideal community, Susan too was nostalgic, tying these feelings to her role as a new parent:

> Uh, hm. An ideal community? Well, growing up I lived here in Austin and I think that was a pretty good ideal community. Everyone uh, looked out for everyone else's kids. Kids could play in the neighborhood without fear of being ran over or abducted or anything. You could sleep with your doors open.

Far from Freie's disdain for the suburban "counterfeit communities" like the fast growing suburb where her company is located, Susan felt encapsulated in the community aspects she remembers from her own small-town childhood, a very real community indeed.

Mitch is a consultant, doctoral candidate, and self-described freelance "data jockey." He created the online graduate school exit survey for his university when he discovered that they were not tracking the progress of graduate students after they left campus. He consults on the sustainability of public information systems deployed by the Telecommunications Infrastructure Fund and prefers to "crank out code" on one of his many laptops from the far corner of Mozart's coffeehouse overlooking Lake Austin. Mitch has long hair and a goatee and prefers cutoffs and Birkenstocks to more traditional business attire. He disdains the thought of having to keep regular hours and always has three or four projects working at the same time. He prides himself on doing pro bono technical work for a variety of AIDS organizations while charging corporate clients to make up the difference. He is constantly scribbling notes for as-yet-unwritten screenplays, books, and technology company business plans. He is an accomplished photographer and is "just one long weekend" from finishing his dissertation on scientists who sought refuge in the United States during the Holocaust. Mitch thrives on these apparent contradictions and shows great passion for the range of his pursuits: "Man, interviewing Teller [the director of Lawrence Livermore National Laboratory and a refugee scientist] was one of the coolest moments of my life!"

Sandy works for one of the most high-profile technology companies in Austin's "Silicon Hills." He is a tall and intense man of 28, often described as a "genius." Although mid-level and hands-on, he has ridden the stock option wave and timed his financial plans well enough that he has the mobility of elites, often jetting away for weekends of blackjack in Las Vegas: "I'm quite a gambler really. I love blackjack. I mean I love the math of it. You can actually win." Despite his somewhat eccentric hobbies—gambling, online bridge games—he probably most closely reflects Putnam's views of social capital. When asked some classic questions about social trust, he drew distinctions between different levels of relationships but added a sharp insight into how these networks of associations together had built community capacity and webs of trust in his own life:

> I would not consider myself a super helpful person to the external world. It's definitely a function of how important those people are to me. . . . [An] interesting way to think about it is there are groups of people that I'm going to identify very closely with. That I'll help a lot. And then I think then there are those that I'm not going to identify with at all that I would pretty much rather be left alone and do my own thing . . . I think different people identify with bigger groups more often. For example, I mean, I think I, you know, there are a group of friends at work or uh, people I deal with a lot or consider myself to have a lot in common with I'd be more than willing to help out. I think there's people that kind of identify with the whole world if that makes any sense. . . . And sort of consider themselves a part of this really big thing and everybody's and they're more than willing to help just anybody on the random street. . . . [but I have] a hierarchy of how important . . . I think that if I'm in a situation with a bunch of people that I don't know at all I'm not very inclined to be very helpful in general. Uh, change that to a group of people that I identify with. And it doesn't have to be good friends. It could be the people that sit next to me with my UT football tickets, right. But it's still a group of people that I see on a weekly basis and know. And all things equal am I going to call the guy to get a mortgage loan or something, absolutely . . . the main thing is that there's some sort of thing going on there that I can identify with.

Despite his passion for technological interaction, Sandy displayed a keen understanding of the concentric circles comprising the web of social capital.

Jennifer is a tall, red-headed Web designer. While she loves "elegant code" and is eternally frustrated by those who will "fuck with perfectly good navigation out of pure laziness," she views herself as more artistic than technological and brings with that view a highly individualized and self-reliant conception of one's duty to one's community: "I believe that we have a responsibility to self-manage—not to be a burden to anyone." Politics always seemed foreign and removed from

Jennifer's life until she took on a temporary project redesigning the Texas governor's Web site. She was surprised by the intellectual quality of some of the people she met but was dismayed by some of the "mindless bureaucracy" and "political bullshit" she found during her weeks on a government contract. Like several other young people I talked with for this study, Jennifer grew up in a small town but, curiously, did not equate notions of the idyllic community with small-town life as several of the other respondents did. Quite the contrary. She saw her move to Austin as a way to escape the stifling and struggling community that did not understand her dreams and eccentricities. Today, she enjoys the hustle and bustle of the "big city" of Austin and sees it crackling with social capital:

> JENNIFER: I find generally people here in Austin and in this job and in the industry that I'm in very helpful. I think there comes a point where people realize that the more we scrabble to bring everyone up on the raft the better off we'll all be. And I think its very evident in this community.
> SS: Uh, in your other community as well? I mean, where you came from? Where you grew up?
> JENNIFER: No, it didn't seem that way at all. Uh, it was a very closed, tight conservative community. It seems much different than here. Of course, perhaps I still have on my rose colored glasses . . . [back there] I worked in the non-profit art community so I was up on that. Up on how the city operated and it was just a very uh, tough city. It was always struggling. Everybody was always struggling.

Like her Generation X compatriots, Jennifer's formative years were marred by difficult times that had instilled in her a strong sense of and need for independence.

Paul is the oldest of the group and the most disengaged from politics, countering the lifestyle effects hypothesis. Although deliberately removed from the happenings of public life, he does not use the language of cynicism or irony to explain his lack of engagement in politics. Instead, he sees politics the way he sees any other profession—one that is best left to the experts. "They don't need me to tell them where the taxes go. They have people who know much better than me about that." Paul is not without a sense of personal efficacy. He is confident enough in his skills and intellect to "freelance" from technology project to technology project in order to maintain his freedom, but he does not see himself as a part of a polity imbued with duties and responsibilities related to democratic self-governance. Adding to his paradoxical view of efficacy is his passion for his current project, which at the time of our interview was connected with a struggling dot-com business in the midst of a postbubble coup d'etat to regain control of its software and other intellectual property he helped create. Paul's company, which will be discussed more fully in the next chapter, is one focused on using Web technologies to facilitate greater philanthropic giving. Somehow he reconciled withdrawing from public engagement because experts already run things with a desire to use his technological skills to make the world a better place through building philanthropy.

As with others in Generation X, Paul was reluctant to prescribe specific conduct to citizens. He repeatedly characterized the primary duty of citizenship as "not to disrupt things," perhaps reflecting his generation's discomfort with conflict. While he did not believe that there was any transcendent duty to participate in community life, Paul was quite clear when enunciating the duty he believed all citizens have—the duty to *respond*:

> I don't think that take an average neighborhood people are sitting in their houses and they're having you know, they're living their lives individually. I think there's absolutely nothing wrong with that but on the other hand if there were a flood I think it would be everybody's responsibility to get out there with sandbags.

Paul's interview was conducted several months before the World Trade Center attacks of September 11, 2001. Sentiments about this duty to respond were implicit in the interviews with all members of my sample, but they became much more explicit during the interviews conducted after the attacks.

John is a freelance technologist, an introvert by nature. Although he is over 30, his first foray into political participation was in the Ralph Nader presidential campaign in 2000. He was drawn to the campaign through his interest in environmental protection and he accessed the campaign through the Web. After reading about the Nader effort, he moved away from his computer and out into the community to help gather signatures on petitions to get Nader on the ballot in Texas. Through these activities, John's worldview evolved, both about the implications for technology on the community and about his vision of what an ideal community would ultimately look like:

> JOHN: Uh, I don't know if it's just it seems to me like we're really at a seesaw point. Where uh, I don't know if this is true of every moment in history but it seems like the connectedness and the communities— the virtual communities that are being built and all that sort of thing

uh, I'm not sure what impact they're going to have. I don't know if they're going to lead to anarchy or community. I think they sort of have the ability to go either direction.

SS: And what will determine which way it goes in your mind?

JOHN: Uh, I think to some extent human nature. Kind of in there. Sort of the communal need of human beings and then also the personal needs and I don't know what's going to be stronger given more and more connectedness. Uh, it really depends on what people want to do.

SS: Are you optimistic or pessimistic?

JOHN: Uh, I'm optimistic.

John's optimism in the wake of his political involvement affirms Herbst's (1998) findings about partisan activists and raises interesting questions about the next-election effects of young people involved in the failed Dean campaign—that even when they lose, their participation increases both their optimism about the political system and their own sense of personal efficacy.

Jim works in technology support for the business school at a large university. His windowless basement office is filled with the persistent hum generated by the bank of servers running the state-of-the-art network needed to make his school a top drawer of potential entrepreneurial talent. Jim's thick glasses distorted the shape of his eyes and he wore a variety of technology devices on his belt, perhaps ushering in the twenty-first-century fashion equivalent of the pocket protector and slide rule. Also a parent, Jim's notions of community and service were drawn from his father, a military officer. When asked about service, he echoed the familiar refrains of Army recruitment commercials. Although Jim thinks of service and obligation in terms of the military, he joins his Wirehead colleagues in prescribing a duty to respond if called.

Pablo works for a local technology company that focuses on hardware and software deployments in the public sector. In other words, he helps design and install new computer systems into old state agencies. He is a very religious man; his views of community are, like Susan's, very much tied to his role as a parent. His beliefs about service to community, though, are deeply rooted in his Christian faith. In that sense, Pablo is very different from the rest of his Wirehead colleagues queried for this study, bearing greater resemblance to Dirk, the Cyber-democrat who spent several years as a Catholic brother before joining the political fray. Pablo perfectly enunciated the dynamic of reciprocity when describing the community most important to him: "To me this [the ideal] community would be very personal for me. The church. My church. The people I interact with. There's that definition of community and I would be very inclined to help others. I help others and they help me." On the government and technology front, Pablo joins his Wirehead colleagues' belief in the public sector's inherent inefficiency and in technology's potential to mitigate these inefficiencies:

> Well, I mean, the consultant comes out in me there. . . . I'm more analytical than political . . . [I ask] how efficiently and effectively is the money being used? Is it meeting its intended purpose? How do you measure performance? How do you measure outcomes? Is the money allocated that's meeting those intended performance measures? Can government be more efficient in terms of how it manages its money? How it administers its programs? How can technology be used more efficiently and effectively? Uh, so it would [be] much more of an analytical management look at the money rather than a political argument.

Here Pablo underscores a persistent Wirehead belief—that politics is inherently inefficient and would be made better by the application of both business analytics and contemporary technology.

More than the other groups in my sample, Wireheads physically and demographically reflect the depictions of Generation X in the literature. They are generally well educated but have waited longer to settle down, buy homes, marry, and start families. They are more inclined to seek flexibility in their work and community in their workplace (Brooks, 2000; Halstead and Lind, 2001). The workplace (or at least their *workstation*, wherever it may exist) is the center of their lives (Brooks, 2000; Florida, 2002). The realms of work, home, and community become blurred into one. This conflation of different spheres underscores the weakness in Putnam's measures of old-style social capital. When work and community are the same, measures that only count activities "away from work" as social capital-building activities miss the main conduit for building and sustaining human relationships among this cohort—the work they commonly produce.

While the larger question of measuring social capital is an important one (and will be addressed in chapter 8 of this book), the more interesting Wirehead story is the way in which they think about what it means to be a good citizen and how this definition has moved from the public realm to the cubicle at work.

Economic Virtue as Good Citizenship

While Wireheads generally conveyed negative impressions of politics and largely eschewed involvement in and knowledge of the political system, their *economic* values were consistent with those of the civic minimalist.

For example, Wireheads were asked to rank a list of human traits in order of their importance (Almond and Verba, 1960), and they were surprisingly uniform in their views. At the top of each person's list was "does his job well," conveying the primacy of the work ethic and of making an economic contribution. However, in all but one case, *Generous* was the trait that they ranked second, which would seem to convey a sense of social responsibility, hardly the lazy slackers depicted in most Generation X accounts. This is important since, as Almond and Verba (1960) found, those who valued generosity were most likely to form groups to try to effect change. Surprisingly, each Wirehead ranked "thrifty" at the bottom of the list.

These anomalies are curious and have implications for citizenship. Their preferences reflect a strong sense of *economic* values—"does his job well" and "shares with those he knows." However, could the low rating of thriftiness convey a cynicism about the future? Do well and be generous today, because who knows what will happen tomorrow? Smith and Clurman (1997), Howe and Strauss (1993), Hicks and Hicks (1999) found that Generation X tended to have more negative views about the future, perhaps because of youthful experiences with the economic strife of the 1970s (through the mid-1980s) and because of the high levels of divorce among their cohort's parents. However, these respondents do not reflect the *selfishness*, described in the literature but rather a strong need for *flexibility*, perhaps reflecting a need for an exit strategy to assure them the freedom to leave a bad situation, whether professional or personal.

Professionally, the dynamic of serial employment has been accelerating for Generation X. According to Halstead and Lind (2001), the median job tenure for Americans over the age of 25 was down to 5 years. However, isolating the Generation X age groups, males aged 25–34 have an average tenure of 2.7 years on the job and for males aged 20–24, the average is 1.2 years. Like Wolfe's (1998) advocates of moral freedom, Wireheads therefore feel that the highest value is one of self-reliance and that any collective actions endorsed should be a matter of *personal choice*. Even when they explicitly discussed notions of citizenship and governance, they did so in the context of their workplace and in the language of business.

Choice

Inherent in the language of business is the primacy of *choice*. To Wireheads, choice maximizes their freedom and fuels competition, which leads to greater efficiency and added value for all. Without choice, they implicitly argue, things are *by definition* inefficient. This inherent definition helps explain that, despite their self-reported liberalism about social issues (especially environmental issues and public education), they view the government negatively. In their view, the government makes excessive demands, the government takes away choices, and is therefore inefficient. Government also takes money without asking. In the Wireheads' view, citizens resent the fact that they have no choice but to pay taxes. When asked about the ways in which government affected his life, Byron displays a resentment born of limited efficacy:

> It (the government) decided what the level of taxes that I pay. Every dollar that I earn a certain percentage is taken out. It gives me a sense of national security. It pays for the military to keep me safe in my home. Away from the intrusion of foreign governments be it real or imagined. Uh, goes into social and socio- economic programs. Uh, boots up. Keeps everybody up. Uh, goes to give money to people who do not make as much money as I do. Maybe some of the elderly, the unemployable, the handicapped, etc. Uh, ways that it directly impacts my life. I would say are fairly minimal other than taking the money out of my pocket. Putting the money back in my pocket it does a very poor job of . . . But uh, again I see very little impact as to where my tax money is being spent and how it affects me.

Further, in the mechanism by which they might exercise choice with respect to the government—the vote—Wireheads see it as too often a choice between two options they do not like (and hence not really a choice) or as a choice that has no ultimate effect on the performance of their government (and hence a choice that has no meaning).

Security and Dependence

Moving from the systemic level to a more personal view, Wireheads perceive governmental *people*—both civil servants and politicians—as having an inferior work ethic, an affront to the critical economic virtue in their worldview of citizenship. In addition to government being dominated by inefficient institutions, Wireheads see it as populated by people bereft of the economic values that Wireheads believe all good *economic* citizens should posses. Comments describing characterizations of "lazy bureaucrats" reflect Wirehead opinions about the dearth of economic virtue among public sector actors:

> I believe that the salary system that we have now is big and bloated.

There are probably too many employees working in the governmental space right now to get the job done. It's not being run as lean as a corporation is being run. Also, uh, again the government has a certain system where you can probably say it better than I can but there's [something] in the government where if you've been there so long. I won't say you're exempt from being fired but it's a very difficult thing to be laid off or to be fired.

*   *   *

I'm also familiar with the people that just like government jobs because they're secure and what not.

*   *   *

I can't say I was terribly impressed with the whole judicial system. Is it really going to help me at all? Because it's like organized chaos. And the permitting system is sort of silly because it's just a way, I think, for the city to generate income. . . . Because some of it to a point was so superfluous to what we were trying to do.

Adaptability to Change

Closely related to the value of the work ethic is the economic attribute of adaptability to technological and economic change. Wireheads disdain public sector workers for their perceived reliance on job security and their resistance to change, risk, and citizen choice. To Wireheads, government workers could not possibly be good citizens because they do not posses the economic values they believe are integral to making a positive societal contribution.

> BYRON: Uh, government people it depends uh, politicians I don't have that much personal experience with them. Other than what is on television. On a nightly basis and I'm sure that's colored and not 100% objective. As far as bureauticians [sic] are concerned or people that work under the politicians or bureaucracy I would say those people [are a mix]. . . . There are certain people who are very devoted towards their work. Uh, they're very devoted towards their job. Then there are other people who are the converse of that. They are certain people who serve between 8:00 am

to 5:00 and at 5:01 they're gone. . . . They simply milk the bureaucracy for what its worth. They put their 30 years in there. They retire. They're out.

SS: You say some are devoted and others are not. How does that compare to your experience in the private sector?

BYRON: I would say in the private sector it's a little bit more difficult because again at the end of the day you run a business and your business is created to make money. There's not a business out there other than the .coms that are going bust with business cases that expressly say we're going to lose money. All business cases say we're going to make money at doing whatever we do. The bottom line is the bottom line with the company. Government, of course, has no bottom line. Government is not . . . directly responsible because there is no measurable bottom line to the government. So when we're talking about employees who are dedicated those are usually people who are dedicated through personal motivations. Uh, when you have people who are non-dedicated uh, put in the 40 hours a week. Not the 41 hours a week. Then you're talking about the people who are just doing enough to get by. And how that is compared with the private sector since the private sector you can be hired or fired any day of the week. 5 days a week, 7 days a week, 365 a year. You do not have job security where you do working for a federal bureaucracy . . . So, of course, not having job security you have to work that much harder, you have to be better than the guy sitting next to you. Better than the gal sitting next to you. You have to be able to show your economic worth every day.

Here, we see Byron being drawn to the simplicity of business. For him, success is "the bottom line," a far cry from the complex interplay of ideas and values inherent in political deliberations.

Wireheads on Technology and Politics

Wireheads are stunningly uniform in their technological capabilities, possessions, and access patterns. Each one owns at least one computer and has broadband, high-speed Internet access at home and in the workplace. They all are connected to the Internet through their entire workday and spend a substantial amount of time at home engaging in various online activities, from e-mail to research, from games to chat rooms. They exchange electronic mail as part of their work routine and as part of their family life and social lives as well—often 100 messages a day or more.

While their technological habits were common, their political orientations were more varied. One of my interviewees was identified as a Republican, one as a Democrat, one as a Nader-supporting Independent, while the remainder claimed that such a question was "not applicable." Wireheads were also split in their voting behaviors—half voted in the 2000 election while half did not. This percentage reflects the typical voter turnout numbers of all Americans, not the abysmally low turnout numbers reported for Generation X as a whole (Lijphart, 1997; Bennett, 1997; Miller, 1992; Cassel and Luskin, 1988). Despite this diversity in political self-identification and their higher-than-typical Generation X voter turnout, they reflected the literature on political efficacy. I asked them three questions that are mainstays of political science, questions relating to efficacy and cynicism (Almond and Verba, 1960; Delli Carpini, 1996): For example, "The way people vote is what determines the way things get run in this country." Each of my interviewees disagreed with that statement. Yet when reacting to the statements, "A few good leaders would do more for this country than all the laws and talk," and "All candidates sound good in their speeches, but you can never tell what they will do once they are elected," all agreed.

These responses raise interesting questions about this group of middle-class young people. Broadly, they do not see that their vote—or for that matter, anyone's vote—really has an impact on how the country operates. Yet, half of them still vote, and most of them of them say that it gives them a sense of satisfaction to do so. Why is that so? Why would someone get a sense of satisfaction out of doing something that allegedly has no impact? Each one also agreed that a few good leaders would be better for the country than "all the laws and talk."

These responses reveal a quirky sort of optimism tinged with a low level of political sophistication. The respondents feel good about voting, yet they do not believe at this point that their vote matters. However, if better candidates existed—and they believe that those candidates do exist (although they are not currently in politics—more on that later), then government would function as they believe it should. My respondents' lack of political sophistication is reflected most explicitly in the "laws and talk" question, a question that taps the commercial bias inherent in this group. For them, the business of the political class is "laws and talk" or more accurately, *debate* that results in the making of laws. For them, this is a tedious process indeed.

The technology community has been observed to have an "action-bias," a preference for doing over talking. This helps to explain the

Wireheads' frustration with politics. They feel that (1) *talk* equals inaction; (2) inaction equals inefficiency; and (3) inefficiency is bad. Add to this mindset the Generation X predisposition to avoid conflict (Smith and Clurman, 1997) and to view conflict as disrespectful (Sanford, 2000) and the picture of Wirehead disengagement from traditional political life becomes clearer.

They view political life as separate and inactive, ineffectual and inefficient, and they avoid it for precisely these reasons. *However, their avoidance of traditional forms of politics does not mean that they see themselves as poor citizens.* Quite the contrary. The Wireheads have quite an explicit view of what good citizens do. They see themselves and their coworkers displaying this conduct every day within the context of their professional work. Their vision casts an intriguing light on the idea of the active minimalist. They agree with many of that category's tenets but the *context* of those values is very different than that contemplated by democratic theorists and social capital thinkers.

Wireheads possess and value these traits in the *workplace* and largely see their bosses and colleagues adhering to these principles each day. However, they do not attach these same values to the current political system or to those who are currently serving in government. Further, they doubt that these traits of quality citizenship are *political* virtues at all. Instead, they believe that politicians and government workers hold up these standards for others but do not adhere to these precepts themselves. As a result, their disdain is both palpable and a vivid example of what Wolfe (1998) found about the American middle class, a community in which many commandments are up for grabs and one commandment is inviolable—thou shalt not be a hypocrite.

In essence, these politically disengaged Wireheads subscribe to the virtues of classic citizenship, but they transfer these virtues to the workplace, giving a thoroughly contemporary cast to the sentiment, "I gave at the office." This transmogrification makes for interesting paradoxes in the arena of social capital.

To Wireheads, vitality, ingenuity, passion, and fun all exist in the work world. This group especially comports to Richard Florida's (2000) notion of the economic geography of talent. While geography is not a limitation, as in one respondent's passion for late-night bridge games that span the globe, geography very much applies to Wirehead work. They seek to be next to vital people and they see this happening at work, *not* in the public sphere. Certainly not in government.

In the Wirehead worldview, *work equals community.* Therefore, they express, value, and exhibit the virtues required for good citizenship and strong social capital but they channel those virtues into their work environments, that is, their communities. This unique definition raises some interesting insights into the current nature of reciprocity, a key ingredient to social capital (Putnam, 2000).

Wirehead Citizenship and the Problem of Reciprocity

The notion of "citizen as free rider" (Olson, 1965) was recently explored by Raadschelders (1995), who claimed that contemporary citizen participation, particularly the demand and rights-oriented activism of special interest groups, highlight the "true problem of our time"—a lack of reciprocity between government and citizen. In his view, the violation of reciprocity norms was the *citizen's* fault. This dearth of reciprocity, he argued, explained dissatisfaction with government, declining participation and demand overload for governments. In a sense, he argued the welfare state (so maligned by Wireheads) that provides communal benefits yet asks little from citizens in return has changed citizen participation from a moral duty to a civil right, something far different from a mutual responsibility. In light of other research concerning reciprocity, I have argued that this perspective helps explain why Americans feel so dissatisfied with their government: by providing services without asking anything in return, the arrangement feels unjust, perhaps giving people a vague sense of freeloading. Putnam's data refute the claim that the expansion of the welfare state has been a primary cause for the decline in social capital, but his data do not address the spiritual angst that people feel when reciprocity norms have been violated. Thus, while AFDC (now TANF) programs may not have depleted social capital, the sense of entitlement that "rights talk" has created may contribute to the cynicism and unease that Americans have about government and politics. This is not a new argument. However, Wireheads see reciprocity between citizen and government quite differently.

Wireheads sense that reciprocity norms have been violated *in the opposite direction*. From their perspective, they are asked—required—to give, and yet see little in return. One may argue that the Wireheads' impression is incorrect, that they are products of public schools and the beneficiaries of student grants and loans and a range of other collective infrastructure goods. Surprisingly, they seem to understand that. However, echoing a refrain from the 1980's, their sentiment is closer to "What have you done for me lately?" as they enter the ranks of taxpayers. This angst underscores the need to delineate between notions of *government as service delivery* and *politics as self-governance*. The reciprocity of service delivery is similar to that of business—I give you money, you give me a product. Simple. However, reciprocity in the social and self-governance sense is more akin to Rucinski's (1991) "shared knowledge of the perspectives of others and the interests underlying those perspectives."

This definition describes the ways in which Wireheads view their workplace colleagues. Rather than a tit-for-tat arrangement between individuals, Rucinski operationalized reciprocity as the "ratio of perspective and underlying interests known to the members of a collectivity." In a sense, she argued that political knowledge—especially political knowledge of others' views—is a necessary condition for societal reciprocity. Here, rather than a gut-level norm, reciprocity becomes a knowledge-based negotiation of shared political power and influence among social actors, individuals, and groups. Wireheads implicitly understand this dynamic and embody it in their *professional* lives. Note, for example, how Sandy describes the capacities of his boss and the amorphous nature of his obligation to the larger world:

> I think you should be semi-informed and vote your preference. Uh, you know, there's simple things you can, you know, you can volunteer or work on a campaign or you could uh, do something for your church or you could uh, you know, clean up the street. There's those basic kind of volunteer help out things. But I think that I don't even think that's the right thing for a lot of people to do. I mean, you take my boss . . . [he is a] very wealthy man. Very successful man. Uh, I think he would hate it and it would be an absolute waste of his time to do any of those things. I think he can add a ton more value uh, even if it's just continue to work in the area he works in and give the money which is certainly helpful to all these. He can do other things. He could uh, he could try and lead a big effort. He could try to find somebody to lead a big effort, you know . . . I think to say something like everybody should spend 10 hours kind of volunteering or walking around is just not the right thing for everybody to do. . . . Not everybody's going to want to do that and some people could be very more effective for the community by doing it their own way. Again, maybe it's just I'm going to work harder at my job and give you money.

However, Wireheads have not yet internalized the more complex type of reciprocity into their conceptions of *political* life. One significant barrier to that understanding is the Wireheads' preoccupation with perceived *bias*.

The Curious Issue of "Bias"

While Wireheads display commercial versions of civic attributes, they do not translate those attributes into action in the public sphere. When they explicitly reject politics and government, it is generally because they perceive it as "biased." Nearly all of the Wireheads with whom I spoke opined at length about the *bias* in the news media and from politicians. All but one largely eschewed newspapers, noting that they followed the news through the newspapers only from "time to time." More followed the news on television but only half did so "from time to time" and only one "watched every day." But all of them reported that they searched for news on the Web. Wireheads described the bias they found in a number of ways:

> Because we only know what the media presents to us really and at that point its colored by how its presented to us. Uh, you know, I had a friend travel to Europe and I forget at what point it was or what was going on. There was something political going on and they were amazed at the difference between how it was spun there and how it was spun here. And there were things that we just absolutely did not know about here.

*   *   *

> Uh, I like the idea of something really appeals to me about reading the Supreme Court decision as opposed to listening to your biased news reporter talk to you about it.

*   *   *

> I have access to what the press will give me access to. However, I don't have any inclination about the political problems going on.

This dynamic of bias is a curious one. Where Wireheads claim to see untenable subjectivity from reporters and news sources in the newspaper and on television, they felt that the only "objective" news was to be found on the Web. Yet, where on the Web did they go for their news? Not to the Jenni-Cam or the old renegade sites of the early Mosaic days. With the exception of one respondent who claimed to get his news primarily from the *Drudge Report*, the remainder got their "objective news" from the sites hosted by the *New York Times*, CNN, and the other mainstream news outlets. They saw no irony in disbelieving what they saw on television and in newsprint, and yet believing what they saw on the computer screen *even if the information came from the same source*.

As with their conceptions of efficiency, this dynamic of bias is tied up with notions of "choice." There was a sense among them that the newspaper is delivered to your home and hence you have no choice as to where you get your news. Television news is the same. You get the same format at the same time each day, regardless of your personal schedule or your peculiar values and interests. Wireheads perceived an enhanced credibility of a news source that you can choose on your own time, on your own schedule, and read at your own depth. Only one mentioned the importance of getting to primary sources (an alleged value of using the Web to become informed) rather than newspapers or television. He was fascinated by the aftermath of the Bush versus Gore case that ultimately decided the 2000 presidential election:

> Sitting on my couch watching CNN and I had my laptop. I have a wireless network card so I can just sit on my couch. . . . And connect it to the Internet via cable modem with a wireless cord. When the decision came out I went to the [Supreme Court] website. I had read the thing before what's her name from CNN. . . . They're all standing around [in front of the camera] and they haven't read it. I just sat there and read it. I read the real decision. I didn't listen. First of all, they didn't even know what it said for like 2 hours. . . . They didn't really get it. Because it was complicated. It was very complicated. . . . So I was like wow! I didn't know this was so complicated. Look! This is what they say. It was very interesting. It was a lot more complicated that I think most people give it credit and the information's all completely there . . . you don't have to like go to the library and archives and all that stuff. Right? You can just sit on your couch and read it.

Another curious facet of the Wirehead worldview is that they do not see *bias* in the business world. This points perhaps to their idiosyncratic definition of bias. Rather than bias meaning a distorted point of view, it means having a point of view but *claiming that you are objective*.

Television and Efficiency

This is the only group of Generation X technologists that admits to watching a lot of television. Wireheads had two interesting views on the vast wasteland. One said that TV was the one way he could relax and be entertained. He claimed to watch TV as a source of news as well, although, echoing the sentiments of others, he found TV news hopelessly biased. While unable to answer the question, "Biased towards what?" this respondent (Byron) was convinced that he knew of *politicians'* biases from "personal experience." When pressed, he supplied a near perfect affirmation of the seduction of television argued by Hart (1994): that his so-called personal experience came from watching reporters and politicians on television. Byron believed that he was participating because he was watching, that he was informed because he was watching, and that he was *superior* to those he was watching. He was therefore the perpetually cynical monitoring citizen—among the three most cynical respondents, helping to support both Postman's and Putnam's concerns about the effects of television on public life:

> Now what you hear, of course, on the news which again is probably the negative things and not so much positive things. But on a daily basis are all the great politicians that we have uh, that cheat and skirt the system. The people that have the checking accounts that never get paid. The people that expect the express limo service. The people taking rides across the country in F-15 fighter planes. Uh, the people with the two different mistresses because, of course, they can afford to . . . if you're really going to try to do something of a service you ought to not get anything out of it other than the intangibles that at the end of the day you did a good job and you were a service and benefit to your country.

Among the many ironies and contradictions in Byron's views, perhaps the most curious was his privileging of business imperatives, yet opining that anyone who would go into elective office should not be paid for his or her work. As Postman might have noted, Byron's embrace of television's realities had convinced him that all problems are simultaneously intractable and yet as simple to solve as a typical television advertising dilemma. Where Byron worked to make his computer more like his television, an instrument designed to entertain him, Sandy took a different approach.

Sandy used his television to choose his politics and to participate in community—including politics. Although he too used television as a means of entertainment, he used his computer to make his relaxation more efficient and to maximize control over his entertainment choices:

> Right now I don't watch anything [in real time]. First of all I save 15 minutes an hour by not watching the commercials . . . [and] I watch the little things I want to watch without having to sit through the big things . . . [now] I can cut back on all these extra HBO's and all this because now I just go and it (the TiVO) figures out what I want to record and so there's always something set that I want to record. But I'm actually bothered by it because there's so many more great things they could do with this that they haven't done yet. . . . The technology's basically there. Like, for example, all they need to do is put an Ethernet card in the thing and assume everybody has a cable modem and now I can send shows to those who didn't tape them, right? Like I didn't tape Friends. Oh, here it is. Boom. Just send it to them. All it needs to be doing is hooked up to the network connection at people's homes are going to eventually going to be hooked up to and you could do that . . . or some simple more editing capabilities so I could cut out the 15 minutes tonight's the MTV video music awards. . . . And there's the Brittany's singing her new song that she does on the thing and all that so someone's going to want to see that. Cut out the 10 minutes send it to them and . . . [p]ut it on your computer even. Take a show and put it on. . . . I could take the *West Wing* and put it on my laptop, watch it on the plane . . . my hard drive has enough space for 4 *West Wings* so as long as I always kept a little free I could always put one 1 hour show on my computer . . . [so] I waste less time watching TV than I did when I was a kid. That's a good thing, right?

Choice, Control, and the Changing Nature of What Constitutes News

When it comes to news, Wireheads are a confusing lot. On the one hand, generally (with a couple of notable exceptions) they watched less television than do typical Americans, although more than in the rest of my sample. On the other hand, the Wireheads displayed a uniform distrust of traditional news sources, perhaps signaling the end of the "Golden Age" of journalism. While explicitly rejecting mediated news, they were also uncomfortable with the notion of a cadre of "experts" who filter and explain current events to them (with the notable exception of Paul, who expected experts to run everything). The disintermediation of all sorts of commercial activities has changed expectations for public information. While journalists and scholars lament this state of affairs, there is room for optimism in many of the

Wireheads' responses. In addition to their actively seeking information on the Web, looking at the catalysts that *send them* to the Web uncovers a potentially important set of questions and potential indicators about new definitions of political information.

A provocative article by Bruce Williams and Michael Delli Carpini (2002) put a pro-Wirehead spin on 20 years of declining news audiences and newspaper circulation. Beyond just the proliferation of news outlets, and news formats, these researchers note, we may be seeing a new definition of what *news actually is*. Rather than echo the common critique of news in decline as a result of increasing entertainment imperatives, Williams and Delli Carpini argue that we need a new definition of "politically relevant information." The Golden Age of journalism was more a Golden Age of journalistic *privilege*, which Wireheads would say was undermined by bias, centralization, and a subtle form of condescension for the public.

Now, perhaps the proliferation of potential sources—whether cynical offerings like the *Drudge Report*, late-night television or talk radio or quality fare like the *West Wing*—indicates a *state of flux* in the definition of politically relevant information. In political information as in social capital: does this flux necessarily signal a decline? Many scholars have argued that "hard news" journalism has done an abysmal job of informing the nation about issues relevant to self-governance. Certainly mainstream television news, with its incoherent nonlinear list of tragedies from around the world (Postman, 1985), episodic frame (Cappella and Jamieson, 1997), and conflict bias (Fallows, 1997) has hastened the decline of cerebral television news. As a result, Wireheads now turn to other sources. Might this democratization of sources lead to greater quality? Because news and entertainment have converged, one might observe, there is a need to find new ways of defining politically relevant media and how people should consume them. By Wirehead commercial logic, more choice yields superior outcomes, so a proliferation of sources for politically relevant information could reduce bias as they define it, leading to greater Wirehead interest in politics.

Williams and Delli Carpini (2002) argue that for this debate about politically relevant information to be useful, political media should no longer be stovepiped by genre (news versus drama), content (fact versus fiction), and source (journalist versus actor). Instead, they compellingly argue that they should be categorized by *utility*: "The extent to which any communication is politically relevant depends on what it does—its potential use—rather than on who says it and how it is said.

In a democratic polity, politically useful communications are those that shape: (1) the conditions of one's everyday life; (2) the lives of fellow community members; and (3) the norms and structures that influence those relationships."

This insight is reflected in how Wireheads think about citizenship. For example, Susan overheard a coworker talking on the other side of her cube wall. That piqued her interest about a city council race, so she launched Google on her desktop to find out more about the issue being discussed. She described this strategy as a sort of information economizing: "We don't get the newspaper. I don't watch the evening news. Uh, I only hear about major things. People at work and then I go and do some research on them if they interest me but I'm just too busy to keep up with everything that's going on."

As with larger political issues, Susan employed a similar strategy closer to home. Her family had a dispute with a neighbor about an easement for their new pool, so she researched the planning commission and permitting process in her town. She made a trip to the commission meeting and was surprised to meet "people who were really helpful" (these are the same bureaucrats who, when they were anonymous, were apparently all that was wrong with America). To be sure, the television and the local paper would not have featured such practical public information. But having an informal source, a choice, technology skills, and an immediate need drew Susan into community life. All of this raises the question: which source is better for building social capital? An informal web of interactions based on choice and chance or a mediated version of what matters decided in a newsroom miles (or half a country) away?

From the standpoint of social capital, there are hopeful signs on the entertainment front as well. Three times as many people watched *West Wing's* special episode on terrorism after 9/11 than the local news that same evening. Could that popular episode, one that was discussed in chat rooms and around dot-com water coolers the next day, be a better source of political and civic understanding than the around-the-clock cacophony hosted by Fox News ("America at War!")? Could new insights be drawn from comedian Jon Stewart's *Daily Show* counterpunch to Fox's excess ("America Freaks Out!") if we approached these sources in the thoughtful, critical way that Williams and Delli Carpini prescribe?

In the same way that Wireheads avoid routine and security in their work, they are suspicious of single sources and prefer to generate questions and data on their own. That analytical and creative activity is at the heart of their work—and Florida (2002) argues, increasingly the heart of most American knowledge work. It is not surprising then, that these creative-class actors would want to create their own definition of what it means to be a good citizen as well. And they do. But they stop short of prescribing a definition for anyone else. Whereas Wolfe (2001) worried that the age of moral freedom would force everyone to become his or her own personal moral philosopher, Wireheads seem to believe that they should be their own *civics teacher* and *news director*. The key question is: *will they?*

Democratic communication requires that audiences know who is speaking to them, that a range of viewpoints is made available, that the information is truthful, and, most importantly for this exploration, that such information facilitates *action*. Recall that to animate reciprocity, an act between two people or between a person and a community must take place. In Putnam's version of social reciprocity, the affirmative act of doing good launches a virtuous cycle of service and obligation that builds social capital. In the Generation X version, as we have seen in both the generational literature and the aftermath of 9/11, the duty to serve is actually eclipsed by the *duty to respond*. In the parlance of Chris Matthews (1999) paraphrasing Machiavelli, if you want to gain someone's loyalty ask them for a favor. Might these less obvious sources of politically relevant information observed by Wireheads on television, on the Web, and in the cubicle next door, move these young people to respond, to act?

In my small sample, the answer appears to be yes. While recent studies have documented the low levels of voter turnout and a slim grasp of the "facts" of civics among young people, other work indicates that volunteerism is up (Halstead and Lind, 2001), blood donations have dramatically increased, and a conservative president has called for every American to donate 4,000 hours of service to their communities. Something is going on, and it is going on in places other than traditional news sources. Political science literature posits that political interest leads to greater media exposure. (Recall Sandy's enthusiastic embrace of *Bush v. Gore.*) It also argues that people form political opinions learned from interpersonal interactions. (Recall Susan and her cube mates talking about elections or the machinations of the Planning Commission.) In those cases, atypical news sources precipitated greater political awareness, knowledge, and activity.

Think of the capabilities of the Web in this context. The Web does not (yet) possess the structural biases of TV news but does have streaming video and other visually sophisticated methods by which to deliver political information.

The Web does not (yet) face the "mediator problem" of reporters who feel entitled to their own agenda and the space limitations faced by modern newspapers and 30-minute evening news casts (Patterson, 1994). The Web also allows multiple types of interaction, both synchronous and asynchronous. And unlike both television and newspapers (to a lesser degree) the Web does require *attention* rather than mere *exposure*, which is shown to have little effect on political learning. The key here is political interest. How does one broadly instill political interest in others and, eventually, political learning and participation?

While collectivity is important in long-term creation and maintenance of social capital, the more pressing issue is to uncover the catalytic event(s) or mechanisms that will initially draw individuals back into social and political interactions. Research shows, after all, that once one dips a toe in the civic pool, one tends to stay in the water.

The Jesse Ventura campaign in 1998, the 2000 presidential campaigns of U.S. Senator John McCain (R-AZ) and Ralph Nader, and most notably the 2004 campaign of Vermont Governor Howard Dean provide evidence for cautious optimism that the Web has this catalytic ability. However, the explosion of e-commerce and the dominance of market logic over democratic logic in both the real and virtual worlds may be gradually eroding that potential (Sclove, 2000). The current conflation of the concepts of capitalism and democracy mask the inherent tension between democratic and market logic. Common wisdom implores leaders to "run government like a business and treat the citizen as customer." Wireheads have certainly embraced this ethos with gusto. However, making the distinction between running an efficient public sector service delivery organization—in which business processes would be appropriate and useful—must be distinguished from the collective thinking and discussion that must take place for a healthy liberal democracy to function. Understanding the differences between these two constructs is critical if civic space on the Internet is to become the catalyst for social capital that some early examples indicate it can become.

Conclusion

Although they reflect some of the more negative traits ascribed to Generation X and technology workers, Wireheads tell a more complex story of citizenship than the one-dimensional diatribes found in most accounts. Despite their relative ignorance of political and civic matters, they are technologically sophisticated, hardworking, and often engaged in a range of virtual, interpersonal, and community activities. *In the context of their work*, they reflect and advocate many of the virtues and behaviors embodied in the attentive minimalist view of democratic citizenship. Based on a matrix of Galston's virtues and classic notions of democracy, attentive minimalists believe in democratic values, trust in the legitimacy of the regime, vote, obey the law, are tolerant of other's views, make few demands on the state, are aware of political affairs, and join or contribute to organizations. Wireheads do nearly all of these things but they do them *at work* rather than in politics. In essence, they are *economic* attentive minimalists who privilege self-reliance and economic contribution but who also display the attitudes toward each other and toward their country necessary for quality citizenship.

The civic challenge with this cohort will be to diffuse the negative impressions of government solidified by years of political grandstanding and "gotcha" journalism that Wireheads have witnessed and to counter their antipathies for the inefficiencies of the public service delivery. Web technologies, which are heavily used by this cohort and increasingly embraced in both government and civic life, could be the tools that help thaw the chilly relationship between Wireheads and the public sphere.

Another possible catalyst to greater involvement may be found in a surprising place—the corner office of the Wirehead workplace—daytime home to the Tech Elites. As the next chapter will show, the Wireheads' bosses are working on a delicate balance with respect to civic life: respecting the old, while helping create the new.

6

Tech Elites: Bridging Old and New Social Capital

The picture of a high-tech CEO in the early twenty-first century is a mythic one. Leibovich (2002) characterized the big five Information Age entrepreneurs that dominated the euphoria of the "New Economy" as the "New Imperialists" and argued that these "five restless kids grew up to virtually rule your world." Proving that recovering *Washington Post* journalists can lapse into fits of hyperbole just as much as Silicon Valley CEOs can, Leibovich constructs a compelling behind-the-curtain glimpse of the postindustrial titans of commerce: Steve Case of AOL, John Chambers of Cisco; Jeff Bezos of Amazon.com; Bill Gates of Microsoft, and Larry Ellison of Oracle. While the New Imperialists (with the exception of Bezos) are Baby Boomers, the Generation X Tech Elites of Austin, Texas, have dreamed big dreams as well. Their scale has been smaller and their fortunes more ephemeral. However, their passion for their entrepreneurial enterprises and their evolution from young outliers with big ideas to civic and cultural leaders helping to define economic and social changes parallel the trajectories of these mythic leaders.

Like the titans, the Tech Elites I have interviewed are generally from comfortable suburban backgrounds, described being outliers as children and saw the commercial implications of technological advance well before mainstream America did. Further, many of them sacrificed some elements of traditional life along the way and tend to wrestle with their futures, both in business and in the community broadly construed. Sociologist Peter Berger (1986) observed that capitalism is "particularly deprived of mythic potency." That status will change, he writes, only "on the day when poets sing the praises of the Dow Jones and when large numbers of people are ready to risk their lives in defense of the Fortune 500." Berger does not assign high probability to either thing happening, proving that he has not spent much time with technology entrepreneurs. Tech Elites display a range of tensions and contradictions, passion, and pragmatism. They often echo Steve Case's description of himself: "I am equal parts capitalist (building a big successful business); an anarchist (enjoy blowing things up and starting over), and populist (really hoping to make the benefits of this medium available for everyone)" (Leibovich, 2002, p. 191).

My first Tech Elite interview reflected these seemingly conflicting characterizations. It took place on the deck of a rickety old duplex above downtown Austin. I met with the respondent at her "home" where she was both living and had relocated her fledgling start-up that had fallen just as dramatically as it had risen just a couple of years before. She suggested that I bring beer and that she would provide snacks; we could sit outside overlooking the Cheapo Records Store at the corner of 10th and Lamar—an Austin landmark for its trafficking in the local musical fare and for being the first place in Austin where Shoal Creek overflows its banks during the rains that deluge the area every 10 years or so. The creek then crests several feet over the major downtown thoroughfare, flooding the resilient small businesses that line that infamous boulevard. It is a quintessentially Austin location, the sort of authentic, original space that Richard Florida argues serves as a magnet for creative talent.

There was no rain the night we talked, only the sultry September air and the faint neon shimmer of the Cheapo sign that cast an eerie red light over the Austin skyline. We could not sit inside because, in her effort to support a clandestine enterprise in blatant violation of neighborhood zoning, she had stuffed her personal effects into the 500 square feet of the old duplex while reserving the lower apartment for the server farms and tiny workstations salvaged from the wreckage of her company's turbulent acquisition by a Silicon Valley rival. Keeping the technology cool and operational meant that her living space bore the full brunt of Austin's stifling September climate. In effect, she lived without air-conditioning to keep her dot-com labor of love in the black. There is perhaps no better metaphor for the commitment these Tech Elites bring to their ventures. Far from the Ferrari-driving laissez-faire Capitalists from Hell described by Borsook (2000), the entrepreneurs I interviewed proved closer to archetypal figures of the creative class (Florida, 2002) while balancing that individualism with thoughtful responses to community needs. Their views on issues related to social capital show the Tech Elites to be a *transitional* elite, one that is actually helping to make the transition from old social capital institutions described by Putnam (2000) to the newer forms animated by Cyber-democrats and Wireheads, also aptly identified by Florida (2002).

Defining Tech Elites

Tech Elites are leaders and entrepreneurs. In this sample, respondents ranged in age from 26 to 41. All had either started companies or worked at the highest managerial and strategic levels of technology enterprises. Two other "gray eminences" from the tech community provided helpful insights and access to these leaders. They had raised significant amounts of venture capital, and many of them had posted impressive "burn rates" literally spending tens of millions of dollars on marketing and growth, chasing the ephemeral promise of the tech bubble ("fundamentals don't matter"). During the course of my study, fortunes were literally made, raised, and in several cases, lost. This meteoric rise and fall demands comparisons with two other recent periods in American history—the Gilded Age at the turn of the past century and the New Deal Era, ushered in on the heals of the great stock market crash of 1929. The Gilded Age brought forth an explosion of social creativity, yielding the creation of many of America's most venerable social institutions. These institutions were the ones joined generations later by the post–World War II cohort. It is the decline in participation in these institutions that Putnam (2000) laments extensively in *Bowling Alone*. Curiously, Putnam gives comparatively little credit to the turn of the century social capitalists who did the heavy civic lifting to actually *create* those institutions later joined by the Greatest Generation.

The New Deal Era was one of the most significant bursts of *governmental* activity and social policy creativity that American politics has ever seen, launching social security, Medicare, and a host of other governmental responses to social problems. This period is useful to consider here because (1) it followed a period of furious capitalistic activity that ultimately collapsed amid corporate greed and malfeasance; and (2) the New Deal "bureaucratized"—that is, brought into government—many of the functions that previously were addressed by many of the community organizations created during the Progressive Era.

Putnam and Skocpol both observed that a potential unintended consequence of increased government action is the crowding out of civic participation in the wake of bureaucratic service delivery (although Putnam explicitly rejects "expansion of the welfare state" as a causal factor in his description of the decline of American civic life). Today, America is recovering from the economic "hangover" from our own version of the Gilded Age, and the Tech Elites have been in the midst of both the rise and fall and rise again of the Digital Age. The jury is still out on what all of this might mean for contemporary social and political creativity in our own time. But given the considerable talent, imagination, and perhaps most importantly *community self-reflection* displayed by these elites, it is not unreasonable to predict a deliberate evolution from old ways of expressing our collective social will and political conscience to a mix of old and new that may encourage younger people into collective enterprise to address community needs.

The Tech Elite group I interviewed includes seven males, three females, one African American, and the remainder Anglo. Ironically, this most professionally "senior" of my generational sample actually contained more women than the other professional subsets. Because these elites are largely entrepreneurs, having started their own companies, they seem not to notice a "glass ceiling" limiting the leadership roles of women. None of the women complained of discrimination, problems with access to capital or the other gender-based barriers often cast at the feet of the tech industry. These women realized that such biases were actually more prevalent in mainline enterprises, whether companies, unions, or social organizations, that relied on seniority or "paying dues" over performance. In addition to the elite cohort being apparently more open to women, it was also more *deliberate in its location*. More than the rest of my sample, these respondents hailed from all parts of the country, from small towns in Oklahoma to dying hamlets of the rust belt. Whether fleeing the cold of Chicago, the boredom of Shreveport or the ugliness of Newark, these Tech Elites all deliberately selected Texas, and especially Austin, as a place where they wanted to live, work, and start companies.

Even before Brooks (2000) christened *Bobos in Paradise* or Florida (2002) named the creative class and crafted a set of indices that predicted that Austin would be a top entrepreneurial destination, these elites saw Texas as a place of opportunity. All but two held a master's degree, with three holding prestigious MBA's from Harvard Business School. All of them owned computers, had broadband Internet access at work, and at home. They exchanged a minimum of 50 e-mails per day, interacted with family, friends, and conducted their business. Perhaps most interestingly, they all found life exciting despite the tumultuous economic fortunes that had marketed the technology sector during the past three years. Tech Elites follow public affairs regularly, although not as voraciously and through as many channels as Cyberdemocrats. Also parting company with members of their generation who generally eschewed partisan labels, this group largely identified themselves as Republicans (including apparently socially progressive professional women), although in subsequent questions only half claimed to be "conservative." This partisan uniformity is especially curious for a number of reasons. First, Tech Elites are generally considered to be more progressive than traditional business leaders. Second, Austin is a traditionally progressive community, known as an island of liberalism in an increasingly conservative state. These apparent contradictions may reflect the transitional nature of this group with respect to civic activity. As I will discuss later, they displayed some of the characteristics of their generational brethren, but they were also considerably more involved in the traditional civic institutions described by Putnam. Before delving more deeply into the attributes and behaviors of these young entrepreneurs, let us meet them.

Meet the Tech Elites

Ali is an archetypal figure of the technology world, having started companies and currently serving as a principal in both local Venture Capital (VC) firms. When asked about the recent economic boom and bust, he was not dismayed by the current state of affairs: "There are a whole bunch of guys out there that think that being a businessman is 'I have an idea. Give me money.' There's more to it than that."

Sam was one of the most high-profile of those on Austin's dot-com scene. A boyish multimillionaire, he was a principal architect of the Alpha 360 Summit, the new elites' first collective foray into public deliberations about their communal roles and responsibilities. Over the course of this study, that gathering evolved from a self-congratulatory high-end automobile and light show to a somber reflection about what went wrong.

Don had been an entrepreneur all of his life. He grew up blue-collar in upstate New York, and through hard work graduated from Harvard Business School in the late 1980s. After a couple of frustrating years in large companies, he struck out on his own, building and then selling a range of technology companies over his 15-year career. He acknowledged that "things have gotten really tough out there" but, like Ali, welcomed the return of financial "fundamentals" to the business world: "I built companies when you actually had to show profits. . . . I hope I don't get tarred with the rest of those [dot-com] guys." Don has a wife and three daughters and spends much of his civic energy on two personal causes—the Girl Scouts and the Austin Youth Theater Company, where his daughters are active participants.

Chuck is the youngest of the elites—26. Recently married, he is slight and intense, currently a principal at a local venture capital firm that was funded by his first successful technology enterprise. The tech boom and bust was a compressed roller-coaster ride for this young thinker. He got rich in one enterprise, and unlike many of his colleagues, became involved in politics, trying to organize young technologists for the Bush gubernatorial reelection campaign in 1998. He also holds piles of worthless stock options of one of the most legendary tech busts in the Austin area. He studied political science in Plan II (the highly selective honors program) at University of Texas and his responses to political questions asked of him still display a disciplinary sophistication not found among other elites. In response to the statement, "A few strong leaders would do a lot more for this country than all the laws and talk," he replied, "Nope. We are a constitutional republic—dictators need not apply."

Arthur was made the poster boy for tech boom backlash by the local newspaper. Although many companies were high-flying successes and then stunning failures, none was followed with as much apparent glee by the local media as was the demise of his online retail company. A boyish math whiz who bears resemblance to old Buddy Holly photos, Arthur built three successful dot-com companies before his twenty-fifth birthday, but it was his foray into the family business that brought his downfall. Convinced that he could "webify" his father's furniture business, he raised $50 million in venture capital to launch his company. In the high-flying early days of the company, he was known for his cool and spacious loft downtown and his A-list parties for the under-30 set. But things went poorly when it was discovered that (1) few people would actually buy couches online; and (2) for those who did, the old economy machinations of mail order, warehouses and delivery were more complicated than e-commerce hype had made them seem. As a result, his dot-com tanked, and pulled a 100-year-old family furniture business in North Carolina down with it. The newspaper coverage resembled that surrounding a political scandal, with new angles explored and rehashed for weeks after the announcement.

Ruth lived over Cheapo records and the night that we met on her deck, she had just raised a homemade "Come and Take it" flag over her illegal duplex that housed the servers, intellectual property, and two diehard volunteers. They were determined to foster online charitable donations in which the recipient could select the charity to whom the contribution would be sent. In a matter of months, she slipped from the laudatory pages of *Tech Weekly* to a part-time CEO who paid the bills by consulting for the Austin Entrepreneurs' Foundation, another group trying to act on its philanthropic impulse while holding dot-com "preliquidity event" stock paper from local companies.

Linda is a 32-year-old African American woman who is the top-ranking minority member of a large, old-line electronics retail company that has been working to recast itself as a technology company. A more traditional member of the corporate elite, she is actively involved in a range of community activities as a result of her job, and thus she feels somewhat removed from the norms of her generation: "It's real interesting because I don't really associate with very many people in my specific age group. My inclination is that they would be on the bottom of the volunteerism and giving back perspective . . . both personally and professionally I am usually around people who are around mid-40's or older. And so my experience would be probably more in line with that particular demographic than my own."

Cheryl, like Linda, displayed the characteristics of the traditional elite. Currently the CEO of a technology-related consulting firm she started several years ago, Cheryl then chaired the Chamber of Commerce. Despite this traditional business community role, her offices bear the distinctive contemporary stamp of the scrappy start-up and she wolfed down a sandwich at her desk "for lunch" as we talked at half past three in the afternoon. She described the fundamental difference she saw between traditional business elites and this new technology group:

> [P]eople from traditional, if you will, kinds of businesses and economies were brought up whether they liked it or not with the expectation that they were going to provide and have interaction with their communities. So there is no banker in the world that ever made it to administration or assistant vice-president without being told they had to be involved in the community . . . there are lots of tech people who were never told that because it was not a part of their business culture. So that's the first thing. The second thing is, you know, so you may say that bankers or some bankers are doing it for the wrong reason. They're not doing it because they want to be involved or because they enjoy being involved but because they were told to be involved. But nevertheless they're involved.

This ambivalence about the sincerity of business people's community work is a theme noted by Leibovich (2002), who drew distinctions between New Imperialists Bill Gates and Larry Ellison. He chronicled Gates's philanthropic obsession with third world health, then contrasted that sincerity with Ellison's sarcastic dismissal of all philanthropy and cause-based marketing as nothing more than "historically expensive PR campaigns." Each of these Austin elite leaders wrestled with this concern at some point during their interviews with me.

James came to Austin for the music scene in his early twenties and at 27, quite by accident, ended up CEO of a successful Web services artistic design company. He has a high school diploma and a vocational music certification. He started his company, which at the height of the boom employed over 50 people and commanded some of the highest design fees in the city, as a way to raise money to build and market a prototype invention that came to him one afternoon while hanging out on the Drag (the main thoroughfare that runs through the center of The University of Texas at Austin). "I saw all of these artists out there selling their beaded necklaces. It seemed to me that it wasn't cost effective to spend so much time making each one. So I thought I would make an automatic bead stringer . . . when I checked out what it would cost to get a prototype made, they said it would take $100,000! So I thought I'd better figure out a way to make some money." He and a fellow musician friend with no business experience then launched their Web design company hoping to raise the funds necessary to develop the automatic bead stringer. In just two years, they generated literally millions of dollars in revenue, and James became one of the most thoughtful yet outspoken advocates for greater civic participation by the technology sector. In the same organic fashion in which he became an entrepreneur, he also became a sort of technology-related civic activist, building a site to bring local political information to his Generation X brethren.

Scott is a Minnesota native and was drawn to Austin for its entrepreneurial potential but also because of its reputation as an open and caring community. Smilingly, he attributed that openness in part to "mild winters," but also reflected a key component of Florida's creative-class Meccas and an important component to an updated theory of social capital—a place where there exists multiple social and professional entry points for newcomers. Another member of the elite who rode the roller coaster of boom and bust, his company's waiting room boasted the logos of large corporate partners and clients and framed magazine covers of the good old days. Despite such upside artifacts, the receptionist desk sat empty, one of many staffing casualties of the recent recession.

Collectively, my interviewees are creative and ambitious and younger than traditional business and political elites (Mills, 1956; Whyte, 1956; Domhoff, 1998). Yet by occupation, sensibility, and income, they behave like civic actors much older than themselves. Further, despite their leadership in the fast-moving contemporary technology world, Tech Elites display the most traditional attitudes about the obligations of citizenship of any of my respondents. In essence, they serve as a bridge between traditional civic leaders and their institutions and the more contemporary approaches favored by those in the Generation X high-tech community.

Defining Traditional Civic Leaders

From my taxonomy of citizenship, civic leaders are the closest to ideal democratic citizens, possessing a sense of civic obligation and actively participating in public affairs. The responsibility of citizens to *participate* in public affairs—civic virtue—is imbedded in the classical tradition of democratic theory. This conceptualization moves beyond the passive citizen who abides by the law and who ratifies the action of the state and demands *intellectual activity* on the part of citizens (Oliver and Heater, 1994). The classical tradition also emphasizes a sense of citizen *obligation* not contemplated by the social model of democracy, which focuses on the state's provision of goods and services. Civic leaders share power and are actively involved in the decisions and processes that govern a democracy. Fishkin and Luskin (1999) provided a specific operationalization of citizenship, while Tech Elites generally subscribe to Fishkin and Luskin's (1999) beliefs that citizens should (1) become educated on political topics; (2) deliberate about current events; and (3) act as a recommending force to political decision makers.

Whereas Fishkin focused on national politics, the elites I interviewed were much more focused on *local* issues. Scholars evaluating the outcomes of Fishkin and Luskin's National Issues Convention found various effects, but two of the most promising were as follows: first, that participants' views became more moderate as a result of their deliberations; and second, that their language grew appreciably more *collective* the longer they discussed issues with their fellow citizens (Hart and Jarvis, 1999). These Tech Elites sense this outcome of greater involvement and therefore work to engage others in the affairs of the community. But like others in their generation, *involvement for involvement's sake* is not enough to warrant participation. Tech Elites reflect their generation and their profession's worship of *efficiency*. As a result, participation without tangible *outcomes* would be a waste of time. A critical outcome of Tech Elite participation was the quality of *local* leadership.

Controversial elite theorist Sartori (1994) argued that the quality of elites or leaders (what he calls the *vertical* dimension of democracy) was the more important goal of democratic processes, as opposed to the mobilization or participatory models that feature increased voter participation (horizontal aspects) as the ultimate goal of political involvement. While high levels of voting and participation are important, Sartori asserted, it is more important to the functioning of a democratic state that participation yield *the selection of competent and effective leaders*. Tech Elites were keenly focused on the quality of local elected leaders and their resulting effectiveness in addressing pressing local issues.

Curiously, this most professionally senior group of respondents was much more focused on *local* issues and the people involved in those issues than any of my other respondents. For them, politics and civic participation were not abstract notions or a passive set of "issues" or a process to be observed through a television screen, as Schudson's (1998) "monitoral citizen" would. Rather, Tech Elite involvement was concrete, specific, and local: transportation and traffic; the feasibility of light rail; highway construction; the next school bond issue.

Tech Elites were not disconnected from politics like the Wireheads, although neither were they passionate consumers of political news like Cyber-democrats. Rather, they were the closest thing that Generation X has to Putnam-vintage social capitalists. They are Generation X civic leaders, displaying a mix of traditional civic leader behaviors, with a creative-class Generation X commitment to flexibility, efficiency, and measurable outcomes as a result of their civic labors.

Returning to my taxonomy of levels of citizenship, *traditional* civic leaders display the following attitudes and behaviors (see table 6.1).

In contrast to this classical characterization, the Tech Elites reflect a synthesis between the traditional attributes and behaviors and Generation X sensibility, yielding a model of a different, young, transitional civic leader (see table 6.2).

Table 6.1   Classic Civic Leaders

Attributes	Behaviors
• Law-abidingness • Open-mindedness • Independence • Work ethic • Ability to evaluate the performance of leaders • Willingness to engage in public discourse	• Vote • Awareness of political affairs • Contribute to organizations • Lead community and political organizations • Select competent leaders

Table 6.2   Tech Elites: Generation X Civic Leaders

Attributes	Behaviors
• Law-abidingness • Open-mindedness • Independence to organizations • Work ethic • Ability to evaluate the performance of leaders • *Commitment to mentoring young leaders*	• Vote • Awareness of *local* political affairs • *Respond to requests* to contribute • *Respond to requests* to lead community and political organizations • Select and *interact with* competent leaders *to produce tangible outcomes* • *Conceptualize new kinds of community leadership and responsibility*

Tech Elites as Transitional Civic Leaders

Tech Elites were not as *generationally* distinctive in their attitudes and behaviors as Wireheads and Cyber-democrats. Florida's observations about the creative class might help explain why. While Cyber-democrats and Wireheads both *create* things—code, software, campaigns—these elites now *lead* and *run* things. For them, creating a company was more about growth and management of an enterprise than the ongoing creation of products or ideas for them *personally*.

Tech Elites are leaders and managers, occupying *traditional* roles albeit in *contemporary enterprises*. By virtue of this mix, these elites provide a sort of bridge between old notions of civic involvement and the more contemporary types advanced by the more quintessentially Generation X Cyber-democrats and Wireheads. Cyber-democrats, for example, like their social capital "just in time" to respond to a specific community need. Wireheads eschew political involvement but display their civic virtue in their work. Tech Elites do both of these things but they also represent their generation in more classic civic institutions and have undertaken a more deliberate and public effort to define what their community roles *should* be.

This distinction could be explained through the Generation X *duty to respond*. Because Tech Elites lead companies, they face community expectations that others in their age cohort do not. As the generational literature clearly illustrated, expectations of Generation X were incredibly low, if not fatalistic (recall Howe and Strauss's (1993) treatise on the group in *13th Generation: Abort, Retry, Fail?* and Linklater's *Slacker* [1991]).

However, as leaders of enterprises, their employees, the media, community organizations looked to them for things that those in such positions have historically provided: charitable contributions, board memberships, event sponsorships, and political endorsements. In essence, Tech Elites were *asked* to participate in ways that their other age peers were not. Echoing the persistent Generation X sense of obligation, they have *responded* to the civic requests.

Recall that across all Generation X cohorts, these young people reflect Wolfe's (2001) insights about moral freedom: they feel little transcendent obligation to existing institutions or the larger community. However, they feel a strong duty to *respond*—either to large tragedy, as in the case of September 11—or to specific *requests* for help in the smaller community context. Perhaps because these Elites were *asked* more often, they *responded* more often, thereby resulting in greater community activity, even if they initially shared the sensibilities of their generation. These responses to specific requests then became catalytic events, animating what Putnam calls the "virtuous cycle" of social capital. These activities set in motion the norms of reciprocity, which in turn lead to ongoing acts of social capital. They respond to such requests, which emboldens others to ask even more of them, which promotes still more responses. That dynamic is essentially Putnam's virtual cycle turned inside out

Putnam and other authors considering reciprocity posit that doing a favor elicits a sense of obligation (Cialdini, 1984). Tech Elites listened more closely to modern-day Machiavelli Chris Matthews (1999)—if you want someone's support, then ask them for a favor. While Tech Elite notions of reciprocity situate them firmly within Generation X, they also affirm Putnam's hypothesis that social capital begets social capital. Sam epitomized the Tech Elite view on civic activity and the role of philanthropy: "Essentially spending resources on it (a problem). In other words don't exist just for the sake of existing. And if you're using people's time and energy, then you need to respect that and part of respecting that is doing a good job in using the resources."

Unlike others in Generation X (both in my sample and in the generational literature), all of the elites I interviewed were actively involved with some sort of *existing* community entity. They served on boards, such as the Girl Scouts or the Boys and Girl's Club. They were involved in the Chamber of Commerce and, as in the case of Cheryl, actually became chair. They also chaired community events, such as the annual fund-raiser for the local community theater. However, unlike the Protestant banker elite who came before them, they are diverse, both by gender and race; they are self-reflective, actively pondering ways to make these institutions more inclusive and appeal to a broader and younger range of citizens; and finally, they contemplate both publicly and privately what their role *should* be in the community. Tech Elite thoughts and attitudes reflect the state of *flux*, rather than *decline* of civic engagement in twenty-first-century America.

The Nineteenth- and Twenty-First-Century Tension: Progressives and Postmodern Robber Barons

In documenting what he saw as the decline of American civic life, Putnam compared the 1990s to the 1950s, judging rightly, in my view, that if the 1950s present the ideal picture of healthy social capital, then the 1990s do not measure up. In the 1950s, people joined a set of institutions. Today, people do not join these institutions or socialize in those same ways. That time was perhaps a spasm of civic activity, perpetuated by the stark separation between men and women, and between home and work. Whyte's gray "organization men" reflected the industrial corporate culture of the day and the social capital institutions that Putnam described also reflected those sensibilities. They included standing, hierarchical organizations that held regular meetings of certain duration. Certain people were expected to participate in certain ways, largely dictated by hierarchical social and professional norms. This description is not meant to discount the considerable good that the Rotarians, Lions, Elks, and United Way provided for their communities in those days. Rather, it is to underscore that, as Florida observed, *the nature of work is changing, and these changes are fostering a comparable and related evolution in social and civic institutions.*

This state of flux requires a new generation of civic leaders to do more complicated work than that performed by Putnam's social capitalists. Tech Elites must create consensus and involvement around a host of positive (or at least varied) causes and interests, reflect the fluid professional norms prevalent in the contemporary workplace, work toward measurable results from their civic endeavors, and help groom a new group of young people to lead companies and civic endeavors to build the sort of community they wish to live in. Putnam's social capitalists simply joined existing institutions created by industrial elites and progressive civic leaders decades before. Ruth, in contrast, wrestled with these complex responsibilities of respecting the old but also working to craft more contemporary lessons:

[P]robably the best example is one of the original investors in [my company] . . . he's an older guy who I've always looked up to. I met him when he was a Regent at UT. And uh, you know, he's been a business leader. He's got to be close to 80 now. He's definitely in his seventies and I mean, there's just nothing that he hasn't done. I mean, from the beginning of time when I met the guy. I mean, I can see that he believed in me. He's always encouraged me and when he said he was going to put money into this deal (he did). When he said he was going to offer support, he did. Whenever he's said he's going to make a phone call he does. Uh, when he deals with other business people and attorneys and so forth he's totally what you see is what you get. He's extremely trustworthy. Which is why he has the network that he does. You know, he sits on all kinds of boards. . . . You know, he's the guy when things are terrible calls you and says don't give up . . . like when [my company] was falling apart. . . . He was the guy that said when I called him to tell him what had happened. He just said well, this is when you should get excited. You know, make lemons out of lemonade . . . one of the issues that we dealt with was trying to figure out how to force a better deal from charitable agents. And yet he connected me with an attorney to help me take care of that and this attorney was telling stories about when my investor had had business problems and just how easy it was to go to banks all the time because he was so trustworthy. So when your reputation, I mean, you know, I think he's so great. But I thought he was great before but now that I've seen him and see how he was totally trustworthy uh, I don't know. As we're talking about these particular individuals I'm starting to think there are some people that I couldn't trust also. But I'd rather not dwell on them. (Laughter.) Things like this are really complicated.

Where the social capitalists of the 1950s *joined and proliferated* formal clubs (Lions, Elks, etc.), bridge clubs, and other informal local social and philanthropic gatherings, their civic forebears of the Progressive Era reacted to rapid social and economic change by *creating* new social and democratic entities. The long civic generation of the 1950s and 1960s joined and expanded those institutions but did not have to *create* institutions from whole cloth. If the prophets of the Information Age are correct that the current changes are the sociological equivalent of the Industrial Revolution, the Progressives have much more to teach us than those of the 1950s. Ruth's rambling response above not only illustrates both the appeal of television's Cleavers, but also the new challenges that face local communities and business enterprises.

Looking back to the turn of the past century, when things civic were also in flux, two opposed groups competed for the soul of American communities: the Progressives and the Robber Barons. Today's technology aristocracy has occasionally been christened "Post Modern Robber Barons," after the titans of the Gilded Age of industrialization at the end of the nineteenth century. J. P. Morgan, John D. Rockefeller, and others were both revered and loathed for their wealth and influence. Yet, they also funded enormous philanthropies and gave birth to many of the civic institutions that still exist today. In a sense, they helped bridge the civic transition from agrarian to industrial America. In Austin, Tech Elites were doing similar work in 2002.

In building a bridge between twentieth- and twenty-first-century social capital, Tech Elites reflected sensibilities of both sides of that Industrial Era conflict between the Progressives and the Robber Barons. The times bear some stunning similarities. West (2000) observed the phenomenon most succinctly: "On one side, the Progressives saw the market dominance and ruthless efficiency of the new corporate giants as a sinister threat to individual liberty. Railroads and industrial leviathans were charging monopoly prices, driving competitors out of business, removing control of local enterprise from resident communities, ignoring labor's demands for fair wages and humane working conditions, and earning enormous amounts of money. Flagrant abuses of corporate power . . . and the steady flow of commercial cash that purchased political favors, substantiated the popular conviction that big business violated the natural order of exchange in a free society." On the other side were those who saw the natural order of things in a different light. The United States was no longer a Jeffersonian nation of farmers and small producers working "perfect" competitive markets. "With no governmental guidance or regulation, private enterprise was opening up jobs and fostering social mobility on an unprecedented scale, and private bankers were raising previously unimaginable amounts of money. The industrialists and financiers who were shaping this new economic order regarded it as natural and inevitable, and wanted that freedom to continue." Sound familiar? These sentiments could have been drawn from last weekend's edition of the *New York Times*.

Today, as in the aftermath of the American Civil War, these tensions were playing themselves out in the nation's collective psyche. Where old industrialists are in some cases becoming isolationist relics, Tech Elites, more than Wireheads and Cyber-democrats, seem to be making a conscious transition between the old and the new while still certainly embracing their newfound privilege. Recall Postman's insight that every new technological innovation has implicit biases; each produces winners and losers. Certainly, Tech Elites, like other young, technologically sophisticated people, are winners in the wake of recent innovations. However, Tech Elites seem more aware of the changes wrought by innovation and are self-consciously reflecting on what these changes mean for the health of their community.

More than others in their generational cohort, Tech Elites have joined some institutions (often specifically invited by those in the older generation), acting as representatives of the young in their parent's civic organizations. Several of them commented that they are often the youngest at these meetings in terms of age, that they hear the laments of the old-line civic leaders, wondering why the younger generation does not join the range of lodges and critter clubs they so enjoy.

But like the Progressives, this group is thinking hard about the changes that are bubbling through their communities. Indeed, I would argue that they are thinking *better* now that the euphoria of the dot-com bubble has burst. They are less self-congratulatory. They take all enterprises more seriously than they did during the first Alpha 360 Summit in 1999.

Tech Elites allude to their nineteenth-century predecessors in other ways as well. For example, Robber Barons did not generally run for office. Instead, they worked in their communities, created philanthropies, and effected change through means other than direct public service. They viewed the costs as just too high and their efficacy as better used in ways outside the political system. One of the most politically active Tech Elites (who is regularly asked if he is interested in running for mayor of Austin) expressed the prevailing view:

> I think politicians are treated very poorly. I think you really have to have thick skin to go into that. I mean, as a result and this isn't a knock on current politicians. I think it discourages a lot of people who may be would get involved in that from doing it because why? I know for me a lot of people come to me and say hey, why don't you go get involved? Why don't you be on the city council? Why do I want to put myself through that? There's no way. I can't be the only one.

Like the Robber Barons, Tech Elites also held the somewhat dubious view that what was good for them and good for business was ultimately good for the community as a whole. This view was tempered, however, by an explicit *sense of gratitude* toward the larger community. Surprisingly, given the libertarian reputation of the technology sector, they credited it with creating conditions needed to help them achieve their successes. Notice the parsing of their language of obligation, a fusion of Generation X and the ethos of Wolfe's (2001) moral freedom:

> Believe it or not I lump in community with business . . . that's part of my business life. But my feeling on that is that, you know . . . I look at that more on that as a give and take thing. Which is that I as long as I'm the beneficiary of a city or a community or whatever it is that enabled me to have a certain amount of success then I ought to give back . . . [but I don't] necessarily have an obligation . . . but [do feel like I should] preserve the equilibrium of giving and taking to then give back. So because I tell you realistically if I had come here and had failed in business like right out of gate, the odds of me actually being involved in the community are pretty slim. . . . There's an environment here, though. Someone before me was active and did something good that allowed me [to succeed] . . . it's like [they] built this market for me to be able to come in and be successful. So I ought to do something in return since that was there for me . . . it's like planting a tree . . . so that future generations have the same benefit of what you had. . . . But that is my choice not an obligation. . . . I just think you ought to do it.

Another Tech Elite conveyed a similar sentiment, but more explicitly tying community involvement to good business practice:

> [Elites participate in the community] because they have the resources to do it and because while they may not recognize that to a very large degree almost always their success has been made in part by the

community around them. Whether that community is just their customers or whether the community is the people who are providing the infrastructure to allow their business to be successful or whether that is the environmentalists who are building a, you know, nice place to live so their employees want to come there.

That good business practices and community involvement go hand in hand was a key way in which Tech Elites were more like old business elites than like their fellow Gen Xers. Another respondent noted this parallel but expressed frustration with comparing public enterprises to the technology sector:

> There's also the whole technology culture is built around moving very quickly. Expectations and short product life cycles or short design cycles. You know, time to market efficiencies and things like that—that creates two problems. One it creates a problem where people feel as if they don't have time to give back to the community. In fact, they do if they choose to make that time. But second it creates an expectation that all of life should react to these kinds of life cycles and therefore, a frustration in getting involved in community or political issues because for instance, you know, it doesn't matter how fast Internet product life cycles are that doesn't get a road built any faster. It still takes 10 years . . . to build Highway 130. So if somebody who has an expectation of 6-month product cycles is going to have a very difficult time getting involved in the right of way funding for 130.

Cheryl's comments above convey the most distinctive feature that sets Tech Elites apart from my other Generation X respondents. Tech Elites were actively and concretely involved in the happenings of the *local* community. They were involved in deliberation about and implementation of public policies in the Austin area.

Cyber-democrats saw notions of citizenship as inherently tied up with politics, especially the division of scarce resources at the federal and state level and the belief in the importance of voting, being aware of political issues, and joining in the public debates of the day. Wireheads saw economic versions of political virtues at play in their companies day in and day out, but felt that the public sector was all about talk (not action), and thereby inherently inefficient. In contrast, the Tech Elites are leaders and pragmatists.

Several Tech Elites mentioned talking with city council members, county commissioners, and the local congressman about development issues critical to the city. Nearly all of them made reference to the transportation needs of the area, often talking in impressive detail about various options and trade-offs between light rail, more highways, smart growth and economic development and quality of life, energy, utilities, and water rights. These were not abstract "public debates." These were real issues and projects on which the Tech Elites had invested time and energy pursuing—and expected to see real, measurable results.

Addressing Putnam's Forgotten Two Culprits

This focus of the elites I interviewed should provide Putnam cause for optimism about the future of social capital, both as he defined it and the more contemporary versions that I am describing. Recall that Putnam's four culprits for the decline of social capital were as follows: pressures of time and money; suburbanization and the related issues of commuting time and sprawl; the role of electronic entertainment, particularly television; and generational change. While much scholarly literature has focused on the culprits of television and generational change, the Tech Elites actually address the two often overlooked culprits: sprawl and time/money pressure.

Generally speaking, Tech Elites are using technology as a catalyst to transform the nature of work. This ethos permits greater schedule flexibility at all levels, and this leads to greater mobility, less reliance on the "8 to 5" workday, and the ability to work from home or just about anyplace else. At the heart of this "knowledge work" lies the possibility that it can be accomplished anywhere. In this sense, Tech Elites are consistent with their Cyber-democrat and Wirehead colleagues, but they are different in one critical respect. Whereas Wireheads and Cyber-democrats are often mavericks or free agents, Tech Elites are at the helm of substantial enterprises and therefore have the ability to *institutionalize* these practices, making them the norm rather than the exception. Broad-based adoption of these strategies could be a catalyst to greater levels of social capital as employees at all levels have greater autonomy, control over their schedules, and ownership of their work.

The other forgotten culprit is suburban sprawl. In this area, the Tech Elites are flexing their social capital muscles. The leaders of the sector are becoming actively involved in local issues surrounding quality of life—open spaces, public transportation, traffic, and the like. Each respondent made at least one reference to transportation, parks, and other quality-of-life amenities that both drew them to Austin and were issues on which they were actively working. All of these elements point to the capacity of network technologies to mitigate financial and geographical pressures that have contributed to the decline in social capital. To counteract sprawl, Tech Elites are serving as advisers, underwriting campaigns, and locating their enterprises—and often their homes—in the close-in old Austin neighborhoods.

While their greatest impact is in the leadership area, the Tech Elites also reflect implications for generational effects. While this new High-Tech Elite has some of the civic apathy chronicled by Putnam and the generational marketing literature (Hicks and Hicks, 1999; Smith and Clurman, 1997; Thau and Heflin, 1997; Howe and Strauss, 1993), they are beginning to search for a civic identity and to use their new tools and social influence to construct new kinds of philanthropy. While many Tech Elites are involved in leadership roles in new institutions like Alpha 360, TechNet, and the Austin Entrepreneur's Foundation, they are also members of and helping to modernize many of the old social capital institutions, such as the Chamber of Commerce, the United Way, and the Girl Scouts, to name a few.

These transitional activities, mixed with the more contemporary approaches that these elites are taking to philanthropy, represent many of the same ingredients found in the Progressive Era—innovative civic pursuits, creation of new entities and movements that suited the new ways of life, and the emergence of a new generation of leadership. From these nineteenth-century efforts sprung lasting civic institutions. That, of course, is good. But what also sprung from them was a crush of bureaucratic encrustations that institutionalized many of the aims of the social movements of the day. While these laws represent the foundation of the modern welfare state and are fixtures of our contemporary public sector, the "professionalization" of social capital leads to ultimate disengagement of volunteers and the inert professionalization that Lippman, among others, addressed.

Putnam also points to the proliferation of "special interest lobbies" that equate writing a check with participating politically. An especially challenging component of these transitional activities will be to use technology tools and an openness to mixing old and new to create civic institutions that can resist bureaucratization, and yet be robust enough to be long-lasting.

Putnam laudably ends *Bowling Alone* with a series of recommendations—or calls to civic action—to create social capital for a new age:

> My message is that we desperately need an era of civic inventiveness to create a renewed set of institutions and channels for reinvigorating civic life that will fit the way we have come to live. Our challenge now is to

reinvigorate the 21st century equivalent of the Boy Scouts or the settlement house or the playground or Hadassah or the United Mine Workers or the NAACP. . . . We need to be as ready to experiment as the Progressives were. Willingness to err—and then correct our aim—is the price of success for social reform. (p. 401)

Moving away from the nostalgia for the tranquil 1950s with its often oppressive limitations for women and minorities, Putnam calls us back to the lessons of our last moments of civic entrepreneurship—the Progressive Era. He calls for new institutions, not yet invented or conceptualized and a spirit of experimentation with new forms and organizations. This call is probably the greatest cause for optimism about Tech Elites as catalysts for building new kinds of civic capacity. It is a sector that thrives on risk and experimentation. One of its core ethics is "if you're not failing, you're not trying hard enough." As Florida (2002) convincingly argued, the new creative class that comprises increasing numbers of young people who are paid to think does not draw the hard line between work, play, and community. They blur these lines into a more organic approach to work, fueled by the whims of the creative impulse rather than the sunrise Rotary Club, the three-martini lunch or the Saturday Little League game.

However, lest we believe that the Tech Elites are merely building a temporary bridge between old and new social capital with the aim of ultimately stamping out the old forms, note Leibovich's surprising finding about the New Imperialists. Even those young men at the top of the world's most influential technology companies still look for the approval of those who came before. One of my background respondents plays such a role in Austin to such a degree that it made the local paper when he finally relinquished his old corporate e-mail address, a final move toward retirement. That phenomenon—the need for a sort of entrepreneurial "parental acceptance"—could help explain why this elite cohort, much more so than Wireheads and Cyber-democrats, feels compelled to do the creative work of animating a thoroughly modern social capital more appropriate to Generation X "creative-class" norms, while still maintaining some attachment to the past generation's collective institutions.

In a sense, Tech Elites appear to be engaged in a sort of Digital Age expectations management (Schudson, 1998). John Mueller (1999) made an engaging case for the image problems faced by capitalism and democracy, one promising that anyone can get rich and the other promising a vibrant marketplace of ideas and genuine self-governance.

Both of those hyperboles pale in comparison to the expectations mismatch of new technologies—now especially the Web. The Web will not—any more than TV or the telegraph—solve any important problems on its own. As Williams (1970) and more recently Lessig (1999) provocatively remind us, all technological development is the result of human thought and agency, which means that technologies are created by humans, used by humans, and ultimately leave sociological changes in their wake. Tech Elites are embracing this agency.

Conclusion

Tech Elites appear to serve as a generational bridge between old definitions of social capital and more contemporary ones. In defining citizenship, they are surprisingly local and interpersonal: in their minds, good citizens do many of the things that classic theorists believe they should, but they also believe that good Tech Elites respond to requests from both new and traditional community sources. Further, they believe that good citizens respect the old guard while preparing their age peers and those younger to become involved in the concrete work of maintaining the attributes of their chosen community that drew them there in the first place. They talk explicitly about mentoring other young leaders and engaging them in community work; but it is not the perpetuation of institutions that is their aim. Rather their goals are to solve problems, affect measurable outcomes, respond to the community, and perhaps, most importantly, create new entities reflecting those values.

Returning to the stories of the New Imperialists and their priorities may offer some indication of things to come. Bill and Melinda Gates have become philanthropists of unprecedented proportions, determined to revolutionize third world health care delivery, eradicate AIDS from the planet, and dramatically improve the college-ready graduation rates and college attendance for poor and minority young people in the United States. Steve Case and his wife Jean have brought their wealth and energy to philanthropic pursuits and have shown great willingness to put the full rhetorical resources of AOL/Time Warner behind them. Leibovich (2002) observes, "This is a common transformation among big ticket technology CEOs. Once they reach a certain level of titanhood, they strive for statesmanhood" (p. 218). And in that transition, their Austin-area progeny are helping to bring the tools and values of a younger generation into the current public sphere, while still supporting—and perhaps paradoxically seeking the approval of—the comparatively stodgy aristocracy that fostered the great social institutions of the mid-twentieth century.

7

Trailing Xers, Rising Millennials, and Two Clichés

Introduction

The final group of respondents I interviewed is the youngest Generation X cohort—those born between 1975 and 1981 and, in this case, undergraduates living in Austin, Texas. During the writing of this study, Gen X critics Howe and Strauss (2000) found a cohort to laud as effusively as their Baby Boomer comrades—the so-called Millennial or "Generation Y". Unlike Generation X, in their view, these young people born after 1981 were "rising" to become the "next greatest generation" of "optimistic joiners." That claim will remain untested in this study, but my analysis of these Trailing Xers does not show an appreciable uptick in optimism, knowledge, or participation compared to my older Gen X respondents. In fact, this younger group generally proved somewhat more cynical about their fellow men than the older respondents. They generally consumed less news from traditional sources. However, they did vote—many voted for the first time when they became eligible. Like other Xers, they were uncomfortable with notions of transcendent obligation but felt a strong duty to respond to requests for help. Their cynicism was in some cases quite explicitly tied to perceived unfairness of their parents or of their schools or universities, and they had a sense that national politicians at best ignore them, at worst disdain them. Rather than being blithely and irrationally cynical, in their view, they were adopting a perfectly rational posture to the world they were entering—negative.

Curiously, my overall sample illustrates that Gen X seems to grow less cynical as it ages. Could there be something about schooling at the secondary and postsecondary level that animates cynicism and decreases efficacy? Lifestyle effects literature claims that young people eschew political involvement in their teens and twenties because they are too busy (with the activities of building an adult life) to concern themselves with the weighty issues of the state. However, in this study, those *least* busy with life's demands were the *most* cynical, and generally the least engaged in their communities. In my view, this observation demands further study of lifestyle effects, particularly around the effects of current methods of schooling on feelings of efficacy and reciprocity, key variables in the building of social capital. Clearly in this sample, young people recently out of high school or in college were cynical, but this cynicism seemed to dissipate once they were out of school and working in their chosen field.

Are our schools and colleges helping to create cynics? Early in this century, John Dewey (1938) predicted that the "traditional" teaching norms of obedience to authority, passive learning, and the primacy of silence and obedience could cause students to "lose their appreciation of things worthwhile, of those values which things are relative and above all [lose] the ability to extract meaning from experiences" (p. 49). The truth of Dewey's claim is debatable, but perhaps helpful in considering ways to help engage young people more actively in their educations by engaging them more actively in their communities. For now, though, back to the Trailing Xers.

General Observations

What do we hear from them? What are their conceptions of good citizenship and community? Certainly, we hear the Reagan echo, "government is not the solution to the problem, government *is* the problem." Where older Generation X respondents reflected these views in terms of governmental inefficiency, the younger Gen Xers parroted Reagan's contempt for government much more deeply and generally. Older Xers recalled waiting in line at a DMV office peopled by diffident, slow-moving clerks and watch-the-clock ticket punchers. The young people were not only more vague in their distastes, but also more negative. To many of them, the government *was* waste, fraud, and abuse regardless of their described political or ideological affiliation. Their attitudes are consistent with the Gen X marketing literature, which observed that these youngest members have internalized the orthodoxy of their first president-of-memory—Ronald Reagan. Even those who self-identify as Democrats or liberals point to mythic inefficiencies in government, the lazy bureaucrat (a common enemy among all respondents), the wasteful, venal politician, and the strapped and helpless taxpayer. One respondent wrestled with his childhood recollection of Reagan's words in this way:

> When I think of government I think more of bureaucracy of Washington. Uh, they offer here in civics class that we are the government but I don't really see it that way. I think there's more of a disconnect. I think what Ronald Reagan said when he was in office if we stop referring to the government . . . when we start referring to government as us we've been here too long or something.

Here we find a sentiment that Reagan reflected repeatedly, most specifically at a White House reception for new political appointees in 1982: "Each day as you go into your offices, remember, we came to this place to pare the unmanageable size of government, to reduce its massive bulk, its powers, and its waste, to free our people and our economy from its oppressive hand. The minute that any of you start to think of government as 'we' instead of 'they,' we've been here too long."[1]

While many of the Trailing Xers I interviewed have internalized disaffection with *government*, they also seemed to be searching for some notion of the "common good." Like the new Millennials, self-interest and money seemed to be secondary concerns to this group. Contrary to Hill (1997), who found that Generation X was less tolerant of differences than Baby Boomers, this group expressed concerns about the larger community, about suburban sprawl and gated communities, and about equal opportunities for all. In a sense, they put a unique spin on Wolfe's (2001) concept of moral freedom. Like their generational peers in this study, they stopped short of prescribing specific conduct or even specifying what "good" conduct is. Far from the recent characterization offered by the Education Commission of the States (Boston and Gomez, 2000), which claimed that current civic life was "eroding the soul of young people," these Trailing Xers were clearly trying to find a place for themselves in an adult world that seemed quite removed from what they had experienced thus far in their short lives.

The most obvious way of distinguishing this group from the older members of my sample was to consider their collective attitudes toward technology and its effects on life, work, and citizenship.

---

[1] Further, according to information provided by the Ronald Reagan Presidential Library, he made similar statements (which were included in his presidential papers) in 1973, 1982, and twice in 1985.

Whereas older respondents saw changes bubbling around them and often marveled at the freedoms and capabilities afforded by contemporary technologies, these undergraduates had little to say when asked how technology was changing their lives. They saw electronic appliances as tools, much like any other tool. They used it day-to-day for a range of reasons. They communicated with family and friends, did schoolwork, and used technology in their part-time jobs. For them, technology was no big deal. They neither worshiped nor feared it or, in many cases, even noticed it. Asking those born middle class in the United States after 1980 how technology affected their lives proved to be a trivial question. When I pressed to get them to really think about this question, only two respondents became engaged. One 23-year-old mused optimistically:

> Let me think. There's no doubt that technology is pervasive and anything that's pervasive requires you to re-examine at least subconsciously what you think about certain things and helps craft your vision of certain things like community. Like citizenship. Like all those things. There's no doubt it can have an impact. It's just a question of how knowledgeable people are going to be of it. How aware are they going to be of the impact that it does have, that it will have, that it can have? Of the opportunities it can have. The opportunity of making their vision, their opinion of community, of citizenship. All that stuff the opportunity of making those things better and closer to their ideal. And less so taking those things from a traditional sense of this is what they have always been to this is what they could be . . . I'm basically optimistic [because] with new technologies its going to enable more good things before it can enable bad things. And if people don't become aware of issues and understand what they're doing and understand the world around them there's no reason to think that the good things will outpace the bad things. Or that the bad things can't come around and still take control. But I think in the long run there's no reason to think that the good doesn't have a step up.

Undergraduates as Weak Cynics and Emerging Active Minimalists

This group of respondents included four women and five men, ranging in age from 20 to 26. All were spending their summer in Austin, Texas, and all but two were undergraduates at the University of Texas (UT). Of the two who were not UT students, one was a student at Texas

A&M and the other attended the University of California at Berkeley. Three were interns at the Office of the Governor of Texas, and the others were drawn from a political communication course at the University of Texas (they were given minimal extra credit for completing the survey and participating in an hour-long interview). The group included three Hispanics, one Asian, and six Anglos. From their written surveys, a picture emerged of a somewhat cynical group. Once they were in the interviews, however, their gratuitous cynicism seemed fleeting, strongest during the early parts of the interview (when they appeared to try and convey a sense of worldly sophistication to their older interviewer). Their cynical comments largely dissipated over the course of the interviews—with two exceptions. Two respondents could be considered "alienated" in that they saw a great deal of cynical manipulation in the world, much of which was specifically directed at them.

These interviews uncovered an important distinction often over-looked in the generational literature. One kind of cynicism mimics media and cultural messages such as "government is the problem." Then there is the more corrosive cynicism that sees sinister forces that specifically maligned oneself or one's group. Most literature on Generation X makes no effort to distinguish between those two types of cynicism. One type of cynicism is perhaps a stylistic posture that one abandons as one grows older. The other seems to be a deeper seeded sentiment that can be paralyzing.

While some of my respondents displayed their generation's much documented (if unspecified) cynicism from time to time, they were certainly not inarticulate. Most of them were reasonably well informed about political matters and were happy to discuss their political worldviews. The eldest, Blake, was quite alienated, found life to be profoundly dull (the only respondent in this entire study to respond thusly), and answered many of my questions with a Bill Maher weary sophistication and glib cynicism. However, as I will explore in more depth later, he was certainly *not* ignorant about public issues, but had come to some exceedingly negative conclusions about the motives and behaviors of political actors. Most curiously, each time I would follow one of his cynical responses with a serious question, Blake would grow visibly uncomfortable, as though I were breaking some sort of unspoken social norm—that is, when one talks about politics, one must talk about it cynically (Hart, 1994). Similarly, the youngest, Caitlin, self-identified as a Republican, spent much of our interview tying all questions of citizenship and social involvement back to the topic of her single-issue activism: animal rights. Both Blake and Caitlin were the only respondents in this study to reply that life was "not too happy." Because these two represent the picture more typically drawn of the Gen X, I will spend extra time exploring their views and responses later in this chapter.

Technologically, these respondents affirmed my reason for wanting to include them in this study; each had grown up with a computer in their home. The average age of their owning their first computer was eight—the fourth grade. Each currently owned at least one computer at home, including Internet access, with the majority having some sort of high-speed access and all but one had access at work as well. While their level of e-mail usage mirrored the older respondents in my sample, this youngest group reported their e-mail use as more explicitly *social* than the other groups, foreshadowing the late 2005 findings of the Pew Internet in American Life project which showed significant differences in online habits by age. Only two respondents mentioned using e-mail for work or for school: most said they used it to stay in touch with family and friends. This finding might preview an evolving kind of technology usage that is more personal and social than professional. However, this could also be attributed to a technological manifestation of the political lifestyle effects hypothesis—that younger adults are preoccupied with social and personal pursuits than political or more professional ones.

Contrary to the lifestyle hypothesis, however, this group reported voting at much higher levels than the literature reports. Only one respondent did not vote in the last national election and the first time they were eligible. These data could be the result of a number of factors, from social desirability within a political town (Austin) to the effect of a great political communication course (in which the majority of them were enrolled). Further, even those who were cynical and disengaged were still surprisingly informed about political topics and had rather well-considered views on civic matters.

Interestingly, they were evenly divided in their ideological self-identification—three moderates, three conservatives, and three liberals, with one observing, "It is highly dependent on issues. I tend to be fiscally conservative and socially liberal." All but one said they followed public affairs "from time to time." All thought that politicians could be trusted some of the time and had mixed levels of trust when asked about the president, the Congress, and the Supreme Court. All but one claimed to feel a sense of satisfaction from voting. All in all, the group did not display the wide alienation and inarticulate disengagement described in the Generation X literature.

That said, every one of them agreed with the statement, "if you don't watch out for yourself, people will take advantage of you." That is a much higher level of cynicism than displayed by older respondents. The most distinctive feature of the full group of Trailing Xers was the way in which they responded to the statement about *political* cynicism: "All candidates sound good in their speeches, but you can never tell what they will do once they are elected." Seven out of ten disagreed with the statement. Most curiously, each respondent (in contrast to other members of the broader sample) felt the need to equivocate and explained their response on the written survey instrument. In the case of Blake the Cynic, he displayed considerable affect in conveying his disagreement: "I think all politicians are unscrupulous bastards and I'm rarely disappointed." Also in disagreement, Beau saw things quite differently: "Disagree. Obviously, candidates have to cast a wide net to get elected, but I don't perceive that many completely abandon their platforms to the point that you have no idea how they'll govern. The leadership desired in the above statement often requires policy makers to modify their position based on new circumstances." Another respondent echoed this same sentiment: "Agree. Most politicians waffle. That does not mean that if they change it is bad, they have the right to review their opinions. However, blatant lying is common as well."

As a group, these Trailing Xers used more cynical language than their older peers, although in most cases, that cynicism dissipated over the course of our conversation, adding heft to Hart's arguments about the inherent weakness of cynicism. However, their story does not end with cynicism, as most accounts argue. Actually, a closer reading of the young people's responses show that with the exception of the two extreme examples I will examine separately, even these Trailing Xers emerged as solid active minimalists. Recall that active minimalists

- Believe in democratic values
- Trust the legitimacy of the regime
- Vote
- Obey the law
- Are tolerant of other views
- Make few demands on the state
- Are aware of political affairs
- Join/contribute to organizations

As their responses will show, these young people embrace the above feelings most completely and without the modifications seen in the older groups. Simply, behind the youthful posturing sit some fairly typical budding young citizens.

Meet the Trailing Xers

Beau is a thoughtful and funny redhead from Texas A&M university who started—and still sings in—an a capella group in College Station. Although he began his university studies in engineering, he has developed an interest in political science and plans to attend the George Bush School of Public Service next year. Like Third Millennium and other Generation X "advocacy groups," Beau was concerned about entitlement spending. When asked how he would change the fiscal priorities of the country, he affirmed Schier's (1998) and accounts of Gen X worries about the impending Baby Boomer retirement:

> Probably less overall entitlement spending. I am a product of my generation and it's just hard to say that but I'm just not a big fan of the notion of entitlement. . . . I don't think that the federal government should be there to provide any kind of retirement savings for the people. I would like it to be philosophically more of a true social safety net rather than give us your money for a few years. And we'll give it back to you in the future. And obviously structurally that's not the case. I mean, it's not your money you're getting back . . . it's some 24 year old today sending you money . . . I don't think that's a very good way. I mean, there's no reason why my parents who have plenty of money need to get, you know, $500 a month from social security. . . . I mean, ideologically I would in a perfect world I would like it to be just a pure safety net if you need it but not something that you expect whether you need it or not.

Like the older members of his cohort, Beau has a strong bias toward self-reliance and a belief that individuals should not rely on the state for support except in dire circumstances.

Ben is a handsome, clean-cut senior at the University of California at Berkeley, where he leads a small chapter of College Republicans and serves as editor of an alternative campus newspaper dedicated to "countering the bias" of what he sees as stifling campus liberalism among both faculty and students. Unlike the recent spate of "conservatives as truth tellers" typified by the theatrically caustic (Coulter, 2002), Ben is candid about his role as activist rather than journalist:

> BEN: We recognize that we're freaks. Our interest in politics is way beyond what's normal for our peers . . . they might know the issues

or whatever but they're not nearly as partisan as we are. . . . I helped start a conservative publication on campus . . . being at Berkeley I wasn't much of a voice alone. . . . So I got together with some friends of mine and we started a paper there on campus. . . . I saw a need there and I think there were quite a few conservatives on campus but they really didn't have a voice. . . . There was no way to counter the liberal biases going on so I thought that there was a void to be filled. And so that's why I did it.

SS: Did you create the publication to put out the conservative view or was it to put out ostensibly an unbiased view to counteract a liberal bias?

BEN: No, we were biased in our own direction . . . that's the way to counter the liberal bias. I mean, we'd try to be honest and consistent with what we said because a lot of the time the liberals were not only biased but, you know, there was hypocrisy and there was deception and we were wanting to expose that. . . . So we weren't really interested in pointing out what's wrong with conservatism or being objective. We were more interested in discrediting the other side.

Ben attributes his interest in politics to his father's influence and admitted to preferring *Meet the Press* to cartoons on weekend mornings as a child.

Caroline is a willowy 20-year-old who interned last year at the Office of the Governor of Texas and has since moved to Washington, DC, to work on Capitol Hill. Ironically, while among the most politically motivated professionally, she was among the least reflective about political life. However, she mimicked her Baby Boomer parents' disdain for those older than her, arguing that older people deceive each other as they work their way up in business and work to achieve. While cynical about those older than she, Caroline was an active member of the campus community, joining a number of campus social groups including the Kappa Delta sorority and served as president of Bevo's Babes, a group of women who tend to the school's mascot.

Raj is active in gay rights groups on campus. He was especially engaged and passionate in our interview, often taking tangents to talk about other political issues of the day. He also served as an intern in a state representative's office during the most recent 140-day legislative session. He was the only respondent to seriously consider the question of the ultimate necessity of government, being drawn to the abstract appeal of anarchy, but perhaps missing the larger irony of his observation: "No one has really tried an anarchic government." He had a sense that government was engaged in a range of "corporate boondoggles" like the superconducting supercollider and corporate bailouts such as the S&L scandal (a formative memory) and the airline bailout that was then under consideration in the wake of the attacks of September 11. Further, he recommended Blake as a respondent for this study. Despite the closeness of their friendship, which according to both involved "a lot of talk about politics," they could not have been more different in their attitudes toward political issues and people. Like others in his generation, Raj internalized the need for independence and an exit strategy: "It's like, you know, how you can trust somebody but only so far and you always have to I guess, always have a way out. You know, and just rely on yourself better."

Blake was the oldest and most cynical of my respondents. At 26, he was still searching for an academic major, working a series of service jobs, and chain-smoking. Physically and demographically, he most closely resembled the Generation X characters in Coupland's (1992) tome that christened this generation as disengaged, angry and under-achieving.

Caitlin was the youngest of my respondents—she had just turned 20—and among the most active. She was a profound outlier among my respondents. Passionately active in a narrow-issue community, she was corrosively cynical about the larger world and about human beings in general. She had an almost maniacal obsession with animal rights, finding an animal rights angle or example to answer *every single question* in my interview protocol. Where Blake was disengaged and cynical, Caitlin was hyperengaged and cynical. I will address these two vivid cases later in this chapter.

Drew is a self-described news junkie who subscribes to the *New York Times* and has his multiple televisions tuned to Fox News, CNN, and CSPAN. He credits his interest in public affairs to conversations with his parents, grandparents, and great grandparents as he was growing up: "We always seem to talk about current issues and so there's part of my motivation that you want to get in on the conversation. Even at a young age I wanted to be a part of those conversations and I think uh, that's why I wanted to be informed. So I made sure that was so."

Sheila sees herself as "gullible," moving as she did from a small town to the big university. She finds herself applying small-town values to everyday transactions, and then ending up being "cheated." From roommates who fail to return borrowed garments to persistently being the "designated driver," the transition from rural childhood to urban college experience was a trying one for her—and one that has stretched her optimistic nature:

Well, in my personal stance I've always been uh, too trusting of a person. My parents both told me that I'm very gullible. I [tend to believe] what other people say [and get burned] so I've tried to make a conscious effort to be a little more wary around people. When, you know, because I get easily taken advantage of . . . So uh, I guess my own stance on that is that I'd rather prefer to be too trusting than too, I guess, I don't even know the word for it. Uh, too not trusting I guess. As opposed to it. I can't think of the word but, you know, because I'd rather give people the benefit of the doubt. . . . I'm always the one who's driving in an instance. You know, somebody just happens to be, you know, oh my car. Something else happened and something else happened and something else happened and I'm like OK. I'll drive. I'll drive. No problem. Next time it will happen, you know, when I wind up spending like twice as much gas as that person.

Gerry, like Sheila, had a difficult transition from small town to large university, again using dorm-life examples to illustrate cold realities about social trust: "And so that kind of happens sometimes in the dorm. Lending clothes out to girls that I didn't really know that well. Like oh, that's a cute shirt. Can I borrow it? And then its kind of like oh, can I have my shirt back? And they'd always come up with excuses and afterwards I moved out and never heard from them again. . . . And just little things like that started adding up so now I'm a little more cautious." Affirming elements of lifestyle effects research, Gerry had little time for thinking about politics. The activities of coping with a new culture and a new town simply crowded out civic pursuits: "I mean, I just feel that I'm not informed enough. I try to become informed but I have daily activities that I start doing and so I'll stop reading the newspaper at one point or I'll turn off the TV. Or I just won't go out in search for the information as much as I should be doing."

Unlike the other groups examined for this study, the members of this group of respondents had less in common with one another than the Cyber-democrats, Wireheads, or Tech Elites. In part that is because they were selected from a broader, more general pool of potential participants. The other groups were more monolithic in their respective professional pursuits. Although all of these respondents were undergraduates living in the same town at the same time, they did not share vocational pursuits. That said, this group of Trailing Xers does convey some compelling insights into notions of citizenship and technology among young people, and perhaps points to some elements of Generation X and rising Millennial attitudes toward civic life. Further, the most vivid cases—the cynic and the activist—raise a host of questions about conventional wisdom regarding cynicism in general.

Thus, we turn to the fundamental questions explored throughout this study—What kind of citizens are these young people? What sort of social capital do they depend upon or generate? And what role does technology play in their worldviews?

Affirming their Generation: Doing Something versus Voting

These undergraduates are consistent with both older members of their generation and of the technology sector—they place a premium on *action* rather than talk, and they do not see voting as a necessary act of good citizenship. However, reflecting Wolfe's concept of moral freedom, most did vote but refused to prescribe voting as a condition of being a good citizen. Said one,

> So there are other ways you can be a good citizen. I think people my age group are pretty good citizens assuming that, you know, they volunteer and I've seen it in my own school. People who may not necessarily be involved in politics or care what's going on at the national level, you know, they're volunteering or they're doing outreach work or, you know, they're volunteering at a hospital or they're tutoring kids. I mean, there's all kinds of ways you can show your citizenship. It can be a real generic thing. Just as simple as caring about other people or volunteering your time to help someone else in need. It can be pretty basic. It doesn't have to be anything that elaborate.

Taking that idea one step further, Beau described Schudson's (1998) "monitoring citizen" and echoed the Cyber-democratic belief that being informed is actually a civic precursor to voting:

> SS: Can you be a good citizen if you don't [vote]?
> BEAU: By not voting, yes. By not getting in the game mentally, I'd say no. So I mean, on the other hand if you never say a bad word about anything. If you just ask nothing and expect nothing other than basic personal respect and not being killed in public then there is some philosophical coherence with that. I mean, if you don't ever complain about the government then in some sense it's OK if you don't get involved in their activity and choose to have an opinion. The problem is when you feel entitled to have an opinion but don't feel responsible enough to educate yourself.

This theme of being uncomfortable with the uninformed existed in many of the interviews. Trailing Xer respondents thought people should be informed and "do something" and felt that there were many people who were not informed enough politically. Ironically, many of them did not see their elders as sufficiently informed, akin to Cyberdemocratic views about the shortcomings of the news media. Raj conveyed this view most succinctly:

> Some people who vote scare me. . . . I don't think they're truly representative of the population. I mean, you know, if you vote you tend to be older. You tend to be more conservative, you know . . . you know, I don't know. They're just not representative. They're more responsible, you know, in that they actually put down the remote control and go vote. Yeah, but I mean, sometimes their views are, you know, just worrisome, I guess. I don't think they're populous. I think they're more slanted to one way or the other. Left or right. Most people are polarized, I guess.

Again, they embraced the real work of communities, reflecting the insight of Shearer et al. (1998) in their description of "Doers"— nonvoters who are active in their communities and upbeat about life in general, but removed from the act of voting:

> Citizens would have to, I think, uh, be active in their local communities. Be community leaders. Identify and react to issues uh, that concern them and their communities. I think that, you know, voting is the tiniest part of it. I mean, there's a lot more to being a good citizen—a new construct of citizen we're developing here, I guess, would be someone who is active. More active than just a general voter. Going beyond, I mean, letting the public officials know how they feel. Letting their views be known. Engaging in public forum and debates. Uh, you know, going to a protest if something they don't like, you know, just generally speaking their minds and working towards uh, what they think is good for the country.

Hearing the Reagan Echo

Like the older members of Generation X, this group internalized many of the antigovernment messages launched by their first president of memory, Ronald Reagan. Concurring with their counterparts, they see government as being inherently inefficient, although typically this view was stated in general terms rather than being based on specific experiences or examples. Several respondents wrestled with this idea of government being inefficient, yet being at a loss for why they felt that way. Mused Raj,

[Many people are] in government and they like that field. A lot of them are limited . . . a lot of them have their hands tied by the . . . I don't want to say bureaucracy. Well, I guess bureaucracy. The way things are. The way things are set up and it doesn't . . . it doesn't . . . government really reward I don't think innovation.

Independent, but Active

Like other respondents, this group put a premium on independence, relying on the state for little and having disdain for those who made such demands for public aid. However, they were also conscious of reciprocity and the notion that what one person did could affect what other people did. They expressed this notion in different ways, but generally it manifested itself in thoughts of having a duty to respond and a need to be aware of other points of view. Beau expressed this sentiment most concisely:

> BEAU: That's plenty. Just be aware. It's a big one. Never have enough education. Never have enough awareness of the world around you. Uh, know what you know and try and know what other people know and so that when the other people try and do things you can determine whether or not it's in your interest and other people's interest.
> SS: Would you say that there is one most important responsibility of citizenship?
> BEAU: I would say that you need to have an awareness that what you do impacts other people. That you subscribe to any social contract whether it be a complex local system or thou shall not kill then you know that you can't be truly independent. Not matter how far away from the city you try to live or on a farm you try and live or anything like that. If you expect other people to respect you and your interest you need to have the same for them.

We see here the active minimalist credo: know what is going on around you and do something—large or small—to make the world better. Not as interesting a headline as "Generation X imperils democracy," but more accurate and more useful.

Technology: No Big Deal

Finally, this group differed sharply from their older colleagues in their views of technology. Most of them looked at me blankly when I asked how technology was changing their lives or that of their communities. They had always used these technology tools, so there was little sense of "change" or technological innovation. Rather, information technology was for them just part of the landscape of their educational, professional, and social lives. When asked about technology's effects on democracy, Raj was unimpressed with the legislature's use of technology thus far:

> And there's all type of stuff. I wish it were more interactive though in that you could offer some feedback, you know. I mean, I know you can send someone an e-mail but if you don't get a reply for a week . . . you know, or a month, you know, whoopee. . . . Another avenue of free speech, expression. I think that can't hurt.

Ultimately, these Trailing Xers were more a collection of individuals rather than representative of any sort of monolithic collective. They reflected some of the literature's findings about Generation X and also affirmed some of the qualities found in the older Generation X technology sector participants. Like their Wirehead colleagues, they fell closest to active minimalists in their civic behavior, but unlike the older groups had not yet begun to conceptualize specific *new* ways to participate. The most interesting single finding was that, across the board, they saw no "technological revolution" bubbling around them. They saw computers, the Internet, cell phones, and e-mail as ho-hum appliances of everyday life, not as great catalysts for communicating, organizing, or practicing democracy in new ways.

However, two of my respondents had such curious notions of citizenship that they deserve special attention. As I have immersed myself in their interview protocols, I am still stunned by their responses. In essence, they emerge as caricatures—one as an activist, the other as a Gen X cynic. To my mind, their responses provide fascinating insights into the two extremes of this generation, extremes that are often used to malign the entire cohort. Simply, these caricatures were the closest thing I found to the actors that the Generation X literature describes as typical.

The Cynical Activist and the Disaffected Cynic: Opposites that Affirm the Clichés

Out of 40 respondents in this study, Caitlin and Blake were the only two to say they were unhappy and that their lives were dull, reflecting the "classic" Generation X sensibility. Recall that Bennett and Rademacher (1997) found Generation X to be indifferent to public affairs, unlikely to vote, disinclined to follow media accounts of public happenings, and uniformed about politics. Hill (1997) went even further, charging that this generation was both intolerant and an anomaly: "atavistic, reactionary group of Americans who have thus far been unable to cope with the mostly positive changes occurring in a nation now run for the most part both politically and financially by boomers." Owen (1998) observed that Xers tend to believe that politicians are inaccessible, out of touch, and corrupted by power. Generally, throughout this study, I have found little evidence to support much of the pejorative cast that Baby Boomer academics and journalists have heaped on those born between 1960 and 1981.

However, Blake and Caitlin do exhibit many of these characteristics, setting them apart from others, and this makes them particularly interesting to this study.

But before embracing the negative descriptions of the generation fully, it is important to note that even in this cynical dyad, monolithic responses were not offered. In fact, one could be described as Shearer et al.'s (1998) nonvoting "unplugged," a person who was aggressively disengaged (and quick to distance himself from all things political) while the other could fall squarely in the behavioral camp of the classic activist, involved passionately in a single social movement but myopic about other political issues. For example, note Blake's extracurricular comments when answering Almond and Verba's question about the qualities he most admired in people:

1. Generous
2. Active
3. Does his job well
4. Lets no one take advantage of him
5. Respectful
6. Keeps to himself
7. Ambitious
8. Thrifty

But you left out most of my favorite personality traits. Fun-loving and humorous is a perennial favorite. Compassionate is better than generous. Insightful is better than any of them. From 6 down I'm just listing how obnoxious I find these traits.

As the above passage reflects, Blake was the glibbest and most persistently cynical of any of my respondents. Curiously, however, he also grew more uncomfortable with each new question asked. Increasingly, he avoided answering questions, becoming visibly uncomfortable each time I did not match his cynical tone. In the sequence below, notice how he gives a glib response and then fumbles when his response was taken seriously:

SS: If you think about national and international issues facing the country how well do you think you understand them?

BLAKE: Not very well. Probably as well as the average American does. I intentionally shelter myself from political thought.

SS: Why is that?

BLAKE: The idea being that the more that I've learned about it in the past historically the more its made me angry on a regular basis.

SS: What kind of stuff makes you angry?

BLAKE: Uh, politics.

SS: What about it?

BLAKE: Conflict of ideas, compromise, uh, corruption, greed, the small mindedness of people. Totally unnecessary conflict.

SS: What would be an example of an unnecessary conflict?

BLAKE: Geez, an example of an unnecessary conflict. Uh, micro or macro?

SS: Whichever one you can think of? But more in the political context.

BLAKE: More in the political context. Well, that's the great thing about my micro and macro. Because the same thing happens. Uh, it's unnecessary prejudice . . . Uh, that leads to misunderstanding, mounting tension and eventually a aggression. There never would have been a Gulf War if those people prayed to the right god . . . that's probably a sweeping generalization on my part.

SS: That's OK. Uh, you say that conflict of ideas is a problem—do you not like a conflict of ideas? Does it make you uncomfortable? Or do you not see a conflict of ideas in other places other than in political stuff?

BLAKE: By and large I don't like people who are absolutely convinced of their own opinion. Uh, a conflict of ideas is just fine as long as nobody's certain that they're . . . OK, OK. It has occurred to me. It has occurred to me. Do I worry about it? Not really. right . . . and if both sides are certain that they're right then that's a good way to get uh, well, a cathartic exercise of that anger and aggression.

SS: So what about state and local issues? Do you feel like you understand them?

BLAKE: Even less than I do national.

SS: Less.

BLAKE: Issues and international issues.

SS: Uh-huh.

BLAKE: I don't pay any attention to them at all. Uh, not only do I uh, feel like I'm being made dirty by learning about them but I'm also wondering about their uh, consequence on a grander scale of things.

SS: Do you worry that if people like you aren't aware or don't participate that things will just get worse?

BLAKE: OK, OK. It has occurred to me. It has occurred to me. Do I worry about it? Not really. Because the world has rambled on for a really long time without me in it and it will be rambling along for a really long time afterwards. . . . And, you know, maybe if uh, everybody in the population is just simply compassionate and realistic of daily life then, you know, that kind of thing will rub off on other people. And they'll get the idea. . . . Gosh, that's simpleminded and overly optimistic.

SS: Some people say that governments are really unnecessary and that people would get along better without them. What do you think?

BLAKE: People being what they are I think governments are absolutely necessary.

SS: Can you kind of unpack that a little bit for me?

BLAKE: People being what they are. As bad as the things that governments do are worse things would happen without them.

SS: Like what?

BLAKE: Uh, a total failure of progress. Uh, industry and commerce as much as, you know, they get a bad rap these days . . . you know, are moving the humans in a certain direction at least. And that totally wouldn't happen. Technology wouldn't happen and advanced culture wouldn't happen without government.

SS: Advanced culture wouldn't happen without government? What does government do to advance culture?

BLAKE: Uh, well, I'm sure there are a few historical points I could come up with. Uh, we'll maintain the art and culture . . . of a good portion of the world before it was sacked by barbarians. . . . Who didn't have a government, right? Without the government of Rome there wouldn't have been that preservation and if there had been a stronger government it wouldn't have all been destroyed.

SS: *The question was "can you give me a more current example?* What about what about now as you think about it? I mean, in sort of a current time.

BLAKE: Now.

SS: In a current time.

BLAKE: Uh, well, art, culture, literature hasn't changed a whole lot in the past 2000 years. I mean, it still is valuable as it was and its still maintaining the same the fragile uh, existence without efforts to preserve it, record it and keep it intact it will be destroyed so the idea of civilization and government helps uh, you know, keep those things together.

SS: Uh, as you think about the taxes you pay what do you think they go for?

BLAKE: ... Building empires. Uh, there's it's a complicated question. I mean, if I listed all of the things it would sound like a government report.

SS: What does that pay for? What do you think?

BLAKE: Salaries of loafers [laughter].

This excerpt is typical of the stop-and-start banter of the interview. I would ask a question, he would give a glib answer, and I would ask him to elaborate on his thinking. He would then lapse into obscure and unrelated examples. When I would try to draw him back to present-day politics, he would revert to retort, growing increasingly uneasy throughout the interview. Could I as an interviewer have been violating some sort of cynicism reciprocity norm? After what was a rather tortuous interview with a cynical, bright, bitter, and articulate young man, I was surprised to receive two follow-up e-mail messages from him. They read as follows:

Do you have a theory as to why Generation X in particular would be resistant to the idea of inherent obligation? I interviewed a few friends at work today. I got one stand-up kinda girl who assured me that she felt obliged to everything from God to government to parents, but I wonder if she wasn't answering out of a textbook. Everyone else felt rather strongly that the idea was repugnant. When I pressed a little further, they replied that would definitely be willing to help but rejected the idea of obligation.

Trying to evaluate the issue from a psychological perspective, I look back at the way I was raised. As is the case for many of my contemporaries, I was raised in a fragmented home by rather fragmented characters who would neither show me the full range of human emotions nor give much promise of benefit or assistance in the future. I don't consider myself as having been raised or groomed so much as fed, watered, caged, and left to my own devices. Nuclear family being society in small, why should I/we feel indebted to people who really didn't do a lot for us?

But the whole approach of modern psychology never impressed me, and it was really an afterthought. When I started thinking about the idea of obligation to society, the first thing that occurred to me was an image of a TV commercial promising no down payments and a low interest rate. Now what the correlation between this image and that idea was mystified me for some time. It seems to me that a rather large number of people (completely unfamiliar to me) have tried to "use" me to the your advantage. It's quite gotten to the point that as soon as I recognize the elements of a sales pitch I stop listening. Either because of the intentionally emotional wording of some sales pitches or simply because these people feel comfortable approaching complete strangers with a proposition, it seems that a segment of the population has been trying to "cash in" on my supposed "obligation" all of my life. That certainly isn't a new condition and I don't see why it should cause a generational phenomenon, but the fact remains that I asked myself a question and that was the answer I got. Of course our generation watches an order of magnitude more television than any that came before and the subsequent exposure to media blitz may have damaged some faculty of our oh so fragile minds.

But maybe I'm on a quest for trite answers.

And four days later,

I've done a little more thinking about the idea of "community." It occurs to me that the way that I was using the idea of living together, the only people that would qualify as my community are those that live with me. Maybe I need to loosen my definition. Maybe I've got a point. I recall once seeing video of a Neolithic South American tribe. There were a number of interesting things about the way that they went about life, but the one that stands out in my mind is that the entire tribe slept together in a heap of more than a hundred bodies. Now I'm not suggesting that this the "ideal" way of life for humans, but it's certainly closer to our roots than the suburbs. The change of social climate from the organic mound and that kind of closeness and affection to the cold exchanges "Would you like fries with that?" and situations where you're constantly surrounded by strangers are (I'm sure) a major factor in the lack of emotional well-being in modern man, but I digress . . . The point I started out to make was the organic mound REALLY constitutes a "community." They're involved with each other's lives. The suburbs are a bunch of people living close enough together to see each other, but too far away to necessarily be involved.

Most curious of all is that during the interview, Blake's responses were only a sentence or two in length. But in these follow-up missives, he asks questions, wrestles with ideas, taps his own experience, and expresses his thoughts in entire paragraphs. He seems to be at the same time justifying his cynical, distant posture adopted during the interview, yet working to show me that he really was not the cynically detached loser he portrayed himself to be when we met in person. Affirming both the marketing literature on Generation X and popular accounts, he blamed his cynicism on the fact that he was from a broken family, raised by television, and launched into a world of limited opportunity.

Further, he affirms Hart's insights that cynicism is a fragile proxy for sophistication among the young. Blake tried mightily through his bombastic responses in the interview to convey a sense of worldliness. However, when faced with sincere question after sincere question from an *un*cynical interlocutor, his confidence in the tool of cynicism weakened.

To his credit, his commitment to cynicism was the mightiest of all respondents in this study. But after nearly two hours it cracked and yielded in print what he felt he could not do in person—talk sincerely about civic life. E-mail became a tool for sincerity but also giving him the immediacy of a phone call. I responded immediately and thanked him for his thoughts. Then, the second missive. Once the cynical wall cracked, its intrinsic weakness was revealed and a flood of thoughtful words (or in this case bits) flowed my way. Could the distance and immediacy of e-mail, a ubiquitous and nearly invisible tool to this young generation, be a catalyst for breaking through the wall of cynicism? Let us hope so.

Like Blake, Caitlin displayed an exceedingly cynical worldview throughout the interview, although curiously, she was the only respondent to lead her list of admirable qualities in people with "respectful." And despite being an activist (by her own admission and meeting my definition of activist), she listed "active" near the bottom of her list:

1. Respectful
2. Generous
3. Does his job well
4. Ambitious
5. Active
6. Lets no one take advantage of him

According to the taxonomy I constructed earlier, activists are those citizens who spend the most time engaged in community and political pursuits, although generally revolving around a narrow, rather than general interest. In Caitlin's case, her passion was animal rights. Where my typical interview transcript ran between 12 and 22 pages, Caitlin's stretched to 42 pages in which a major portion included detailed soliloquies of the many venues and injustices of the animal rights movement. From the very first question about whether she viewed people as generally helpful to the final discussion of technology, every question about community, technology, citizenship, cynicism, philanthropy, or politics warranted an animal-rights-related response.

In her study of political "sophisticates," Herbst (1998) found that while cynicism had increased among most political actors, the most optimistic were partisan political operatives and volunteers. Even those operatives who were in minority parties or chronically on the losing side of elections were found to have a strong sense of optimism and patriotism. This finding is consistent with the literature on social capital, which finds that social involvement breeds increased feelings of efficacy. Brehm and Rahn (1997) found a "tight reciprocal relationship" between participation and interpersonal trust, where the stronger causal effects are from participation to trust (i.e., the more that citizens participate, the greater their levels of interpersonal trust). Interpersonal trust is a critical component of civic culture and social capital. Caitlin's obsession with some of the more arcane offshoots of the animal rights movement certainly situated her squarely in the camp of fringe activists who are often on the losing side of political issues.

Instead of building bonds of social trust, Caitlin's activism seemed to stoke a cynicism and paranoia about the larger political culture. Rather than Herbst's activists, Caitlin seemed more akin to Hart's (1978) atheists, extremely negative and further uses the "smeary worldless language all over the establishment 'we know you for what you are. And you know what we know.' " In Caitlin's case, her involvement in political life seemed to reflect both the "rhetoric of the ostracized" and some of the more unsavory observations and predictions made by elite theorists.

For example, Huntington (1975) argued against the "excess" of democracy and urged a *moderation* of democracy. He and Sartori (1994) cited examples from the United States in the 1960s, when street-level activism was historically high and when governmental *activity* was expanded but governmental *authority* declined, a recipe that damaged the stability of democracy: Huntington's "democratic distemper." The animal rights movement in particular has been one characterized by irrational spasms of violence and an agenda marked by hyperbole and little commitment to meaningful political goals, such as legislation or policy change. Consider Caitlin's wandering arguments against a range of political actors. First, a local elected official:

And so uh, everybody was like we don't want to sell these dogs to these medical schools anymore. It's really horrible. We don't want to sell them to scientific research anymore and uh, he was like at first he was going along with it and then uh, he was like well, maybe I will. Maybe I won't. I don't know what I'll do. At the last minute whatever it was he changed his mind and uh, because there was so much political pressure because he was like yeah, we should kill them. It's fine to keep selling them because the medical schools in Texas would value them and it's a really great source of revenue. And it's really horrible and wrong. I mean, I guess that could have been someone's pet that they never got reunited with. . . . And so uh, so at the last minute under a lot of pressure he had to change his mind to be with the pro animal groups because there was so much pressure. But, I mean, he's sleezy. I mean, he passed that stadium referendum thing. You know, building that and they don't have the money to build that. And it's for private sport. . . . So I don't see why the city should pay the bill to play games but not save animals.

Then, she turns her cynicism to the post–September 11 work of the Red Cross:

And I mean, you know, it's like the Red Cross keeps asking for donations for that (September 11 victims). The government is obligated whether they like it or not to pick up the tab for that . . . So and we pay our taxes . . . So why do we need to also pay for the clean up? To the Red Cross. The Red Cross is really crooked anyway. People think they're so wonderful and I mean, I think it's wonderful that they're helping with that. Those people need all the help they can get but they do a lot of animal research that nobody knows about unless they're actually well versed in the ways of the Red Cross. Because people that run those non-profits usually have huge salaries . . . in the hundreds of thousands.

And this for members of Congress:

SS: When you think about taxes you pay what do you think they go for?

CAITLIN: Mostly crap.

SS: Hm?

CAITLIN: Crap.

SS: Like what?

CAITLIN: Big salaries for politicians. Cars, security that sometimes I don't think is necessary. Uh, I mean, they should have some security but some of them I think like to think they're better than the people that don't even know who they are. . . . They like to give themselves notoriety . . . let's see. I think we pay for their vacations. . . . I think we pay for, I mean, they get a lot of money when they retire and I forgot what kind of fund it is but they can put money into it and then if they don't use it up they get to keep it. . . . I don't think that politicians are ethical at all. I think that they've done all these studies and usually it's the wealthiest candidate wins.

Finally, she offered these reflections about her school, school district, and then secretary of education:

> [Former Houston Independent School District Superintendent and then Secretary of Education] Paige drove a Mercedes. . . . This doesn't seem right to me. When he drove a Mercedes as the superintendent of HISD . . . And he drove a Mercedes but yet all those like kids in those broken down schools, I mean, Houston HISD, I mean, I went through HISD it's a horrible district. It's really dangerous. They have lots of gang problems. . . . I grew up in a really affluent area and I went to what's considered like one of the upper class high schools. I mean, then there were kids that we had kids bringing guns to school. They would do drugs. They were smoking in the hallways. I mean, it's like people have no control. Those classes were bigger than what those teachers could handle. Those teachers weren't any good anyway.

Like Atheists in the 1970s, this proponent of a marginal social movement "meets failure directly—escalating their rhetoric and increasing their obstreperousness, even though such techniques function only to preserve their socially marginal status."

Caitlin was a particularly acute form of activist. My taxonomy of classic activist virtues and behaviors provides a guide to more mainstream limitations of activists as social capitalists. For example, while engaged in political activity, sometimes they do not exhibit the democratic virtues of less active citizens. In the name of resistance and dissent they disobey the law. In pursuit of their views, they can be politically narrow and myopic, closing their minds to the arguments of others. While activists exhibit willingness to engage in political activity, they often ignore the rights of others, make unrealistic demands on the state, and mistake activism for discourse. Thus, activists represent a unique segment of the citizenry—engaged, participatory, and often optimistic— yet, missing other virtues *classically* required for good citizenship.

Caitlin certainly displayed all of those things. What she is *not*, however, is the ignorant, apathetic, disengaged Generation Xer found in much of the generational literature. Although she has taken her rhetoric to a narrow extreme, in her responses to the interview and survey instruments, she displays many of the traits of the classic activist: one who believes in democratic values; votes; is aware of political affairs; organizes citizens in pursuit of political/social change; creates community organizations; actively participates in political/legislative activities in pursuit of a specific agenda. What sets Caitlin apart from Herbst's activists is that in the case of her work on partisan activists, she found that their sense of efficacy increased even when they lost political battles. Animal rights activists are persistent losers in political battles and such losses, rather than increasing a sense of optimism, involvement, and efficacy, seemed to fuel further isolation in persons such as Caitlin.

Caitlin's negativity raises a host of interesting questions about the nature of the fringe activist. If you lose all the time, or are perhaps the object of ridicule for your activism, then does that corrode the civic spirit? Can a narrow, marginal interest, even if it engages one in the larger community, actually deplete social capital by animating reciprocal resistance?

The cynic and the activist manifest their alienation in opposite ways, one by pulling away in ironic detachment, the other by an obsessive involvement in chow rescue and the other travails of PETA. Perhaps most importantly, both feel detached from any notion of community. When asked to describe the ideal community, for example, Caitlin replied,

> Well, I guess, knowing everyone liked animals. Fur would not exist. Fur coats would all be out. And everybody would understand the horror of it. We would stop using animals in medical research and start using horrible murderers and rapists and child molesters. I know people think that sounds crazy but we've got real human subjects, you know.

Recall the recent study identified five categories of nonvoters, two of which comprised Generation X members: Doers and the Unplugged (Shearer et al., 1998). In contrast to the Doers, the Unplugged resemble the more dire "slacker" characterizations found in popular literature. Eighty-one percent of these individuals were under 40. They were less educated, 63 percent with a high school education or less. They rarely followed public affairs, seldom talked about politics with friends or coworkers, and did not regularly volunteer for charities or other community activities. Caitlin appears to be a cynical Doer, while Blake appears to be relatively well educated, Unplugged—two more possibilities to add to the taxonomy of nonvoters.

I opted to give special attention to Caitlin and Blake because of their very different approaches to participation and yet their similarity to classic descriptions of Generation X. Recall that notwithstanding evidence of a more complex reality, this entire generation has been widely maligned for its political apathy (Bennett, 1997), lack of political knowledge (Hays, 1998), limited attention span, unseemly social habits, and dearth of critical thinking skills (Sacks, 1996). This cohort has further been described as demanding and intellectually lazy, largely because of their postmodern philosophical bent (Sacks, 1996). Some even feared that the civic incompetence of this generation could imperil democracy (Hays, 1998), as the reins of leadership pass to an unsocialized generation that shuns political participation. Given the cynic's and activist's disdain for all that Hill (1997) claimed was created and run by Boomers, Caitlin and Blake could be engaging in a sort of retrograde clique maintenance, the tendency of the disengaged of one generation to see every personal disappointment as the fault of the generation ahead of them. At least in that sense, these young "disengaged" may have inherited some Boomer sensibilities after all.

Conclusion

The more thoughtful commentaries made about Generation X reveal a generation that volunteers at a rate considerably higher than their parents. Another recent study found that 72 percent of college freshmen had performed volunteer work in the previous year, and that 38 percent volunteer on a weekly basis (UCLA Higher Education Research Institute, 1998). This generation also senses that it should participate more in political affairs, but feels it is not sophisticated enough in its politics to do so, that political issues are not relevant to their lives (Hays, 1998), and that they get inferior, biased information from the media (Media Studies Center, 1996). I found echoes of all of these sentiments when interviewing this small sample. I also found some support for the more negative characterizations of Generation X—the whining, the negativity, the gratuitous cynicism. However, the sharp distinction between the qualities portrayed in written surveys and the longer interview point to the need for more qualitative approaches to generational research, especially among younger respondents. Social desirability bias becomes a curious and complicated thing with younger respondents. Which is more socially desirable—being the "cool cynic" or pleasing a sincere interviewer?

One thing is certain—the approaches of Sacks, Bennett, Howe, and Strauss et al. truly underestimate the complexity of this generation. In looking at the whole generational cohort so pejoratively, these researchers do young people a disservice. My research shows that these young people represent the full gamut of citizenship, from the fringe activist to the disaffected loner to the mainstream active minimalist. It is also noteworthy that this latter approach to citizenship was the *most common* found in this study.

Based on these interviews, I find ample support for Coupland's accusation of Baby Boomer clique maintenance, where Baby Boomer academics are quick to laud all members of their own generation as those "who changed the course of history" (Hill, 1997) and Generation X as "an atavistic slightly reactionary group of Americans who have thus far been unable to cope with the mostly positive changes occurring in a nation now run for the most part both politically and financially by boomers." Just as such pronouncements ignore the "Me Generation" excesses of Baby Boomer middle age, their descriptions and analyses of Generation X highlight the Blakes and ignore the Beaus and the Bens. Whether because of clique maintenance or the fear of getting old and uncool, Boomer academic and journalistic treatment of Generation X often seems misguided. Worse, their analyses may have negative consequences for the civic involvement of young people in the future by describing them so negatively that they see no alternative other that to fulfill the prophecies made about them.

8

Embracing and Surfing Social Change: Generation X and New Norms of Civic Life and Social Capital

So what does all of this mean? What might a small group of Generation X, high-tech actors in Austin, Texas, tell us about larger issues of citizenship and social capital? Certainly this study took place during a tumultuous time. The euphoria of the tech bubble was at a fevered pitch when I penned my proposal in mid-2000: NASDAQ at 5000, Dow at 11,000. Then, the bust. Then the attacks of September 11—all of which occurred during my data collection. It was quite a time to be studying American civic life, but an especially compelling time to be investigating notions of citizenship and social obligation in the high-tech community—the very ground zero of economic turmoil in the American economy. Dow rebounded to top 12,000 in October of 2006. Boom, Bust, Boom again.

When this project began, scholars, pundits, and journalists were buzzing about *Bowling Alone*, lamenting the civically anemic and cynical "lost generation" X and claiming that "fundamentals don't matter" in business. Two years later, two new offerings hit the shelves: Putnam's *Democracies in Flux: The Evolution of Social Capital in Contemporary Society*, an edited volume that looks at how social capital might be changing rather than simply declining; and *Millennials Rising: The Next Great Generation* by Strauss and Howe, who were not content to malign Generation X from the Boomer perspective, but also to malign it from the perspective of the generation below. Despite that annoying quality, the Strauss and Howe book does do something uncommon in the generational literature: it has positive things to say about young people. They have since penned two well received additional offerings on Millennials—looking at their impact on popular culture and the implications of their generational size and ethos on American institutions of higher education. Between the Millennials rising and the Boomers retiring, in the view of most generational theorists, Generation X remains the Rodney Dangerfield of generational cohorts. It gets no respect. At the beginning of this tome, I began with the observation that Generation X had not typically been taken seriously by scholars or popular writers, with the notable exception of some Gen X thinkers, including Halstead (1999), Bagby (1998), and Liu (1994), although none of these writers produced research-based works. Instead, they discussed public policy, penned celebrity profiles, and anthologized essays by Generation X writers, respectively. All three offerings were interesting, but did little to counteract the negative and increasingly predictable slant of generational work especially with respect to those born between 1960 and 1981. In contrast, I hope that my study has provided a fresh set of insights to those studying generational issues in the areas of political science, communication, and social capital studies. As well, I hope that the insights about changing notions of quality citizenship will provide additional grist for the pundit mill as the oldest Baby Boomers retire and the Generation X begins to occupy a greater proportion of economic and civic roles and increasingly step into positions of leadership. There are now over 55 members of the U.S. Congress born after 1960, and the most well known, Senator Barack Obama, has garnered much early attention for his fresh, authentic approach to contemporary issues, seeming to transcend many of the stale ideological debates raging since the Baby Boomers ascended politically in the late 1960s.

The purpose of this study was to look beyond the typical characterizations of Generation X and Putnam's definitions of social capital. To bring a fresh view to the generational perspective, rather than casting all Generation X actors into a single group, I parsed them based on the nature of their involvement in the technology sector, yielding four distinct groups: Cyber-democrats, Wireheads, Tech Elites, and Trailing Xers. By parsing the sample this way, I was able to explore questions such as:

- Compared to existing accounts of demographically similar actors, how do high-tech actors differ in their civic, social and political attitudes, behaviors and knowledge?
- Within the high-tech community, how do these groups compare with one another?
- While conventional wisdom and popular accounts portray a monolithic high-tech community and unified Generation X, are they, in reality, diverse in their civic attitudes and behaviors?

Rather than accepting the singularly quantitative and generally pejorative descriptions of Generation X and Putnam's well-covered argument that social capital was in decline because younger generations were not joining old institutions, this study asked questions such as: are new citizenship values driving the participation, involvement, and philanthropy of these "cyber" generations and thereby changing how they live, what they value, and how they govern themselves? Have earlier scholars attempted to judge civic life by the scale of old life + new technology, rather than adopting the insight Postman provides, which says that revolutionary technologies introduced into a culture ultimately yield something fundamentally new?

Through written surveys and oral interviews drawn from a range of well-known civic and political instruments, I found that these young respondents generally thought quite deeply about public life and civic involvement when given the opportunity. Generally, they were not the ill-informed, disengaged cynics portrayed in other literature. In fact, they reflected many of the attributes and sensibilities advanced by democratic and social capital theorists. However, affirming Postman's insight, they rearranged and recast many of those behaviors and sensibilities in ways that reflect more contemporary values, lifestyles, and norms. Young high-tech actors in Austin proved to be an especially rich cohort with whom to explore these changing definitions and manifestations of civic spirit.

Certainly the boom-bust business cycle of the recent past was felt strongly in Austin, a city that cast itself as a high-tech center since the late 1980s and which had been identified by a range of observers as one of the top high-tech destinations, which put it in company with Seattle, Silicon Valley in California and Route 128 in Boston (Scott and Sunder, 1998; Florida, 2002; Lisheron and Bishop, 2002). With a high concentration of technology firms and lifestyle amenities attracting "creative-class" workers (groups that are populated largely by Generation X members), Austin was a particularly apt place to study issues of *contemporary* social capital. And, finally, from a civic/political perspective, Austin has a long history of community activism and political involvement, which put it at variance with the more typical institutions producing Putnam-esque social capital. Austin has been a place where Environmentalists chained themselves to the mayor's desk and not a place where a small caste of ruling bluebloods frequented country clubs and Moose Lodges. In short, studying Generation X high-tech actors' conceptions of citizenship and community involvement could not have been undertaken in a better place or at a more interesting time. Obviously, this group does not constitute a generalizable sample and Austin is a political town. However, these findings provide some potentially rich and fresh questions for future research.

This study began with an exploration of the intersection of generational studies, democratic theory, and technology research, an interdisciplinary stew, which can be synthesized into a list of "problems" reflected in current writings about the decline of civic life in America. Those problems were

• Bowling Alone
• Generational change
• The Internet
• Technology and community.
• Politics and young people.

Each of these developments has been lamented by scholars in several disciplines. Identification of these problems was used to support Putnam's thesis that American civic life was in decline, that technological advancement and young people were primarily to blame, and that this state of affairs was causing existential angst and democratic crisis across the United States.

Parting company with those in the Putnam camp, this study asserts that the problems listed above are actually a set of blinders worn by those on what Postman would call the "losing side" of technological advancement. This is *not* to say that all is right with American civic life. Instead, it is to argue that America is in a time of significant economic and generational change. As a result, measuring societal health with traditional measures overlooks the creative evolution of civic relationships and institutions underway among young people, especially those between 20 and 40. Thus, the "problems" listed above and identified earlier in this study are, in fact, not problems per se; rather, they are opportunities, or catalysts perhaps for new sorts of citizenship and civic participation. It therefore seems sensible to revisit these "problems" by taking into account the insights provided by the respondents in this study.

The Problem of Bowling Alone

I would argue that the problem of Bowling Alone is one that is being remedied by many high-tech Generation X actors and those younger— yielding a rich area for future research, mapping and measuring the *new means* of interaction and association with the energy that Putnam mapped the old. Since "Bowling Alone" is a metaphor describing the evolution of a 1950s activity from the way it was practiced at mid-century to the way it is practiced today, I feel at liberty to use a similar construction to make a different point.

Many things have changed since the 1950s. As Florida (2002), Skocpol (2002), and Wuthnow (2002) have recently observed, the social capital institutions of the 1950s were generally homogeneous (especially regarding gender and class) structures that mimicked the hierarchical, regularized, and male-dominated workplaces of the day. Now take Putnam's bowling metaphor—that we used to bowl in leagues but now we bowl alone—and transfer it to existing social institutions. In the 1950s we used to gather with those who shared similar interests, in places and institutions structured like our workplaces. Now, according to my high-tech respondents, we gather in more informal, diverse settings while displaying less regimented, ritualistic fashions—mimicking the evolution of the contemporary workplace. We still bowl. We still gather. But we gather *differently*, in ways that are more consistent with how we live *and work*. Is social capital truly in decline if we do not gather every Tuesday night, with the same people wearing matching shirts, week after week? As work and social patterns have changed and become less regimented, such routinized gatherings are simply not possible. Thus, a "just-in-time" social capital has emerged, one that responds to a community need in a different way. A work-based social activity arises ad hoc rather than on a particular night. Is that decline or evolution? Or could it be even progress?

Skocpol (2002) points out that these kinds of activities are difficult to measure but are akin to the kind of change that occurred during industrialization. Across all the respondents interviewed in this study, evidence of these new means of organizing and socializing were obvious. Cyber-democrats and Wireheads particularly embraced a sort of "just-in-time" social capital, alluding to the team and project orientation found in many contemporary businesses and social groupings. Each of the groups felt a duty to respond to a community need or a request for help—both before and after the events of September 11. In Putnam's parlance, people may not be bowling in leagues, with their homogenous populations and their rigid schedules, but instead playing games of pick-up basketball, playing when a game arises or when someone specifically asks you to play.

The Problem of Generational Change

No doubt, the maligning of Generation X by scholars and popular authors has been evidenced enough in this study. Generation X norms and values, when judged by those of an earlier era, do not measure up. But again, *difference* does not necessarily produce decline. Florida employed a clever technique to illustrate this phenomenon in his introduction to *The Rise of the Creative Class*. There, he offered a "thought experiment" wherein he posited two time travelers, one who traveled from 1900 to 1950 and another who traveled from 1950 *to* the present. He asked which traveler would observe the greatest and most uncomfortable set of changes. On the surface, it would appear that the traveler from 1900 to 1950 would encounter the most: automobiles, airplanes, electricity, telephones—technological tools that would be completely foreign to him. However, his workplace, Florida observes, would be relatively unchanged. If a person worked in a factory, he would likely still work with men much like himself, in tightly scripted routines on a day that started promptly at 9:00 a.m. and ended promptly at 5:00 p.m. Our worker would then go home for dinner with his family, a dinner prepared by his wife who had been at home taking care of the house and children all day. While the technology tools found at home in 1950 would certainly be different, the rhythms of life would be quite familiar.

In contrast, the traveler from 1950 to to the present would encounter updated versions of the same gizmos he used in 1950, with the exception of personal computers and the ubiquitous blackberries and i-pods. Cars would be sleeker and more numerous; phones would need no cord; headphones would have proliferated. Unlike the earlier traveler for whom changes would be obvious in the first few moments spent in the future, it would take longer than a single walk through town for the 1950 time traveler to see the important changes of the past 50 years. It is those changes that are overlooked by Putnam and often attributed negatively to generational change. Florida's characterization is worth including here in full:

> Our second time traveler would be quite unnerved by the dizzying social and cultural changes that had accumulated between 1950 and today. He would find a new dress code, a new schedule and new rules. He would see office workers dressed like folks relaxing on the weekend, in jeans and open necked shirts and be shocked to learn they occupy positions of authority. People at the office would seemingly come and go as they pleased. The younger ones might sport bizarre piercings and tattoos. Women and even nonwhites would be managers. Individualism and self-expression would be valued over conformity to organizational norms— and yet these people would seem strangely puritanical to this time traveler. His ethnic jokes would fall embarrassingly flat. His smoking would get him banished to the parking lot and his two-martini lunches would raise genuine concern. Attitudes and expressions he had never

thought about would cause repeated offense. He would continually suffer the painful feeling of not knowing how to behave. . . . People would seem to be always working, yet never working when they were supposed to. . . . they would seem career conscious, yet fickle—doesn't anyone stay with the company more than 3 years? Caring yet anti-social—what happened to the ladies clubs, Moose lodges and bowling leagues? While the physical surroundings would be relatively familiar, the feel of the place would be bewilderingly different. (pp. 3–4)

As this passage illustrates, lifestyles and worldviews are changing— old orders are breaking down and flux and uncertainty seem to be a growing part of everyday life. From this vantage point, the talk of civic decline seems to be tied to clique maintenance, an effort by the winners of the old technological order fighting to maintain their privilege in the midst of change. The new order confronting them privileges those who are different.

Recall, for example, the upwardly mobile Cyber-democrats doing the work (and making the money) of their parents' peers due to the changes in legislative work occasioned by the Internet. Therefore, the "problem of generational change" depends very much on where one sits. If one is an old, pre-Internet white male member of the corporate elite in an industrial "company town," this evolution is indeed a problem for him. If one is young, independent and technologically savvy, such changes are part of a social revolution where he or she is on the winning side—no problem at all. The respondents in this study certainly appear to be on the winning side of this sociological and generational change contest.

The Problem of the Internet

Certainly, the Web can be viewed as an opportunity rather than just a problem (as television typically is in social capital literature). However, it is too early to pass judgment on the ultimate role of the Internet in civic and political pursuits. From the point of view of this study's respondents, the Internet has proven to be a tool for interpersonal and business communication, a means to activate informal networks to respond to community needs, and a vehicle to customize access to news and information. It is also an increasingly commercial space, a tool for commerce and community rather than for revolution. The two greatest concerns within the "problem of the Internet" identified at the beginning of this study are still unresolved: (1) the inequality of tech-nology access; and (2) the encroachment of entertainment imperatives and norms on what had been a largely text-based, interactive medium.

The Digital Divide remains. Given findings in this study about the Web as a tool of political activism and of social capital formation, and given Skocpol's (2002) and Wuthnow's (2002) findings that social capital has actually declined most acutely among more marginalized groups, unequal access to technology could further exacerbate existing social and political inequalities.

This dynamic makes public access to information technology efforts even more important. The key here is to avoid doing what many have done in the "broadband" debate addressed in chapter 4: using technology as a proxy for all economic and social injustice. Such reductionism makes those larger debates seem trivial. "If we can just get caller ID to Knox city or Broadband to the Fifth Ward of Houston, then we will have done our job" is a dangerous diversion from more weighty and complicated matters of social policy. A cable modem in the hands of a starving child is a sick joke that does nothing to improve that child's chance or survival or success. Governments should not be oversold by the exaggerated promises of technological determinists. Equal access to technology does not mean equal opportunity. However, libraries and philanthropies have worked during the past five years to make technology tools, and training available to the disadvantaged through public access campaigns, hardware and software donations and training. These are not trivial pursuits, and in fact can be social capital-building activities in their own right. But these activities are only a small part of the continuing struggle between the haves and the have-nots in America, a struggle that may be made more difficult by many of the economic changes identified in this and other studies, most recently Tom Friedman's widely read The World is Flat.

There is promising news on the second concern as well. Popular accounts have lamented the decline of "fun" on the Internet, observing that a frontier of silliness has given way to a sort of "mall" comprised of name-brand retail and news offerings. What is unclear is what increased bandwidth might bring by enabling greater convergence between Web-accessed computers and twenty-first-century television. Rumblings abound in the technology trade press about even mainstream companies "cashing in" on the highest yield area of online entertainment—pornography. Librarians who have public access terminals in their facilities lament that many adult patrons spend time surfing X-rated sites rather than reading news or looking for work. Technology companies have begun lobbying for extended broadband capability to support new applications, tools, and products and to capitalize on increased capacity. The "problem of the Internet" is still very much an open question. But in terms of short-term implications for social capital, it has, for high-tech Generation X actors, been a tool for engagement and achievement rather than isolation and alienation. The recent rise of the "blogosphere" is an area ripe for additional study. While it is inherently text-based, requiring engagement rather than passive watching for entertainment, its ferocity and reach in some extremist directions have given rise to legitimate concerns about this new global frontier of free speech.

The Problem of Technology and Community

Akin to the discussions above, technology appears to be, at least among the cohort I interviewed, facilitating community-building activities rather than detracting from them as television has. Recall, for example, that Putnam blamed 25 percent of his decline in social capital on television. In essence, being rather more like the telephone or the telegraph, contemporary technologies further separate notions of communication from those of transportation. The Web has become yet another means by which people can communicate without being face-to-face. As some authors have noted, the decline in face-to-face interaction can have negative effects on social cohesion. However, based on the responses I received in this study, the Web seems to be a way to maintain "weak ties" by letting us communicate with people from a distance as well as a tool to help us organize quickly in response to a community need.

Addressing the more fantastic predictions of the Web made by futurists such as Vlahos (1998) and others, this group of technological leaders *does not* appear to be *replacing* real community activities with virtual ones. As yet, they have not rushed into the Infosphere. Among this study's youngest cohort, I found some evidence of participation in chat rooms and other purely virtual communities (though generally Web-based tools were used to facilitate real-world activity, such as the "virtual field" organization in Jesse Ventura's 1998 campaign).[1] The "problem of technology and community," at least in the short run appears to be a myth. Time in front of a computer monitor appears only to be displacing time in front of a television screen. And

---

[1] The unprecedented strategy (at that time) used the Web to build crowds at campaign stops and used digital photos from those events to help encourage visitors to come back to the site and to attend additional rallies in the "real world." Elements of the strategy have been mimicked in campaigns since, with varying levels of success.

interestingly among the rising Millennials, the networked computer (or now text-messaging cell phone) appears to be an interactive tool that animates other activity rather than simply being a passive entertainment medium.

The Problem of Politics and Young People

Two recent developments are worth noting with respect to the "problem" of politics and young people. The first is that a number of compelling books have been published recently, including Florida's *Creative Class* and Homer-Dixon's the *Ingenuity Gap*, both of which take a serious look at the changing nature of work among the fastest growing professions. Florida noted that the creative-class occupations represent 38 percent of the workforce and the highest paid in the American economy.[2] He and others have also begun to look at animators of economic growth and find the Gen X work ethic and professional norms to be driving the economic growth of the fastest growing urban areas in the 1990s. Curiously, the places with the highest concentrations of creative-class people and the *fastest growing economies* are places that, according to Putnam's measures, *have the lowest levels of social capital*. Further, Florida notes that the places with the highest levels of Putnam-defined social capital are those places with the *lowest levels of economic growth*. *There appears to be an inverse relationship between entrepreneurship and traditional social capital.* Ritualistic gathering seems to dampen the entrepreneurial spirit and fosters conformity rather than innovation. These findings underscore the prescience of Granovetter's (1973) observation about the strength of weak ties and, perhaps, an inverse proposition—the weakness of strong ties.

While the conflation of the economic with the social can be problematic, such conflation can also force a new look at what constitutes social capital and civic life. For young, creative people, quality of life, amenities, and low barriers to social entry into a community are prime attractors of creative talent. Traditional social capital institutions, with their Protestant elite sensibilities, and rigid structures and rules

---

[2] Florida describes a "super creative core" group of professions that includes computer and mathematical occupations; architecture; engineering; life, physical, and social sciences; education, training, and library; arts, design, entertainment, and sports occupations. He then augments this group with "creative professionals" that include management occupations; business and financial operations; legal; health care practitioners and technicians and high-end sales and sales management.

for membership make it more difficult to enter a new community. With Generation X's penchant for mobility (and an exit strategy) and the creative class's primacy of horizontal mobility, such barriers to entry almost guarantee that high-tech Gen X actors would eschew those historical organizations. Again, I ask, does such avoidance indicate a decline or could it be a shift of privilege occasioned by a Postman-like social effect of technological innovation? Those privileged by the new order featuring new technology simply have no interest in belonging to the institutions of those privileged by the old order, particularly if assuming leadership in such hierarchies is based on seniority or time-based "paying your dues."

While the economic engine represented by the Gen X work ethic has driven some to revisit their characterizations of Generation X in recent years, the most potent antidote to the "problem of young people" may be the coming of age of the Boomers' late-in-life children. *Millennials Rising*, Howe and Strauss's first offering of the newest generation entering young adulthood paints a rosy picture of those young people born after 1981. Zemke et al. (2000) go so far as to assert that the Millennial generation, core values are optimism, civic duty, confidence, achievement, sociability, morality, "street smarts," and diversity. Such optimism about young people is a refreshing change from 30 years of complaints about the cultural incompetence of the young. Perhaps the optimism surrounding the "next great generation" will prompt officeholders, teachers, and other civic actors to more fully engage young people in the real work of communities rather than rejecting them out of fear. Note, for example, the sharp distinction between those characterizations of Millennials and Hart's findings regarding the four dominant views of young people found in traditional messages:

Youth as stranger. Millennials are even named the "next great generation": a clear allusion to the generation that survived the depression and fought in WWII.

Youth as ideologue. Rather than having bizarre values, Millennials are civic-minded optimists—young joiners. This study would seem to lead one to predict that Generation X will be the social entrepreneurs who *create* the institutions for the Millennials to join, just as the Progressive era barons and populists created institutions for the previous "Greatest Generation."

Youth as egocentric. Far from being immune to appeals to make society better, accounts of the Millennials explicitly argue that this generation has—and continues to—turn its back on the perceived excesses of the two generations before it and ushers in a new era of social and civic responsibility.

Youth as distracted. Millennials are seen as sheltered, highly scheduled, high achievement young citizens, foreshadowing a return to more conventional morality, the antithesis of the "narcissistic" Boomers and "disengaged" Gen X.

Instead of young people being a problem, I would argue that Generation X's strong work ethic and entrepreneurial impulses, combined with the optimistic energy of Millennials (and Boomer's optimism about them), makes young people today not a problem, but a potential solution to alleged civic apathy.

This study has shown that civic attitudes and behaviors are significantly more complex than NES-based Generation X studies have advanced to date. These young people are at the bleeding edge of social, professional, and economic changes that have been catalyzed by the introduction of disruptive technologies. Ironically, where Postman is generally considered hostile to prophets of technological advance, his arguments and cautions have proved prescient in the context of Generation X high-tech actors. New technologies create winners and losers, privileging new skills, sensibilities, and attributes. Internet technologies, still in their adolescence, have certainly privileged this group of professionals and also helped to drive their values and norms into changing the civic as well as the business sectors. This evolution, by Putnam's measures of the old social order, does show an old civic sector in decline. However, Putnam generally ignores the ascent of the new order and their evolving conceptions of citizenship (see table 8.1).

Before fully advancing my respondents' emerging definition of good citizenship, let us first revisit the taxonomy of classic notions of citizenship that I advanced early in this study. Combining the classic virtues of citizenship and the civic activities in which good citizens engage, I created the following continuum of classic democratic citizens:

Table 8.1   Classic Good Citizenship

Category	Virtues	Civic Activities
Passive minimalist	• Law-abidingness • Open-mindedness	• Vote
Active minimalist	• Law-abidingness • Open-mindedness • Independence • Work ethic • Ability to evaluate the performance of leaders	• Vote • Awareness of political affairs • Contribute to organizations

Table 8.1 Continued

Category	Virtues	Civic Activities

Typical citizens	• Law-abidingness
	• Open-mindedness
	
	• Independence
	
	• Work ethic
	
	• Ability to evaluate the
	   performance of leaders
	
	• Willingness to engage
	   in public discourse
		• Vote
		• Awareness of political
		   affairs
		• Contribute to
		   organizations
		• Personally participate
		   in community affairs
		
		• Personally participate
		   minimally in political
		   matters

Civic leaders	• Law-abidingness
	• Open-mindedness
	
	• Independence
	
	• Work ethic
	
	• Ability to evaluate the
	   performance of leaders
	• Willingness to engage in
	   public discourse
		• Vote
		• Awareness of
		   political affairs
		• Contribute to
		   organizations
		• Lead community and
		   political organizations
		
		• Select competent leaders

Activists	• Willingness to engage in
	   public discourse
		• Vote
		• Awareness of
		   political affairs
		• Contribute to
		   organizations
		• Organize in pursuit
		   of political/social change
		• Create organizations

While the above represent a synthesis of traditional conceptions of citizenship from the most basic levels to the most active, table 8.2 reflects the ways in which my respondents conceptualize quality citizenship.

While table 8.2 reflects their responses-by-cohort, drawing together their responses in the aggregate produces some important insights across all four sets of respondents. For one thing, my interviewees do not see themselves as revolutionaries but as separated from the old social structure. Contrary to some popular treatises, these actors are generally not particularly cynical, ill-informed, or disengaged. And

Table 8.2 High-Tech Generation X Qualities of Good Citizenship by Cohort

Generation X Cohort	Virtues (In Order of Importnace)	Civic Activities (In Order of Importance)
Cyber-democrats	• Willingness to engage in public discourse • Willingness to demand only what can be paid for • Ability to evaluate the performance of those in office • Work ethic • Independence • Open-mindedness • Capacity to delay gratification • Adaptability to economic and technological change	• Awareness/knowledge of political affairs • Vote • Select competent leaders • Respond to a community need/request
Wireheads	• Work ethic • Make few demands of the state • Independence • Open-mindedness	• Respond to a community need/request • Contribute to organizations • Vote • Be aware of public affairs
Tech Elites	• Law abidingness • Open-mindedness • Independence • Work ethic • Ability to gauge the performance of leaders • Willingness to engage in public discourse • Commitment to mentoring young leaders	• Vote • Awareness of local political affairs • Respond to requests to contribute to organizations • Respond to requests to lead community and political organizations • Select and interact with competent leaders to produce tangible outcomes • Conceptualize new kinds of community leadership and responsibility
Trailing Xers	• Open-mindedness • Independence	• Awareness of political affairs • Contribute/participate in organizations • Vote

they certainly do not see themselves as such. Instead, they have a distinct set of values about citizenship and civic virtue. To wit,

They engage in similar activities but have different priorities. The activities of high-tech, Gen X citizenship are similar to classic understandings of civic duties, but the virtues and behaviors they champion fall in a *different order of priority.* Where classic notions of democratic citizenship posit the primacy of the vote, these actors place greater value on the *work ethic and on being informed* and active, affirming recent accounts of "individualization" of politics, from collective activities to more private or individual ones.

They reject formality and structure in favor of greater responsiveness. The institutional arrangements of this age group are less formal, ritualistic, and hierarchical than were civic institutions in the past. Instead, they are more project-/task-/need-based and tend to organize and disband depending on local conditions, all of which reflects both Gen X's creative sensibilities and the changing norms of the contemporary workplace. A standing card game at six in the evening is simply impractical to an increasing number of contemporary workers, where workdays are long and varied and productivity is tied to the creative impulse.

They see technology as a powerful tool but not as revolutionary. Technology provides an organizing and informational tool to make these episodic associations agile and effective—an update of the telephone more than a tool of revolution or a virtual destination replacing, real communities. This is not to say that they see technology as insignificant. Quite the contrary. Technology has enabled them to be more successful and effective in their work and in their communities of interest.

They are creators rather than joiners. High-tech Generation X actors are entrepreneurs, creating new businesses, new policies, and new means of association. This creative process has greater urgency than joining old institutions for this cohort. There are likely both structural and rhetorical reasons for this. In the same way that women avoid the glass ceiling of large corporations by starting their own companies, Gen Xers start their own community efforts to bypass what they view as mindless hierarchies and barriers to entry of old-line institutions. This dynamic may have significant implications for the survival of other seniority-based institutions from civil service occupations to labor unions. Even among Tech Elites, those most concerned with "pleasing their parents' institutions," there is greater energy given to considering new means of service and participation rather than maintaining the old.

They privilege personal choice over transcendent obligation. Activities are increasingly based on *choice rather than duty*, affirming Wolfe's findings about both the American middle class (1998) and moral freedom (2001). As higher levels of education and changing economic norms have resulting in increased mobility, Gen Xers have come to expect increased choice in where they work, how they live, and how they participate in civic life. Respondents across all categories rejected the notion of transcendent or external obligations. However, they felt a strong tug to respond to requests for assistance, both large and small.

They turn traditional reciprocity norms inside out. My respondents affirmed Putnam's view on the critical role that reciprocity norms play in the creation of social capital. However, among this group, reciprocity operates differently from Putnam's description, which assumed that social capital is animated in a general way—that is, do good in the world and others will as well. My respondents, in contrast, embraced a more personal sort of reciprocity somewhat akin to Cialdini's (1984) reciprocity of concession: ask for help to animate a personal cycle rather than do something nice and animate an abstract social cycle.

They embrace weak ties over strong ties. Generation X in the high-tech world live with high levels of professional mobility and therefore look for low social barriers to entry and exit, but also look to technology to help keep weak ties active. And the dynamics that foster the maintenance of weak ties—technology and mobility—are actually drivers of contemporary social cohesion. In Putnam's world, in contrast, those traits deplete social capital by his definition.

They enjoy creative work and therefore blur lines between the job and the community. A strong work ethic was a common theme heard throughout most of my interviews, but *hard work* is also a concept whose definition is evolving. As Florida illustrated in his "thought experiment," work does not take place only in the workplace between the hours of 9:00 a.m. and 5:00 p.m. As a matter of fact, a number of my respondents claimed that such demarcation (or "clock watching" in the lexicon) was actually *bad citizenship.* Lines are blurred between work time, social time, personal time, and community time. As a result, researchers are going to need new ways of defining and measuring civic/social activity—techniques that do not privilege rigid delineations of time and place. Like the primacy of choice and the suspicion of seniority-based reward, these contemporary definitions of what young people see as good citizenship can help explain the decline of interest in unions and public sector occupations among this age cohort.

They want to make a difference but they think work *is the place to do it.* These Generation X actors want their ideas to have an effect on the world, affirming Florida's understandings. But rather than engage in traditional social activism, they see change happening as a result of "working hard on cool stuff with great technology" rather than in the political world. Obviously, the Cyber-democrats are a unique case, but even they have chosen to be political technology *professionals* rather than social activists. More simply, this generation tends to give at the office rather than take to the streets.

Far from being disengaged, nomadic losers or Cyber-selfish narcissists, then, these high-tech Generation X actors are actively involved in their work and, often unconsciously, use their creative impulses to stimulate a new civic life that is more consistent with *their values* and the changes that lie in the wake of technological and social advancement. These means of association are still very much in flux, consistently evolving as technologies and related enterprises advance. Further, as a new younger generation moves into the adult ranks, these distinctions among Boomers, Xers, and Millennials may keep these changes in civic values and behaviors in play for many years ahead. Indeed, Putnam's lament about the passing of standing associations and mid-century socialization patterns will only grow more acute if my respondents prove at all representative. These changes demand a fresh look and conceptualization of what constitutes civic strength. What kinds of organizations exist among this cohort? Do they have the capability to provide the sinew that holds humanity together, whether in Putnam's terms or de Toqueville's? By what means do we evaluate the strength and value of contemporary organizations, from youth Soccer Leagues to Habitat for Humanity to the host of episodic, neighborhood acts of civic response to an immediate and pressing need? Must ongoing, official organizations exist to constitute civic strength or can something more organic better serve communities and engage young people? Have the excesses of contemporary activist groups, whether animal rights or anti-WTO soured thoughtful people on the very idea of "activism" as practiced by now retiring Baby Boomers?

Those are the questions for future researchers and Putnam, to his credit, has engaged thinkers (if not yet methodologists) in exploring these types of questions in *Democracy in Flux* and more recently featured a number of case studies of community activities in *Better Together: Restoring the American Community*. I ask Putnam and his disciples to try and quantify the value of these more episodic groups and activities. While he chronicled the decline of the neighborhood bridge game, he did not explain what inherent civic value those games produced or what specific civic harm was done by their demise. These kinds of questions are especially important in times of broad social and economic change. Without a rigorous look at the real value of these activities, such laments are merely clique maintenance bathed in nostalgia—the generational equivalent of a cynical "family values" debate: code words for maintaining old privilege.

Moving beyond these abstract academic questions of definitions, what might we do with these insights about the evolving nature of economic and civic life? My observations and recommendations fall into two broad categories: (1) things that we can we do as individuals, writers, civic actors, and policy makers to reduce cynicism while increasing the production of new social capital that resonates more clearly with young people today; and (2) observations for what these insights might mean for contemporary social policy issues. These recommendations are broad and have implications for media, educational institutions, and individuals. I offer them to spur further public debate and cast old definitions in a new light.

Promote the Real Efficacy of Young People

Studies of political efficacy show that low levels of efficacy promote disengagement and cynicism. Respondents in this study affirm those findings. The less efficacious and informed respondents were more cynical and disengaged. Recall Byron the TV watcher and Caitlin the frustrated fringe activist and Blake, the disengaged Gen Xer. Blake wrote about the sense of "being sold to." In his mind, he was too clever for politics and civic life. Both he and Byron confused watching politics on TV with real involvement in public life.

Paradoxically, they both claimed to be clever enough to disbelieve the biased media and dishonest advertising appeals, yet obviously completely internalized both the episodic frame of news coverage and the customer focus of advertising. Further, those who felt most clever and were the most cynical were also the least informed, least engaged, and least successful. This finding would seem to argue for promoting the real efficacy of young people, moving them away from the television toward communities and work in an authentic way. However, Blake's lament of "being sold to" affirms this generation's insistence on candor—vacuous bromides of "children are our future" fall flat and simply contribute to greater levels of cynicism among those least engaged. Related to notions of promoting real efficacy among young people is for older adults to be authentic in their interactions with them. This insight was recently affirmed by *Washington Post* columnist David Broder in a panel discussion where he predicted that partisan rancor in the nation's capital could not be solved by those who came of age in the 1960s but would rather take an infusion of a younger generation of leaders more authentic and candid and less ideological, a posture typified by prominent Generation X leader Barak Obama.

Be Authentic

As generational marketers, Harwood (2002) and others have found, Americans are starving for authenticity, and this is especially true among young people. Throughout my interviews, respondents repeatedly remarked how much they enjoyed having a meaningful conversation about important things and how seldom they had the opportunity to do so. Akin to what Hays (1998) observed about college students and the inherent value of focus groups as a mechanism to engage young people in politics, perhaps as individuals we can simply agree to occasionally talk with people about important things, especially about young people. Research in secondary education underscores the power of this simple recommendation. In smaller, thematic learning communities, such as the Minnesota School of Environmental Science, High Tech High, or the MET school in Providence, young people are given a "seriousness of purpose" (the quality most credited with the collegiate success of GI Bill recipients) by couching their academic learning in real work in the adult world. As a result, young people in these schools show lower levels of cynicism, higher levels of community engagement, and eschew the ersatz clique drama, bullying and other pathologies of the traditional American high school. Like the GI Bill recipients showed us half a century ago, in the face of real human challenge and high stakes, the cynical dramas of popular culture adolescence or television fall by the wayside.

Break Down Rigid Barriers between Young People and Adults

Closely related to the arguments for authenticity outlined above, there could be a range of venues for such meaningful conversations, both formal and informal. But perhaps the key component is to try to break down the physical and bureaucratic barriers between young people and the adult world they will be entering. Dewey (1938) observed that removing real experience from the educational processes of children in school would create *an arbitrariness* in study that would invite resistance and a contempt for learning. Given current attitudes about school as something to be endured and politics as something to be avoided, it would appear that Dewey was prescient. There are a range of ways by which the barriers between schools and the community can be made more porous, including internships, externships, mentoring programs, service learning, and alternative certification to allow professionals from a range of adult pursuits the opportunity to interact with students and to help them draw connections between their studies and adult life as it exists in their communities and nation. There are signs that Right has met Left in this realization in recent days. Forty-six-year-old Secretary of Education Margaret Spellings, whom Neil Howe has called the "first Gen X cabinet secretary" (although she is technically slightly older than the typical marker for the beginning of that generation) has called for an Adjunct Teacher Corps, literally tens of thousands of math and science professionals to teach their craft in America's high schools. This puts the United States' most prominent advocate for school accountability shoulder to shoulder with one of the patron saints of Progressive, constructivist education, Deborah Meier, who famously asserted that "young people need to come into contact with a range of adults they can see themselves becoming." Instead of corralling young people on remote campuses away from authentic adult experiences, perhaps accelerating the sense of efficacy and optimism found in older respondents in this study would help inculcate a meaningful civic ownership in younger people.

Help Young People Learn to Be Citizens

While immigrants to America receive a citizenship handbook to help them understand the nation they are joining, native-born young people do not. Just as typical education removes experience from learning (and young people from the larger community) we often expect young people to know how to be citizens without ever teaching them. The landscape of civics education is often typified by insular disciplinary arguments within the education establishment tending to be ideological or discipline-based rather than focused on the larger goal of imbuing young people with the knowledge and sensibilities necessary to being an engaged and productive citizen. Further, much general education has been reduced to mere "workforce development," the narrow teaching of skills designed to prepare someone for a particular job. Job skills are important, but what contemporary enterprises are demanding of young employees today look more like the skills and sensibilities of *citizens* than cogs in the corporate machine. My respondents understood this implicitly and characterized it explicitly—their workplace has become their community and their notions of good citizenship manifest themselves there.

Consider the traits that Oblinger and Verville (1998) found in her survey of senior business people regarding what they looked for in prospective employees: critical thinking skills, the ability to work in teams, excellent oral and written communication skills and multicultural sensitivity—an awareness of different cultural norms and the ability to work with people very different than oneself. That description (or prescription) sounds much more like the Jeffersonian ideal of public education—the creation of a polity capable of self-governance—than the current construction of schooling as inherently a collection of disconnected academic disciplines. I worry about the obvious disconnect between what the "adult world" actually demands that young people need to know and be able to do to be successful in our economy and democracy and what the current educational and political environment often offers school-aged people. Our educational system seems to be in a similar state of flux as our civic conceptions.

While assessment and accountability are absolutely critical to the successful evaluation of schools and school systems, it must be balanced with a notion of "preparation"—that schooling is not simply something to be endured for a certain time, but rather a series of activities and lessons that will prepare young people for the adult worlds— college, work, citizenship—that they will enter once they leave school. Our current approach appears to be further removing relevant experience from young people in exchange for more regimented, abstract, and arbitrary "content coverage." I worry about the sort of reciprocity norm that this hierarchical disrespect may animate. What happens if reciprocity theorists are right, and this powerful norm dictates that one returns what one is given? How might young people respond if we continue a rhetorical posture that claims young people are "hostile others" and advance an educational approach that removes real community efficacy from young adults? What sort of young citizens would such a regime produce? Should we be surprised if the products of such a system had little respect for communal norms (since they would have been physically isolated on campuses and intellectually isolated in test prep)? Should we be surprised that they would not possess the related economic skills demanded by employers? In the current regime, where might they have learned them? This mismatch between the skills for citizenship, the skills for economic success, and the content and methods of schooling would seem to set the stage for the creation of a generation ill prepared for the adult world they enter. This is not an argument for rapping Shakespeare or a move away from rigorous academic standards. Rather, it is a plea to give rigorous content some sort of context in the real world. As Meier observed, perhaps a reciprocal act of citizenship could be that adults in the community become some of the adults—beyond teachers—in schools that young people can indeed see themselves becoming.

This dynamic of current approaches to secondary schooling may help explain the *decline in cynicism* I found in my sample as they got older. The most cynical were the youngest, those still in school and subject to these conflicting cultural and educational messages and removed from authentic and efficacious opportunities to engage in the activities of citizenship and work. Once these Generation X actors reached their late twenties and thirties, their sense of efficacy improved and their levels of cynicism were considerably lower in both the classical survey questions and the more open-ended interviews. There is a lesson to be learned in such data.

As Adults, Animate Reciprocity—Interpersonal and Societal

Respondents in this study affirmed Putnam's argument about the centrality of reciprocity to notions of social capital. What this group also showed is that reciprocity can cut both ways, creating a vicious cycle as well as a virtuous one. Further, this group turned Putnam's notion of societal reciprocity inside out. Rather than doing good and awaiting a generalized social benefit, this group reflected Chris Matthews's (1999) fundamentally political insight—if you want someone to be loyal, ask them for a favor. This dynamic leads naturally to my next broad recommendation.

As Civic Actors, Ask for Help

High-tech Generation X actors feel little transcendent obligation and further, resent the idea than such a thing even exists. However, they feel a strong duty to respond to a need and are often quick to organize and mobilize in order to provide an effective response. Where Putnam and others argued that people should go out and do good to animate social capital, my study suggests that people should go out and ask for help with something. Instead of just volunteering on one's own, perhaps asking friends to join in to help on a project is the more compelling service impulse for young people today. This posture toward organizing is consistent with the entrepreneurial nature of Gen X found by Florida, who argued that this cohort is more likely to start something than to join an organization that already exists.

As Policymakers, Seek Out Innovation in the Civic Sphere (As We Do In the Economic Arena)

Putnam's measures of social capital focused heavily on joining existing institutions or socializing in ways common to the 1950s. The social institutions and practices of those days obviously reflected the norms and values of the times, factors that are now dissipating due to a range of social, economic, and technological changes. In the wake of this change, new skills and people are being privileged and new means of social cohesion are coming to the fore. We need to capitalize on these shifts in emphasis and scholars should seek to identify them and test their effectiveness in the civic sphere. Putnam's *Bowling Alone* follow-up took him to communities to look at community activities today, but he still privileged those things that looked most like what he chronicled from mid century—traditional forms of activism—unions, church groups. This study indicates that the vibrancy of American civic life may be in the creation of new forms and mechanisms of association not "renewal" of old ones, particularly because those old types assume a less mobile population.

As Civic and Economic Thinkers, Embrace Mobility

In the contemporary economy, increased mobility is a fact of life. Increasing educational levels have long been associated not only with higher levels of social involvement but also with higher levels of mobility, all of which create a drag on Putnam's sort of social capital. With many communities working to become the next Seattle or Austin, (and not the next Peoria or Detroit), more "creative-class" or "just-in-time" social capital activities will become the norm. Embracing those means and considering ways to encourage, reward, and (from a scholarly point of view) *measure* those types of social capital activities will help us move from tired laments about the dying past to more productive discussions about the communities of the future.

Such relentless negativism about the current state of communities and sensibilities of Generation X would seem to stoke cynicism rather than reduce it. Putnam clearly identified important social trends and nicely captured the unease people felt as a result of the upheavals occurring in a time of technological advance. But we need to move beyond these concerns by identifying the kinds of social capital suitable to a new age and new people.

As Human Beings, Generation X: Ignore Cynicism and Allow It to Die As Boomers, Live Up to Your Own Press

Florida made another key observation about members of the creative class that captures the sensibilities of respondents in this study. He noted that, increasingly, they are hiring a "staff" akin to the servants who were employed by old elites. This dynamic is true even for those squarely in the middle class, not just the more successful respondents. Granted, these services are purchased by the hour rather than employed on a full-time basis, but there has been a recent explosion in the demand for personal services: cleaning services, gardeners, personal trainers, dog walkers, and personal chefs. Work life has become so busy that people do not have time to tend to the mundane chores of home life. I would add tending to cynicism to the list of mundane chores that should fall by the wayside. Hart has argued that cynicism is a fragile thing, more orchid than ivy. It takes tending and revisiting, feeding and practice. I would posit to the creative class—and perhaps to everyone—to sacrifice the care and feeding of your cynicism to more important work. Like an orchid, when cynicism is left unattended for several days, it will shrivel up and die. That is surely a good thing.

Where I urge Gen Xers to let their cynicism go the way of the sunrise Rotary Club, I urge Boomers to live up to their own publicity as a trend-setting generation. Cialdini (1984) argues that a powerful type of reciprocity is reciprocity of concession—whereby one concession becomes a catalyst (because of the tug of the reciprocity norm) to other concessions. This cycle is a key component to successful negotiation and might well be employed in the area of civic life. From their earliest days of antiwar activism, Boomers have focused on attaining new rights with little thought toward corresponding responsibility. The fruits of such a rhetorical posture are well chronicled by Skocpol, Etzioni, and others. Rights-based interest groups have proliferated and now dominate much of our political debate. As the largest generation and the one that launched this trend, Baby Boomers are perhaps the ones who could reverse that 40-year-old trend. Instead of organizing for more rights and services for themselves, they could organize around a grand concession—and see if their sheer numbers could animate a new kind of political reciprocity for this century—a reciprocity of concession and responsibility. Instead of interest groups simply advocating for maximizing the resources to their own members (reciprocity says they do that because everyone else does), the nation's largest generation could be the catalyst for a new norm.

Eschew Demands and Make a Civic Concession, Redefine the AARP

Throughout recent generational literature, the Boomers have been the 78 million persons who set all American trends. They were architects of the rights-based activism of the 1960s. They were the Me Generation of the 1970s and the self-absorbed yuppies of the 1980s. The reciprocal response to such activities has been increasing levels of rights-based activism, a corresponding proliferation of special interest groups, each of which was out to secure the greatest portion of a finite pie of resources—both special interest and corporate interest. Much of Generation X cynicism has been blamed on Boomer excess and on the perception that those excesses have resulted in fewer economic opportunities for the generation that followed.

A particularly acute example raised by Halstead (1999), Schier (1998), and a number of Generation X political commentators is the pending crisis in federal entitlement programs. If actuarial tables are destiny, the generations that follow the Boomers are in considerable fiscal trouble even with current formulas for Social Security and Medicare. To this is added the recent Boomer political triumph which added a prescription drug benefit to those entitlements, all of which adds literally hundreds of billions of dollars in liabilities to a system already strapped.

Baby Boomers and the elderly are together the wealthiest segment of American society. These universal entitlements as they exist today systematically transfer wealth from poor to rich and from young to old, a fundamentally unfair and certainly unsustainable practice. In the name of civic health, the Boomers could make an important public policy concession that could have both enormous fiscal and rhetorical force: apply their lifetime ideals to redefine the AARP.

The American Association of Retired People is arguably the most powerful special interest group at work in American public life today, reliably successful in maximizing its members' access to publicly and privately funded goods through political power and marketing sophistication. It is not alone in that posture but is unparalleled in its reach and influence and its constituency represents the wealthiest demographic in America today. If Cialdini and Putnam are right, the concession, I recommend, could animate a potentially powerful cycle of policy and social progress. As the largest generation, their concession of universal benefits (in favor of a means test) would seem to be true to their own mythology of fostering social justice. And raising the retirement age would affirm and institutionalize their frequent assertions that old age is not what it used to be. Simply, this unparalleled generation could redefine the most powerful special interest group in its own self image—using their privilege and power to help those with less. What if the AARP became the nation's expression of a general interest? What if it used its considerable clout to advocate on behalf of a broader societal imperative, for both young and old, in the process becoming a powerful force for equity in America?

I make this suggestion only half in jest. I understand the realities of the political process and know that the idea of a generational concession on a matter of entitlement policy would be logistically difficult if not impossible. However, I offer this suggestion in the spirit of Florida's thought experiment in an attempt to crystallize a picture of the nature of change and to promote a potential remedy based in theory. What if the generation who brought us protests for social justice, the Me Generation and "government doesn't solve the problem, government is the problem" made good on all three promises? This redefinition of the AARP could do all of those things. It would bring a dose of authenticity to our politics that thinkers cited in this volume claim we crave, and potentially animate a cycle of generosity (or at least away from unapologetic pursuit of self-interest at the expense of more pressing and obvious needs) in our political culture.

Further Implications for Research and Social Policy

Certainly this group of 40 young people in Austin is not a representative sample of a generation. However, the civic insights that they provide should be fodder for additional research as well as approaches to political and civic engagement and the resonance of ongoing policy debates.

In research, this study certainly points to the need to systemically investigate the effects of mobility on civic involvement. As noted earlier, mobility is only going to increase with higher levels of education, the decline of fixed benefit pensions and increasing globalization. Social capital definitions that rely on more stable residency patterns put them at variance with individual realities and engines of economic growth. In addition to mobility, a key issue uncovered in this study is the ephemeral nature of many community activities—they begin with e-mail trees to organize participants, execute a task in response to a community need, then disband until the next need arises. Research should consider ways to study and quantify such phenomena. Finally, this study found that young adults are often creating their own non-profits and the wealthier creating their own philanthropies, bringing a more outcome-focus and problem-solving sensibility to their work. In essence, this generation does not embrace the fixed hierarchies of tra-ditional civic organizations nor the cause or protest based activism that had its roots in the antiwar movement in the late 1960s. Like Broder's observation about many of the new young members of Congress, the new generation coming to power seems to have eschewed many of the ideological culture wars the Baby Boom political class has been fighting for the last 40 years.

In addition to these research implications, there are also implica-tions for evolution in thorny social policy debates. For example, this generation and the one behind it believe in the primacy of personal choice—and see both a right to have choices and the ability to make them well as cornerstones of contemporary citizenship. While school vouchers have rabidly ideological supporters and critics, the idea of being able to choose the school that is right for your child is an idea that would appear to be highly resonant to Generation X parents. Further, with this generation's preoccupation with accountability, self-reliance, and work ethic, national efforts to improve transparency of school results would also be expected to gain traction. One can imag-ine a Wirehead reaction to the New York teacher union leader's recent response to John Stossel's question in this exchange on the news pro-gram 20/20: "Don't you think that it is a little excessive to demand a 15% raise in exchange for working an additional 10 minutes per day for a total of a 6 hour and 40 minute workday?" To wit the union leader replied, "That's the same as the private sector." To a cohort to whom work ethic is the top civic attribute and "clock watching" is considered bad citizenship, such a claim would seem ludicrous and *unpatriotic*. Given the finding that the middle class, new "blue-collar" elements of Generation X find such "work conditions" rhetoric so offensive, it poses interesting political challenges for unions and other seniority-based occupations, such as federal and state civil service. Already the federal government is making moves toward performance and incentive-based pay to try and recruit and retain younger staff. It is important to note that these respondents did not eschew these dynamics (seniority, union protections, work restrictions, absence of performance reward) as uninteresting or unappealing—they view them fundamentally as *bad citizenship*.

Finally, the postideological bent of these respondents could also have implications for political parties. The popularity of "mavericks" such as John McCain and the excitement of young people for the unsuccessful (some would argue because of his excessive candor and authenticity) candidacy of Howard Dean reflect the findings from this study—a considerable segment of this generation believes in independence, the primacy of the individual, the importance of choices, hard work, and merit. This curious mix of liberalism and libertarianism across all political identifications provides a wealth of areas for additional academic and political research.

Conclusion

The admonitions and observations of this chapter display a shifting unit of analysis in my thinking about citizenship and social capital. These suggestions call for organizational and political changes of the most profound sort, yet they also plaintively ask individuals to act differently in relatively tiny ways. The "shifting unit of analysis" issue is clearly present in the most current definition of social capital:

> The basic idea of social capital is that a person's family, friends and associates constitute an important asset, one that can be called on in a crisis, enjoyed for its own sake, and leveraged for material gain. What is true for individuals, moreover, also holds for groups. Those communities endowed with a diverse stock of social networks, civic associations are in a stronger position to confront poverty and vulnerability, resolve disputes, and take advantage of new opportunities. (Woolcock and Narayan, 2002, quoted in Putnam, 2002, p. 6)

Florida's most recent findings about the inverse relationship between Putnam's forms of traditional social capital and new styles of entrepreneurship call even this most current definition into question, demanding a complete revaluation of what constitutes quality citizenship and a robust civic life. These dynamics underscore the complex interplay of generational and sociological change. While such change feels enormous and disconcerting at times, it is merely the cumulative result of countless acts of altruism, kindness, indifference, creativity, or a host of other human endeavors. Those events do not happen to us, they *are* us.

9

Closing Thoughts

It is now 2006. Much has happened in the years since this inquiry began—from the proposal to data collection and analysis and even from the defense to this final version. I find it ironic that, in a text that posits relentless acceleration of change as a fundamental to the reality of our world, the core insights from these respondents have held up remarkably well since our initial interviews in 2000–2001. Yet that reality is juxtaposed over a funny moment during the homestretch revisions resulting in this book. As I went to look back at my old data saved on three-and-half inch floppies, I discovered that my new computer does not feature a floppy drive, only CD and DVD. The pace of change touches large and small things.

With each year, the Greatest Generation of World War II passes away; the Baby Boomers march through middle age and toward retirement; Generation X occupies a great portion of the workforce and leadership positions; and the oldest Millennials graduate from high school and now enter college in unprecedented numbers. We are in the midst of a profound period of generational change. Since the boom and bust of the late 1990s, the attacks of September 11, and the war in Iraq, uncertainty has been persistent in the American psyche. This uncertainty is compounded by these generational shifts increasingly chronicled by the media and interest groups lamenting pending Baby Boomer retirements from a host of posts and professions. There is an undercurrent of fear and clique maintenance to these stories.

In addition to coverage of these shifts, 2005 and 2006 have also featured stories of enormous tragedy, exacerbated by governmental incompetence and corruption. The summer of 2005 concluded with back-to-back Category 5 hurricanes that pummeled the Gulf Coast and devastated the city of New Orleans and leveled many smaller communities in Mississippi and Alabama. In response, CNN did what CNN does—it focused its 24-hour cameras on the dramas there—the thousands left behind in the New Orleans Super Dome to face unthinkable conditions of filth and violence while they awaited help from the city, the state, the federal government. Failures at each level compounded the tragedy on the ground, the outrage in the country, and the amazement abroad as the "world's only remaining superpower" seemed unable to get food and water to the suffering within its own borders. The Katrina/Rita "one-two" punch and its aftermath seemed to affirm the beliefs held by my respondents—that governmental service and government people are inherently inefficient and ineffective, individual acts of voluntarism are better than public services, and that, ultimately, a "public safety net" is largely a fictional relic. WalMart (much maligned for its labor practices in the activist community) was able to get water on trucks and into the storm-ravaged area as FEMA officials flew over the carnage in helicopters, seemingly unable to effect timely action. While public outrage hardened into a familiar cynicism about government ineptitude, Americans also opened their wallets, got into their cars, and helped private relief efforts in unprecedented levels.

This series of events is an apt microcosm of my respondents' worldview—and perhaps this generation's curious mix of liberalism and libertarianism: the primacy and superiority of individual effort to deal with pressing social problems; the apparent inability of the public sector to handle such tasks; and yet a powerful impulse and willingness to organize to help those in immediate need.

How can the unique sensibilities of a new and largely untapped generation—with its fundamentally different life experiences, values, expectations, and creative impulses—help transcend these dysfunctional and polarized political times? Strauss and Howe posit that each generation makes a unique "bequest" to those that follow—and generally seeks to "correct the excesses" of the previous generation. They argue that Baby Boomer excess is ideology—and the Generation X reaction to that excess involves the distinctly uninspiring notions of transparency, pragmatism, and effectiveness. This is hardly the stuff of goose bumps but perhaps an overdue shift in approach. Such a posture could likely help New Orleans.

Against this backdrop, as candidates begin their nascent moves toward the 2008 presidential election, how might these generational civic insights inform approaches to the most pressing social issues today? The markers of Generation X are mobility, transparency, choice, authenticity. Although there are distinctions by age and occupation, the most common civic virtues admired by this cohort are work ethic, independence, and open-mindedness. Recalling Strauss and Howe's provocative observations, each generation rebels by breaking stylistically from its pop culture makers and correcting the "mistakes" of its parents and leaders to fill a social role vacated by a dying generation. My study suggests that the reaction of the rising generations will have particular implications for how the nation deals with its most pressing public issues of the coming century: education, health care, and entitlements.

Implications for Education

Bill Strauss has observed in recent speeches to education stakeholders that Boomers have been reliving their own favorable recollections through their Millennial children and thus have been seeking a comparable, fairly traditional learning experience for their children. Generation X parents are very different. They are less willing than Boomers to believe that the high achievers of their generation became K-12 teachers and administrators. And they are less willing than Boomers to trust public schools to do a competent job educating their children. Strauss argues that when overseeing their Millennial children's education, Gen Xers will want:

- Transparency
- Accountability
- Real-time performance
- Lack of ideology
- "Top of market" learning
- Cash value.

From this disconnect, it is easy to predict the generational clashes emerging between Boomer-dominated educational interest groups and Generation X parents (and increasingly Generation X-led institutions). Note this excerpt from the American Federation of Teachers Web site:

> Forty-five percent of all government employees are considered Baby Boomers eligible to retire in the next five to 10 years. Baby-Boomer retirements and turnover will be exacerbated by early retirement programs and cutbacks forced by state legislatures, county councils, congress and policy makers. Turnover at every level of government is

increasing. This is an issue for public sector unionists across the United States, as this shortage of workers goes to the very heart of our ability to provide quality public services to the taxpayer. We must collectively research effective recruitment and retention tools for public employment.

The appeal of a career in public services has to be sophisticated and focused, given the different goals and attitudes of young people now entering the workforce. Establishing an effective government recruitment and retention program represents a dramatic shift in operating procedure for most public employers since, historically, little has been done to advertise and promote jobs in government. Leaders in government and in our union can help to change operating procedures and help promote the jobs that build our communities and strengthen our nation.

Through professional polling of our members across the country, we know that, in addition to increasing salaries, AFT public employees feel that their employers should offer professional/career development opportunities and more flexible work schedules. This is attractive to potential employees. Public employees have indicated a strong willingness to help with recruitment efforts. Low-tech job fairs and high-tech Web sites offer opportunities for public employers to inform potential employees about the exciting and important work being done by government agencies across the board.

Effective recruitment and retention programs require a cooperative labor-management partnership that gives employees greater say and more control over their work. A meaningful partnership benefits all parties: employees, government administrators, policy makers and the public at large.

Such institutions see the changes bubbling around them, but they seek to engage the younger generation without disrupting their own leadership or operating norms. They tap a generational zeitgeist against conflict (affirmed by my respondents) by promising a "meaningful partnership that benefits all parties" and nod toward efficacy and mobility through "more flexibility and control over their work," yet they ignore the most resonant elements for this generation—transparency, work ethic, and reward for performance. Note the sharp distinction between the AFT appeal and the approach of rock star status Generation X senator, Democrat Barack Obama, in a speech he entitled "21st Century Schools for a 21st Century Economy":

> If we truly believe in our public schools, then we have a moral responsibility to do better—to break the either-or mentality around the debate over education that asks us to choose between more money or more

reform, and embrace a both/and mentality. Because we know that good schools will require both the structural reform and the resources necessary to prepare our kids for the future.

We can learn from innovation taking place all over the country and right here in Chicago. Chicago public schools are collaborating on a number of innovations with foundations and groups like New Leaders for New Schools, Teach for America, the New Teacher Project, the Chicago Public Education Fund, The Academy for Urban School Leadership and the University of Chicago Urban Education Initiative. The Chicago Teachers Union is also now collaborating on the Fresh Start Schools, and we're watching that experiment with great interest. It's not easy, it's not popular with everyone, and, in the end, some of the experiments may be rejected. But we can't stop trying. We have to keep moving ahead for the sake of our children.

Now, the problem on a national level is that we are not applying what we're learning from these reforms to our national education policy. And so we need new vision for education in America—one where we move past ideology to experiment with the latest reforms, measure the results, and make policy decisions based on what works and what doesn't. These teacher academies are also showing us that it's not enough to just put outstanding teachers in the classroom—we have to place outstanding principals in the schools as well. In districts across the country, the role of principal is being transformed from bureaucratic manager to instructional leader who can set high standards and recruit great talent. With 230 New Leaders serving more than 100,000 kids annually, New Leaders for New Schools has been at the cutting edge of this process—a process we need to expand nationally.

After we recruit great teachers, we need to pay them better. Right now, teaching is one of the only professions where no matter how well you perform at your job, you're almost never rewarded for success. But with six-figure salaries luring away some of our most talented college graduates from some of our neediest schools, this needs to change.

That's why teachers in these Innovation Districts who are successful in improving student achievement would receive substantial pay increases, as would those who choose to teach in the most troubled schools and the highest-need subject areas, like math and science. The city of Denver is trying pay increases in partnership with the local union, and when Chattanooga, Tennessee offered similar incentives for teachers who taught in high-need schools, student reading scores went up by over 10%.

This juxtaposition is at ground zero of generational change in social policy. Union and public sector leadership are trying to appeal to younger workers while holding fast to their core organizing principles—principles that this study would indicate are fundamentally at variance with the values of this generation. While the AFT and other civil service entities work to counteract these generational changes, new leaders from this generation are stepping up to posit new arrangements that transcend these traditional orthodoxies.

Each of the organizations that Senator Obama cites was founded by a Generation X leader and entrepreneur with the specific purpose of bringing new young blood into the educational system and creating competition within the existing hierarchy. Teach for America is perhaps the most well known and established, and its founder Wendy Kopp has become a generational legend, while drawing her share of criticism from older defenders of traditional teacher development programs and Schools of Education. TFA brings top performers into teaching, drawing thousands of applicants from the top echelons of Ivy League colleges to serve in low-performing, high-need schools—a project akin to a education-sector Peace Corps. New Leaders for New Schools was founded by Jon Schnur, a young staffer in the Clinton administration, and is designed to bring fresh leaders into the principalship and to promote the very vision that Obama describes—moving beyond the old bureaucratic building manager to a contemporary educational leader, recruiting and motivating great talent to improve student outcomes. The New Teacher Project is led by TFA alum Michelle Rhee and targets successful mid-career professionals to inject selectivity and performance into mid-career converts to the teaching profession. NTP has recently released a pointed report on teacher assignment practices in key districts designed more to protect seniority rights than to improve teaching and learning. They hope such transparency will help focus adult teacher practices more on student success than on adult power and comfort.

The vibrant young Gen X leaders who crafted these organizations have done so to bypass—or compete with—the calcified and rule-bound civil service selection apparatuses that dominate educational hiring today. They fully reflect the civic ethos found in my respondents and affirm Strauss's observations about what Generation X will demand from the educational system: competition, transparency, performance reward, professional mobility, and individual service. And as Obama observed, such approaches would "allow us to finally break free from the either-or mentality that's put bureaucracy and ideology ahead of what works; ahead of what's best for our kids."

As Generation X ascends to greater civic and professional leadership and begins to represent a larger share of parents with school-aged children, I would expect that these pressures for choice, accountability, transparency, and performance reward will grow much stronger.

Combine this dynamic with the generation's aversion to joining existing institutions and ceding individual authority to collective organizations and one can predict a tough future for teacher unions and other civil service occupations and organizations that seek to maintain old practices that insulate members from accountability and fail to reward better performers. Simply, members of Generation X will be unlikely to join such organizations and will not stand for such practices in the public institutions supported by their tax dollars and charged with educating their offspring. The bold entrepreneurial organizations noted above are just the beginning. The impulses and values that led to their creation could have implications in other pressing social policy arenas as well.

As I described in my opening chapter, Postman (1992) observed that technological advance creates winners and losers amidst a "changed everything." As the "nomadic" generational archetype begins to dominate contemporary institutions, the "prophet's" collective institutions would seem to be on the losing side of such advance. However, the traits that have Generation X rejecting old collective institutions, as in educational interest groups, could create opportunities to make progress on stubborn social issues that if left unaddressed could create considerable hardship for future generations.

Implications for Entitlements and Health Care

My respondents' reaction against "rights talk" would seem to open a window to progress on entitlements. Commitment to mobility and lower expectations for a social safety net would seem to make the tough choices around curbing entitlement costs of fixed benefit pensions in the public sector an easier lift since many members of the generation are changing jobs regularly and have little faith that government promises will be kept anyway. Estimates differ by source, but Halstead, Florida, and others have noted that Generation X members change jobs every two to five years. This reality would seem to indicate that pensions and health coverage should be portable for this group rather than tied to a single employer. This insight could be greeted as welcome news from both the establishment Left and Right. The Left could use this fact as an argument for single payer government heath insurance and the Right could argue for fully privatized, individual insurance responsibility. My respondents' liberal libertarianism would likely reject both of those ideologically pure responses, opting instead to try to solve the key problems: guarding against catastrophic illness or accident that would wipe out a family's savings and assuring some level of portable coverage for all. In pensions and social security, their view would likely be the same—pensions should not require someone to watch the clock in a job for 20 or 30 years but should create incentives to save for retirement, embracing mobility, and providing transparency into investment choices and performance.

The group's insistence on transparency and faith in technological progress to help deliver such transparency would seem to create opportunities to make more clear and candid arguments for actuarial realities of current social security policy and to better demonstrate effectiveness (or not) of public sector expenditures. Ideally these developments would help to tame the ideological excesses that typify today's politics in favor of a more dispassionate look at data and effectiveness. Such transparency combined with candor would appear to be both the resonant politics for this generation and the key to progress on pressing social issues.

Rather than lamenting these developments and trying to mitigate the impact of such things as mobility, would it not be more productive to focus on how we create new institutions to capitalize on these changes rather than trying to slow them? If people are more mobile, then shouldn't their retirement accounts be as well? If younger workers are drawn to performance reward, wouldn't it benefit the social sector if we examined how to capture that impulse to improve performance of the sector and draw more high performing young people into those professions? If young leaders crave technology and transparency, shouldn't we marry those two for greater accountability and effectiveness of collective efforts? If transparency and candor breed social trust, why wouldn't we do more of it? In the words of the Secretary of Education Margaret Spellings, "In God we trust. All others should bring data." That posture bodes well for education policy in the coming years.

We know from social capital literature that social trust leads to greater public engagement and participation—and that participation and cynicism are inversely related. Could these distinctly unromantic impulses—transparency, pragmatism, mobility, work ethic, and open-mindedness—serve as catalysts to greater civic health and social policy progress? The current popularity of such candid and independent leaders as John McCain and Barak Obama would seem to foreshadow such developments.

I suspect that some will read this book as a screed against Baby Boomers. It is not intended to be. Rather, it is designed to look at their generational bequests and the subsequent generation's reaction and correction in the civic sphere, hoping to build on the opportunities that help strengthen our democracy and make sense of the changes percolating around us. Many of the successes of Generation X that I have described in this book are descendents of the more positive elements of the Boomer bequests.

The Boomer rebellions against their Greatest Generation parents gave us greater equity—the Generation X leadership has certainly benefited from broader access to education and the effects of the women's movement and the civil rights movement. It is no accident of fate that some of the greatest vitality in the educational sector is driven by women entrepreneurs such as Kim Smith of the New Schools Venture Fund and Wendy Kopp and Michelle Rhee in the teacher sector. While such social entrepreneurs have occasionally had an uneasy relationship with 1960s era feminists, they have seized the power and opportunities created and are now using their influence to fundamentally alter old power relationships and replace hierarchical institutions with more agile, open, accountable, and effective ones. Their ascension would not have been possible without the rebellions of the 1960s.

One can see similar dynamics at play in the minority community. Recently, PBS personality Tavis Smiley hosted a forum on the State of the Black Union in which discussions focused around a new covenant for African Americans. One of the most compelling sections of the program involved two panels of leaders—the first featured icons of the civil rights era, and the second showcased "emerging leaders" in the African American community. The setup was dramatic. The elders literally turned over their chairs on stage to their civic descendants. The contrast between the two groups reflects many of the findings of this study. The older spoke of movement in religious terms, of struggle, of ideology. The younger group, including lawyers, business people, philanthropists, and even an environmental activist called for accountability, transparency, and educational performance. They lacked the rhetorical fire of those who came before, but they are emerging as pragmatic and effective leaders in their diverse workplaces and communities. This panel showed that the next generation of leaders will come from a broad range of professional ranks, not from the picket lines of 1960s era activism.

In considering these differences, recall these formative memories:

- On November 22, 1963, the first Boomers were turning 17.
- On January 20, 1981, the first Generation X members were turning 20.
- On September 11, 2001, the first Millennials were turning 20.

Today, the oldest Baby Boomers are retiring, and the oldest Xers are getting elected to office and taking the helm of new and old enterprises. As generational theorists have observed, each brings their generational imprint, and each gives the other the generational angst of rebelling against that which came before and working to maintain that which they created. Older people shape events and events shape young people. Together these forces create generational archetypes, and those archetypes ascend and recede in powerful cycles. We are certainly in one of those cycles today.

> Our answer is the world's hope; it is to rely on youth. The cruelties and the obstacles of this swiftly changing planet will not yield to obsolete dogmas and outworn slogans. It cannot be moved by those who cling to a present which is already dying, who prefer the illusion of security to the excitement and danger which comes with even the most peaceful progress. This world demands the qualities of youth: not a time of life but a state of mind, a temper of the will, a quality of imagination, a predominance of courage over timidity, of the appetite for adventure over the life of ease . . . it is the young people who must take the lead. Thus you, and your young compatriots everywhere have had thrust upon you a greater burden of responsibility than any generation that has ever lived.

Robert F. Kennedy offered these words to college students in 1966, the eldest of the Baby Boomers at a time where the oldest of Generation X were learning to tie their shoes. That I use these words here probably most aptly affirms Hart's observation that every generation has its own—and the same—conceit: that it is important and that it is unique. Such a conceit has not yet been embraced by Generation X. Perhaps now is that time.

Appendices

Appendix 1: Interview Protocol Part 1

Written Portion

Demographics

Variable	Response

- Gender
- Race
- Age
- Place of birth
- Educational level
- How long have you lived in this community?
- How many times have you moved in your life?
- How many times have you changed jobs in your adult life?
- How long have you been in your current profession/discipline?
- Do you own a computer?
- How old were you when you first learned to use a computer?
- Do you have internet access at work? At home? Broadband or dial-up access?
- How often do you use e-mail?
- About how e-mails do you exchange per day?
- Generally, with whom do you exchange e-mail?
- How much time per day do you spend on the Internet?
- Taken all together, how would you say things are these days for you personally?

- In general, how do you find life?
- All of us have ideas about what people should be like. Here is a list of characteristics you might find in people. Could you select the quality you admire most? Please rank these attributes in the next column based on your order of preference.
- Does his job well.
- Active in public and social affairs.
- Ambitious, wants to get ahead.
- Generous, considerate of others.
- Thrifty, saving.
- Lets no one take advantage of him.
- Keeps himself to himself.
- Respectful, doesn't overstep his place.

Political Identification

Question	*Response*

- Do you consider yourself a member of a particular political party? If so, which one?
- Did you vote in the last national election?
- Did you vote in the last local election?
- What was the first election that you voted in?
- Do you consider yourself very liberal, liberal, moderate, conservative, very conservative?
- Do you follow the accounts of political and governmental affairs?
- Would you say you follow them regularly, from time to time or never?
- What about newspapers? Do you follow accounts of political or governmental affairs in the *newspapers* nearly every day, about once a week; from time to time, or never?
- What about *radio* or *television*? Do you follow accounts of political or governmental affairs in the radio and on TV nearly every day, about once a week; from time to time, or never?

- What about the *Web*? Do you follow accounts of political or governmental affairs on the Web nearly every day, about once a week; from time to time, or never?
- The following are some institutions in this country. Would you please tell me whether you have Confidence/no confidence in them?
  - President
  - Congress
  - Supreme Court
- Confidence in Government
- Washington can be trusted: Which one of these statements comes closest to describing your feelings when you go to the polls to cast your ballot?

Here are things that people say, and we want to find out how other people feel on these things. Please note whether you agree or disagree with the following statements:

Statement	*Agree/Disagree + Comments*
• The way people vote is the main thing that decides how things are run in this country.	
• If you don't watch yourself, people will take advantage of you.	
• A few strong leaders would do more for this country than all of the laws and talk.	
• All candidates sound good in their speeches but you can never tell what they will do after they are elected.	
• Human nature is fundamentally cooperative.	
• People like me don't have any say about what the government does.	
• The individual owes his first duty to the state and only secondarily to his personal welfare. Some people say that politics and government are so complicated that the average person cannot really understand what is going on.	

Appendix 2: Long Interview Protocol

Survey Questions (First 3 for interview protocol)

- Demographics
- Gender
- Race
- Age
- Place of birth
- Educational level
- Marital status
- How long have you lived in this community?
- How many times have you moved in your life?
- How many times have you changed jobs in your adult life?

NES Variables

- Civic engagement
- Interpersonal trust
- Confidence in government

Political Identification

- Do you consider yourself a member of a particular political party? If so, which one?
- Did you vote in the last election?
- Consider yourself very liberal, liberal, moderate, conservative, very conservative?

Life Satisfaction

- Taken all together, how would you say things are these days? Very happy, pretty happy, or not too happy?
- In general, do you find life exciting, pretty routine, or dull?

Moral Outlook

- All of us have ideas about what people should be like. Here is a list of characteristics you might find in people. Could you select the quality you admire most?
- Does his job well
- Active in public and social affairs
- Ambitious, wants to get ahead
- Generous, considerate of others

- Thrifty, saving
- Lets no one take advantage of him
- Keeps himself to himself
- Respectful, doesn't overstep his place
- Which would be next?

Social Trust and Efficacy

- NES/Interpersonal Trust
  - Some people say that most people can be trusted. Others say you can't be too careful in your dealings with people. How do you feel about it? Can you think of instances that would illustrate this?
  - Some people are inclined to help others. Other people look out for themselves. Thinking again of the people in this community, which statement do you think applies? Are most people helpful or do most look out for themselves?
- Political Efficacy
  - Some people say that politics and government are so complicated that they average man cannot really understand what ii going on. In general, do you agree or disagree?
  - Thinking of the important national and international issues facing the country, how well do you think you understand those issues?
  - How about state and local issues?
- Now I'd like to ask you another kind of question. Here are things that people say, and we want to find out how other people feel on these things. I'll read them one at a time and you just tell me off-hand whether you agree or disagree:
  - The way people vote is the main thing that decides how things are run in this country.
  - If you don't watch yourself, people will take advantage of you.
  - A few strong leaders would do more for this country than all of the laws and talk.
  - All candidates sound good in their speeches but you can never tell what they will do after they are elected.
  - Human nature is fundamentally cooperative.
  - People like me don't have any say about what the government does.
  - The individual owes his first duty to the state and only secondarily to his personal welfare.
  - No one is going to care much what happens to you, when you get right down to it.

Political Interest

- Do you follow the accounts of political and governmental affairs? Would you say you follow them regularly, from time to time or never?

- What about newspapers? Do you follow accounts of political or governmental affairs in the *newspapers* nearly every day, about once a week; from time to time or never?
- What about *radio* or *television*? Do you follow accounts of political or governmental affairs in the radio and on TV nearly every day, about once a week; from time to time, or never?
- What about the Web? Do you follow accounts of political or governmental affairs on the Web nearly every day, about once a week, from time to time, or never?
- Some people say that governments are really unnecessary and that people would get along better without them. What do you think?
- Think about the national government. In what ways do the activities of government affect your life or your family's life?
- State government: in what ways do the activities of government affect your life or your family's life?
- Local Government: in what ways do the activities of government affect your life or your family's life?
- Can you give me examples?
- What sorts of things are the taxes you pay used for?
- Could they be put to better use? If so, in what way?
- Have you ever had any personal contact with anyone in government? If so, which ones? (Elected officials, DMV employees? Political appointees?)

Confidence in Government

- I am going to name some institutions in this country. Confidence/no confidence.
  - President
  - Congress
  - Supreme Court
  - Washington can be trusted:
  - Just about always
  - Most of the time
  - Some of the time
  - None of the time

Duty to Participate

- We know that the typical person has many problems that occupy his/her time. In view of this, what part do you think the ordinary person ought to play in the local affairs of his community? What specifically ought he to do?
- People speak of the obligations that people owe to their country. In your opinion, what are the obligations that every person owes his country?

Social Capital

- Are you the member of any political club or organization? Which one(s)?
- Have you ever been active in a political campaign? That is, have you ever worked for a candidate or party, contributed money, or done any other active work?
- If yes: What about your friends and acquaintances? Would you say that all your friends support the same party that most of them do, that some of them do, or that almost none support the same party?
- Did you vote in the last election?
- Which one of these statements comes closest to describing your feelings when you go to the polls to cast your ballot?
  - I get a feeling of satisfaction out of it.
  - I do it only because it is my duty.
  - I felt annoyed, it is a waste of time.
  - I don't feel anything in particular.
- Are you a member of any organization now? Business groups? Social groups? Veterans, fraternal, athletic clubs, or religious groups? Which one(s)?
- Have you ever been an officer in one of those groups?
- Are any of these groups to which you belong concerned in any way with governmental, political, or public affairs? For instance, do they take stands on or discuss public issues or try to influence governmental actions?

Definition of Citizenship

- When people say they are citizens of a nation, what do you think they mean? That is, what makes someone a citizen of a nation?
- Is citizenship a birthright?
- Does citizenship have to be earned or are we just entitled to it by virtue of our birth or our residence?
- What about when people say they are citizens of a local community, do they mean the same thing as when they say are citizens of a nation?
- How would you define the word "community"?
- What communities are you a part of?
- It is often said that citizens have certain duties.
  - What do you think these duties are?
  - What would you say are the most important duties?
  - Which are the least important?
  - What duties would a very good citizen undertake?
  - What duties would a particularly bad citizen ignore?
  - What exactly do you mean when you say that citizens have certain duties?

- Think about those people who vote regularly, keep up with public affairs, and do volunteer work in the community. Do you think such people are extra good citizens or are they simply behaving as "all" citizens should?
  - If "extra good"—Why can we only expect extra good citizenship to perform this way? In what sense are these activities above the line of duty from what we expect from one another as citizens?
  - If "all": What allows us to expect that all people should behave in these fashions? In what sense are these activities those that we would expect of all citizens?
  - Of all: Do citizens have an obligation to help one another and to help the community as a whole?

Social Capital

- Have you ever started/created a civic/social group? If so, what was it? For what purpose? Why did you create it?
- Are you a member of any organization now? Business groups? Social groups? Veterans, fraternal, athletic clubs, or religious groups? Which one(s)?
- Have you ever been an officer in one of those groups?
- Are any of these groups to which you belong concerned in any way with governmental, political, or public affairs? For instance, do they take stands on, discuss public issues, or try to influence governmental actions?
- Are you the member of any political club or organization? Which one(s)?
- Have you ever been active in a political campaign? That is, have you ever worked for a candidate or party, contributed money, or done any other active work?
- If yes: What about your friends and acquaintances? Would you say that all your friends support the same party, that most of them do, that some of them do, or that almost none support the same party?

Bibliography

Almond, G. A., and Verba, S. (1960). *The Civic Culture: Political Attitudes and Democracy in Five Nations*. Princeton: Princeton University Press.

Aristotle. (1943). *Aristotle's Politics*. Trans. B. Jowett. New York: Random House.

Axelrod, C. (1984). *The Evolution of Cooperation*. New York: Basic Books.

Bagby, M. (1998). *Rational Exuberance: The Influence of Generation X On the New American Economy*. New York: EP Dutton.

Bennett, S. E. (1997). Why Young Americans Hate Politics and What We Should Do about It. *PS: Political Science and Politics, 30*, 47–53.

Bennett, S. E., and Craig, S. C. (1997). Generations and Change: Some Initial Observations. In Craig and Bennett (1997).

Bennett, S. E., and Rademacher, E. W. (1997). The "Age of Indifference" Revisited: Patterns of Political Interest, Media Exposure, and Knowledge among Generation X. In Craig and Bennett (1997).

Berger, P. L. (1986). *The Capitalist Revolution: Fifty Propositions about Prosperity, Equality, and Liberty*. New York: Basic Books.

Bimber, B. (1998). The Internet and Political Transformation: Populism, Community and Accelerated Pluralism. *Polity, 3*, 133–160.

Borsook, P. (2000). *Cyberselfish: A Critical Romp through the Terribly Libertarian Culture of High Tech*. New York: PublicAffairs.

Boston, B., and Gomez, B. (2000). *Every Student a Citizen: Creating the Democratic Self*, retrieved February 24, 2002, from http://www.ecs.org/clearinghouse/ 16/91/1691.htm.

Boyle, E., and Lawler, E. (1991). Resolving Conflict through Bargaining. *Social Forces, 69*(4), 1183–1204.

Brehm, J., and Rahn, W. (1997). Individual-Level Evidence for the Causes and Consequences of Social Capital. *American Journal of Political Science, 41*(3), 999–1024.

Brooks, D. (2000). *Bobos in Paradise: The New American Upper Class and How They Got There*. Washington, DC: Touchstone.

Cappella, J. N., and Jamieson, J. H. (1997). *Spiral of Cynicism: The Press and the Public Good*. New York: Oxford University Press.

Carey, J. W. (1988). *Communication as Culture: Essays on Media and Society (Media and Popular Culture)*. Boston: Unwin Hyman.

——— (1998). The Internet and the End of the National Communications System: Uncertain Predictions of an Uncertain Future. *Journalism and Mass Communication Quarterly, 75*, 28–34.

Cassel, C. A., and Luskin, R. C. (1988). Simple Explanations of Turnout Decline. *American Political Science Review, 82*, 1321–1130.

Cavanagh, T. (1981). Changes in American Voter Turnout, 1964–1976. *Political Science Quarterly, 1*(96), 53–65.

Cialdini, R. B. (1984). *Influence: The Psychology of Persuasion.* New York: Quill William Morrow.

Conover, P. J., Crewe, I. M., and Searing, D. D. (1991). The Nature of Citizenship in the United States and Great Britain: Empirical Comments on Theoretical Themes. *Journal of Politics, 53*, 800–832.

Coulter, A. H. (2002). *Slander: Liberal Lies about the American Right.* New York: Crown.

Coupland, D. (1992). *Generation X: Tales for an Accelerated Culture.* New York: St. Martin's Press.

Craig, S. C., and Bennett, S. E. (Eds.) (1997). *After the Boom: The Politics of Generation X.* Lanham: Rowman & Littlefield.

Dahl, R. A. (1999). *On Democracy.* New Haven: Yale University Press.

Delli Carpini, M. (1996). *What Americans Know about Politics and Why It Matters.* New Haven: Yale University Press.

de Toqueville, A. (2001). *Democracy in America.* New York: Knopf.

Dewey, J. (1938). *Experience and Education.* New York: Macmillan.

Dizard, W. (1999). *Old Media New Media: Mass Communications in the Information Age.* New York: Longman.

Domhoff, G. W. (1998). *Who rules America? Power and Politics in the Year 2000.* Mountain View: Mayfield Publishing Company.

Drew, E. (1994). *On the Edge: The Clinton Presidency.* New York: Simon & Schuster.

Ehrmann, S. C. (1999). Grand Challenges Raised by Technology: Will This Revolution Be a Good One? Academe. *Bulletin of the American Association of University Professors*, 42–46.

Etzioni, A. (1994). *Spirit of Community.* New York: Touchstone.

Fallows, J. (1997). *Breaking the News: How the Media Undermine American Democracy.* New York: Vintage.

Fisher, R., and Ury, W. (1983). *Getting to Yes: Negotiating Agreement without Giving in.* Boston: Penguin.

Fishkin, J. S. (1995). *The Voice of the People: Public Opinion and Democracy.* New Haven: Yale University Press.

Fishkin, J. S., and Luskin, R. C. (1999). Bringing Deliberation to the Democratic Dialogue. In McCombs and Reynolds (1999).

Florida, R. (2000). *Competing in the Age of Talent: Quality of Place and the New Economy.* Report prepared for the R. K. Mellon Foundation, Heinz Endowments and Sustainable Pittsburg.

——— (2002). *The Rise of the Creative Class: And How It's Transforming Work, Leisure, Community and Everyday Life.* New York: Basic Books.

Fountain, J. (1995). Lecture Delivered at the John F. Kennedy School of Government, Harvard University, National Center for Digital Government, Cambridge, Massachusetts.

Freie, J. (1998). *Counterfeit Community.* Lanham: Rowman & Littlefield.

Galston, W. A. (1991). *Liberal Purposes: Goods, Virtues, and Diversity in the Liberal State.* Cambridge and New York: Cambridge University Press.

Gates, B. (1999). *Business @ the Speed of Thought: Using a Digital Nervous System.* New York: Warner Books.

Glaser, B. G., and Strauss, A. L. (1967). *The Discovery of Grounded Theory: Strategies for Qualitative Research.* Chicago: Aldine.

Goulder, A. (1960). The Norm of Reciprocity: A Preliminary Statement. *American Sociological Review, 25,* 161–178.

Granovetter, M. S. (1973). The Strength of Weak Ties. *American Journal of Sociology, 78*(6), 1360–1380.

Groves, R. M., Cialdini, R. B., and Couper, M. P. (1992). Understanding the Decision to Participate in a Survey. *Public Opinion Quarterly, 56*(4), 475–495.

Guernesy, L. (2002). As the Web Matures, Fun is Hard to Find. *The New York Times,* March 28, G1.

Habermas, J. (1991). *The Structural Transformation of the Public Sphere: An Inquiry into a Category of Bourgeois Society.* Trans. F. Lawrence and T. Burger. Cambridge: MIT Press.

Halstead, T. (1999). A Politics for Generation X. *Atlantic Monthly Magazine,* August, 33–42.

Halstead, T., and Lind, M. (2001). *The Radical Center: The Future of American Politics.* New York: Doubleday.

Hart, R. P. (1978). An Unquiet Desperation: Rhetorical Aspects of Popular Atheism in the United States. *Quarterly Journal of Speech, 64,* 33–46.

——— (1994). *Seducing America: How Television Charms the Modern Voter.* New York: Oxford University Press.

——— (2000). *Candidate Toolkit.* Analysis prepared for the Aspen Institute's Young Voter Project, retrieved December 17, 2002, from http://www.campaignyoungvoters.org/toolkit/index.html.

Hart, R. P., and Jarvis, S. (1999). We the People: The Contours of Lay Political Discourse. In McCombs and Reynolds (1999).

Harwood, R. C. (2002). *A New Political Covenant: America's Aspirations for Political Conduct.* Bethesda: Harwood Institute for Public Innovation.

Hays, C. E. (1998). Alienation, Engagement and the College Student: A Focus Group Study. In Johnson et al. (1998).

Herbst, S. (1998). *Reading Public Opinion: How Political Actors View the Democratic Process.* Chicago: University of Chicago Press.

Hicks, K., and Hicks, R. (1999). *Boomers, Xers, and Other Strangers: Understanding the Generational Differences That Divide Us.* Wheaton: Tyndale House.

Hill, K. A. (1997). Generations and Tolerance: Is Youth Really a Liberalizing Factor? In Craig and Bennett (1997).

Homer-Dixon, T. F. (2000). *The Ingenuity Gap.* New York: Knopf.

Hout, M., and Knoke, D. (1975). Change in Voter Turnout, 1952–1972. *Public Opinion Quarterly, 39*(1), 52–68.

Howe, N., and Strauss, W. (1993). *13th Generation: Abort, Retry, Ignore, Fail?* New York: Vintage.

——— (2000). *Millennials Rising: The Next Great Generation.* New York: Vintage.

—— (2003). *Millennials Go to College: Strategies for a New Generation on Campus.* American Association of Collegiate Registrars, February.

—— (2006). *Millennials and Popular Culture.* LifeSource Associates.

Huntington, S. P. (1975). The Democratic Distemper. *The Public Interest, 41*, 9–38.

Jarvis, S. (1998). The Virtual Citizen: Democratic Theory and the New Political Media. Paper prepared as part of application materials to the 1998 NCA Doctoral Honors Conference, Mass Communication Seminar, July 29–August 2, 1998.

Johnson, T. J., Simon, P., Hays, C., and Hays, S. (Eds.) (1998). *Engaging the Public: How Government and the Media can Invigorate American Democracy.* Lanham: Rowman & Littlefield.

Jones, D. (2002). Businesses Not Feeling so Charitable toward Schools. *USA Today*, September 17, retrieved December 17, 2002, from http://www.usatoday.com/money/companies/2002-09-17-school-funding_x.htm.

Jones, S. G. (Ed.) (1994a). *CyberSociety: Computer-Mediated Communication and Community.* Thousand Oaks: Sage.

—— (1994b). Understanding Community in the Information Age. In S. G. Jones (1994a).

Kamarck, E. (1998). Campaigning on the Internet in Off Year Elections of 1998: A Snapshot in Time. In *John F. Kennedy Visions of Governance for the 21st Century.* Bretton Woods.

King, D. (1998). Political and Demographic Characteristics of Web Users in Late 1997. In *John F. Kennedy Visions of Governance for the 21st Century.* Bretton Woods.

Komorita, S. J., and Hilty, C. P. (1991). Reciprocity and Cooperation in Social Dilemmas. *Journal of Conflict Resolution, 62*(4), 607–617.

Kymlicka, W., and Norman, W. (Eds.) (1994). *Citizenship in Culturally Diverse Societies: Issues, Contexts, Concepts.* Oxford and New York: Oxford University Press.

LeBlanc, J. (2000). *Digital Beat Extra—the Digital Divide*, The Benton Foundation, April 6, retrieved December 17, 2002, from http://www.benton.org/News/Extra/.

Leibovich, M. (2002). *The New Imperialists.* Paramus: Prentice Hall.

Lessig, L. (1999). *Code And Other Laws of Cyberspace.* New York: Basic Books.

Lijphart, A. (1997). Unequal Participation: Democracy's Unresolved Dilemma. *American Political Science Review, 91*, 1–14.

Linklater, R. (Writer/Director). (1991). *Slacker.* Motion picture. United States: MGM/United Artists.

Lisheron, M., and Bishop, B. (2002). *Why the Creative Come Here: Austin, a City That has Always Been a Little Bit Different, Is Thriving with a New Class of Inventive, Imaginative Worker*, The Austin-American Statesman Online, May 12, retrieved December 17, 2002, from http://www.austin360.com/aas/special reports/citiesofideas/0512creatives.html.

Liu, E. (1994). *Next: Young American Writers on the New Generation.* New York: W. W. Norton.

Marvin, C. (1988). *When Old Technologies Were New: Thinking about Electric Communication in the Late Nineteenth Century.* New York: Oxford University Press.

Matthews, C. (1999). *Hardball: How Politics is Played—Told by One Who Knows the Game*. New York: Simon & Schuster.

McCombs, M., and Reynolds, A. (Eds.) (1999). *The Poll with a Human Face: The National Issues Convention Experiment in Political Communication*. New Jersey: LEA.

McCracken, G. D. (1988). *The Long Interview*. Newbury Park: Sage.

Media Studies Center. (1996). Young Voters—How Closely Do They Follow the Campaign? *The Media & Campaign 96. Briefing No. 4*. New York: Media Studies Center.

Meloy, J. M. (1994). *Writing the Qualitative Dissertation: Understanding by Doing*. Hillsdale: L. Erlbaum Associates.

Miller, W. E. (1992). The Puzzle Transformed: Explaining Declining Turn Out. *Political Behavior, 14*, 1–43.

Mills, C. W. (1956). *The Power Elite*. New York: Oxford University Press.

Mueller, J. E. (1999). *Democracy, Capitalism and Ralph's Pretty Good Grocery*. Princeton: Princeton University Press.

Noble, P. (1999). Using the Internet to Bring New People into Politics. *Campaigns & Elections, 20*(7), 50.

Oblinger, D. G., and Verville, A. (1998). *What Business Wants from Higher Education*. Phoenix: Oryx Press.

Oliver, D., and Heater, D. (1994). *The Foundations of Citizenship*. New York: Harvester Wheatsheaf.

Olson, M. (1965). *The Logic of Collective Action: Public Goods and the Theory of Groups*. Cambridge, MA: Harvard University Press.

Owen, D. (1998). The Partisanship Puzzle: Identification and Attitudes of Generation X. In Craig and Bennett (1997).

Pateman, C. (1970). *Participation and Democratic Theory*. Cambridge: Cambridge University Press.

Patterson, T. E. (1994). *Out of Order*. New York: Knopf.

Pavlick, J. (1998). New Media Technology: Cultural and Commercial Perspectives. Boston: Allyn & Bacon.

Pew Charitable Trusts. (2000). *Internet and American life*, retrieved December 17, 2002, from http://www.pewinternet.org.

——— (2001). *Society and the Internet: Trust, Civic Engagement and the Internet, May 2001*, retrieved December 17, 2002, from http://www.pewtrusts.com/ideas/ideas_item.cfm?content_item_id=658&content_type_id=21&issue_name=Society%20and%20the%20Internet&issue=10&page=21&name=Summaries%20of%20Reports%20and%20Publications.

——— (2005). *Internet and American Life*, http://www.pewinternet.org/.

Postman, N. (1985). *Amusing Ourselves to Death: Public Discourse in the Age of Show Business*. New York: Viking.

——— (1992). *Technopoly: The Surrender of Culture to Technology*. New York: Knopf.

Putnam, R. D. (2000). *Bowling Alone: The Collapse and Revival of American Community*. New York: Simon & Schuster.

——— (Ed.) (2002). *Democracies in Flux: The Evolution of Social Capital in Contemporary Society*. Oxford and New York: Oxford University Press.

Putnam, R. D. (2003). *Better Together: Restoring the American Community*. New York: Simon & Schuster.

Quigley, K. (1996). Human Bonds and Social Capital. *Foreign Policy Research Institute, 40*(2), 333–350.

Raadschelders, J. (1995). Rediscovering Citizenship: Historical and Contemporary Reflections. *Public Administration, 73*, 611–625.

Rucinski, D. (1991). The Centrality of Reciprocity to Communication and Democracy. *Critical Studies in Mass Communication, 8*(2), 181–194.

Sacks, P. (1996). *Generation X Goes to College: An Eye-Opening Account of Teaching in Post Modern America*. Chicago: Open Court.

Sanford, S. J. (2000). Tech Elites and the Primacy of the Customer. Unpublished paper.

Sartori, G. (1987). *The Theory of Democracy Revisited*. Chatham: Chatham House Publishers.

——— (1994). *Comparative Constitutional Engineering: An Inquiry into Structures, Incentives and Outcomes*. Basingstoke: Macmillan.

Schier, S. E. (1998). Hazards Lie Ahead: Economic Prospects for Generation X. In Craig and Bennett (1997).

Schudson, M. (1998). *The Good Citizen: A History of American Civic Life*. New York: Free Press.

Schumpeter, J. A. (1943). *Capitalism, Socialism, and Democracy*. New York and London: Harper.

Sclove, R. (2000). How a Commercially Driven Internet Threatens Democratic Civil Society and What to Do About It. Paper presented at DIAC 2000, *Shaping the Network Society: The Future of the Public Sphere in Cyberspace*, May 20–23, Seattle, Washington.

Scott, B. R., and Sunder, S. R. (1998). Austin, Texas: Building a High-Tech Economy. *Harvard Business Review*, November.

Selnow, G. W. (1998). *Electronic Whistlestops: The Impact of the Internet on American Politics*. Westport: Praeger Press.

Shearer, E., Morris, D. L., and Doppelt, J. (1998) No-Show 96: Americans Who Do Not Vote. In Johnson et al. (1998).

Skocpol, T. (Ed.) (1999). *Civic Engagement in American Democracy*. Washington, DC: Brookings Institution Press and New York: Russell Sage Foundation.

——— (2002). Bridging the Privileged and the Marginalized? In Putnam (2002).

Smith, J. W., and Clurman, A. (1997). *Rocking the Ages: The Yankelovich Report on Generational Marketing*. New York: HarperBusiness.

Sopher, B. (1994). Concession Behavior in a Bargaining Game: A Laboratory Test of the Risk Dominance Principle. *Journal of Conflict Resolution, 38*(1), 117–137.

Stephens, M. (1998). Which Communications Revolution Is It Anyway? *Journalism and Mass Communication Quarterly, 75*, 9–13.

Strama, M. (1998). Overcoming Cynicism: Youth Participation and Electoral Politics. *National Civic Review, 87*(1), 71–78.

Strike, K. (1988). Democracy, Civic Education, and the Problem of Neutrality. *Theory into Practice, 27*(4), 56–261.

Sunstein, C. R. (2002). *Republic.com*. Princeton: Princeton University Press.

Thau, R. D., and Heflin, J. S. (1997). *Generations Apart: Xers vs. Boomers vs. the Elderly*. New York: Prometheus Books.

UCLA (University of California at Los Angeles) Higher Education Research Institute. (1998). Retrieved December 17, 2002, from http://www.gseis.ucla.edu/heri/heri.html.

Vlahos, M. (1998). Entering the Infosphere. *Journal of International Affairs, 51*, 497–525.

West, W. (2000). The Truth about Robber Barrons. *The Heritage Foundation Policy Review, 99*, 69–77.

Whyte, W. H. (1956). *The Organization Man*. New York: Simon & Schuster.

Williams, B. A., and Delli Carpini, M. X. (2002). Heeeeeeeeeeeere's Democracy! *The Chronicle of Higher Education*, April 19, B14–B15.

Williams, R. (1970). *Television: Technology and Cultural Form*. New York: Schocken Books.

Wolfe, A. (1998). *One Nation, After All: What Middle-Class Americans Really Think About, God, Country, Family, Racism, Welfare, Immigration, Homosexuality, Work, the Right, the Left, and Each Other*. New York: Viking.

——— (2001). *Moral Freedom: The Impossible Idea That Defines the Way We Live Now*. New York: W. W. Norton.

Woodward, B. (1994). *The Agenda: Inside the Clinton White House*. New York: Simon & Schuster.

Woolcock, M., and Narayan, D. (2002). In Putnam (2002).

Wuthnow, R. (2002). From Membership to Advocacy. In Putnam (2002).

Zemke, R., Raines, C., and Filipczak, B. (2002). *Generations at Work: Managing the Clash of Veterans, Boomers, Xers, and Nexters in Your Workplace*. New York: AMACOM.

Index